Love Potions Thro

A Study of Amatory De

Wedeck

Alpha Editions

This edition published in 2023

ISBN : 9789357390408

Design and Setting By
Alpha Editions
www.alphaedis.com
Email - info@alphaedis.com

Contents

INTRODUCTION

The amatory motif is pervasive, timeless, and universal. In some of its phases and manifestations it has presented age-old provocations and, not infrequently, problems that are still unresolved.

Among such problems are involved the faculty of physiological potency, the urge to attract amorously, and, conversely, the problem of preventing such attraction in a designated instance, or of diverting it to another objective.

That, in brief, is the essence of the material means of effecting such a realization. In its various mutations, its protean diversities, it is the love-potion, the philtre, the mystic concoction that, once quaffed, will instil love and passion and desire and lust, that will replenish erotic inadequacies, that will awaken the ancient *fons vitae*, the symbol of animate being, the source, as the antique Hellenes sensed and exemplified, of all cosmic creation, of the totality of living generation.

The potion, then, is at least a hypothetically efficacious instrument for securing and preserving the amorous interests of the desired object. It also serves as an apotropaic device for diverting misplaced love, as the agent sees it, and redirecting it to the proper and preferred channel.

The actual means for the fulfilment of these erotic purposes vary with the ages, with ethnic groups and demographic alignments, with legendary and folk traditions and mores, with the disparate levels of culture of a specific region. They present variations and adaptations in correspondence with climatic and epichorial conditions. But they retain the essentially common characteristic, the unchanging property, of attempting to shape and mould the amatory esurgences, in whatever degree, and whether transitory or of more enduring permanence, by impersonal, palpable, mechanistic and visual means.

It should be observed, as a *terminus a quo*, that the term philtre itself stems from the Greek *philtron*, a love-potion (from *philein*, to love, and *tron*, an instrumental suffix). It means, then, a love-charm.

The term potion is derived immediately from the Latin *potio*, a draught, whether of medicine or even of poison. The ultimate source is the Greek *potos*, a drink. In a general sense, therefore, a love philtre or potion is a concoction, usually liquid in form, but not necessarily so, intended to produce or promote amatory sensibilities. In a wide and comprehensive denotation, the philtre will include any object or charm or periapt that serves the same erotic purpose.

This present survey touches on the use of the potion in the course of the centuries, in varying circumstances and disparate countries: on the fantastic factors that composed the final preparations; and on anecdotes, both apocryphal and authenticated, and episodes and occasional allusions that point up the treatment, its hazards, and even its humors.

With regard to the potions and similar concoctions and preparations of an amatory nature, a caveat must here be entered. All such philtres are considered in this book from an exclusively traditional, historical, and academic viewpoint. They are not recommended in any instance for personal use, as they may involve unpredictable or even catastrophic effects: in no sense, therefore, should such prescriptions be utilized for empirical experimentation.

H.E.W.

CHAPTER I
ANTIQUITY

In ancient Greece, the climatic conditions, the long unending summer days, the broad spaciousness of the sea, wine-dark and loud-sounding, as Homer describes it, the secluded pools and fountains and glades, the remote valleys, the snowy mountain summits were all alive, to the Hellenic perceptive and imaginative mind, with graceful nymphs and shaggy satyrs, with a multitude of anthropomorphic divinities, and with the alluring pipes of Pan.

Under such conditions it was not difficult to conceive human life as dominated by the cosmic creative force, and to do homage and obeisance to the great god Dionysus, divinity of the fruitful wine, protector of all procreative and generative functions.

The generative and sexual activities of the Greeks were, in general, so freed from contrived restrictions, so much in harmony with their instinctive and developed sensitivity to beauty of form, of movement, of rhythm, that artificial aids and inducements to amatory performance were far less necessary than they are in a highly complex and competitive and in a sense exhausted contemporary social frame.

Hence we do not constantly hear of the *ad hoc* use of philtres, potions, and analogous means of stimulation. Yet their existence is established, and in particular cases they were brought into effective use. Xenocrates, a Greek physician of the first century A.D., as Pliny the Elder records, advised drinking the sap of mallows as a love-potion. Such a philtre, together with three mallow roots tied into a bunch, would inflame the erotic passions of women.

Again, Dioscorides of Cilicia, in Asia Minor, an army physician who flourished in the first century A.D., produced a *Materia Medica* that treated drugs, remedies, ingredients in a rational, systematic manner. His text became a standard work, used for centuries, in both the East and the West. He recommends the roots of boy-cabbage, soaked in fresh goat's milk. A good draught of this drink would be productive of intense excitation of the sexual impulse.

Many spices, plants, herbs that were described, either by the encyclopedists and historians or incidentally mentioned in dramatic literature, in occasional poems, anecdotes or in epitomes of legends and folklore, were of such obscurity and rarity that it is no longer possible to ascertain the corresponding modern equivalent. There was, as an instance, satyrion. It is frequently mentioned, both in Greek and Roman contexts. Actually unidentifiable botanically, it may have been analogous to the orchis. In Greek and also Roman antiquity it was reputed to constitute a potent aphrodisiac, and is mentioned in an accepted and traditional sense by writers such as Petronius, who casually alludes to it in the course of his *Satyricon* as a common erotic aid.

The name satyrion is evidently associated with the Greek satyr, a wood spirit, partly goat-like, and partly human. Attendants to the rustic god Pan, the satyrs were known as bestial and lustful creatures, symbolic of the basic sexual passion of man.

Botanically, satyrion is a plant with smooth leaves, red-tinted, and equipped with a two-fold root. The lower part of this root was credited anciently with promoting male conception, while the other part was conducive to female conception. In its modern counterpart, satyrion has been associated with the Iris florantina.

There is another variety of satyrion, called Serapias. This has pear-shaped leaves and a tall elongated stem. Its root consists of two tubers that have the appearance of testes. Unquestionably, the association of the plant as an aphrodisiac derives from the orchidaceous configuration of the root.

Remarkable properties were attributed to the root of satyrion. When it was dissolved in goat's milk, the erotic effect was so vigorous and urgent that, as the Greek philosopher Theophrastus asserts in his *Enquiry into Plants*, the potion produced, on a particular occasion, some seventy consecutive coital performances.

Still another species of satyrion was erithraicon. This plant had a peculiar virtue. The mere holding of it, or carrying it, in the hand, occasioned a lustful desire. This fact is attested by Pliny, in his *Natural History*, in Book 26, 96 and 98, as well as by Dioscorides in his *Materia Medica* 3. 134. When the libido became too intense, lettuce was eaten to mitigate the effect, to allay the erotic provocation.

Greek mythology abounds in references to satyrion as an efficacious stimulant. The prowess of Hercules, the lusty warrior, as the Roman Petronius, Arbiter Elegantiarum, calls him, is attested in an amatory sense by the story of his visit to a certain Thespius. Entertained lavishly as a guest, Hercules, fortified by satyrion, repaid the host's entertainment by having intercourse with all fifty daughters of Thespius.

In Roman times the effectiveness of the root in arousing erotic excitation was common knowledge. Petronius, the voluptuary attached to the court of the Emperor Nero and the author of the remarkable picaresque novel entitled the *Satyricon*, alludes to the matter. One of his characters, describing the frenzied activities in a brothel, remarks:

We saw many persons of both sexes, at work in the cells, so much every one of them seemed to have taken satyrion.

In a more general direction, important testimonies to manipulative and mechanistic means of arousing vigor are the references in Petronius, particularly the episode involving Quartilla:

Quartilla came up to me to cure me of the ague, but finding her self disappointed, flew off in a rage, and returning in a little while, told us, there were certain persons unknown, had a design upon us, and therefore commanded to remove us into a noble palace.

Here all our courage fail'd us, and nothing but certain death seem'd to appear before us.

When I began, "If, madam, you design to be more severe with us, be yet so kind as to dispatch it quickly; for whate'er our offence be, it is not so heinous that we ought to be rack'd to death for it": Upon which her woman, whose name was Psyche, spread a coverlet on the floor. Sollicitavit inguina mea mille iam mortibus frigida. Ascyltos muffled his head in his coat, as having had a hint given him, how dangerous it was to take notice of what did not concern him: In the mean time Psyche took off her garters, and with one of them bound my feet, and with the other my hands.

Thus fetter'd as I lay, "This, madam," said I, "is not the way to rid you of your ague."

"I grant it," answer'd Psyche, "but I have a Dose at hand will infallibly do it" and therefore brought me a lusty bowl of satyricon and so merrily ran over the wonderful effects of it, that I had well-nigh suck'd it all off; but because Ascyltos had slighted her courtship, she finding his back toward her, threw the bottom of it on him.

Ascyltos perceiving the chat was at an end, "Am not I worthy," said he, "to get a sup?" And Psyche fearing my laughter might discover her, clapped her hands, and told him, "Young man, I made you an offer of it, but your friend here has drunk it all out."

"Is it so," quoth Quartilla, smiling very agreeably, "and has Encolpius gugg'd it all down?" At last also even Gito laught for company, at what time the young wench flung her arms about his neck, and meeting no resistance, half smother'd him with kisses.

A peculiar situation in which erotic provocation or inducement to passion is conditioned by the concept of social prestige, or, in the contemporary idiom, status, is exemplified in a later passage in Petronius' *Satyricon*:

Going out full of these thoughts to divert my concern, I resolv'd on a walk, but I had scarce got into a publick one, e're a pretty girl made up to me, and calling me Polyaemus, told me her lady wou'd be proud of an opportunity to speak with me.

"You're mistaken, sweet-heart," return'd I, in a little heat, "I'm but a servant, of another country too, and not worthy of so great a favor."

"No, sir," said she, "I have commands to you; but because you know what you can do, you're proud; and if a lady wou'd receive a favor from you, I see she must buy it: For to what end are all those allurements, forsooth? the curl'd hair, the complexion advanc'd by a wash, and the wanton roll of your eyes, the study'd air of your gate? unless by shewing your parts, to invite a purchaser? For my part I am neither a witch, nor a conjurer, yet can guess at a man by his physiognomy. And when I find a spark walking, I know his contemplation. To be short, sir, if so be you are one of them that sell their ware, I'll procure you a merchant; but if you're a courteous lender, confer the benefit. As for your being a servant, and below, as you say, such a favor, it increases the flames of her that's dying for you. 'Tis the wild extravagance of some women to be in love with filth, nor can be rais'd to an appetite but by the charms, forsooth of some slave or lacquy; some can be pleased with nothing but the strutting of a prize-fighter with a hacktface, and a red ribbon in his shirt: Or an actor betray'd to prostitute himself on th' stage, by the vanity of showing his pretty shapes there; of this sort is my lady; who indeed," added she, "prefers the paultry lover of the upper gallery, with his dirty face, and oaken staff, to all the fine gentlemen of the boxes, with their patches, gunpowder-spots, and toothpickers."

When pleas'd with the humor of her talk, "I beseech you, child," said I, "are you the she that's so in love with my person?" Upon which the maid fell into a fit of laughing.

"I wou'd not," return'd she, "have you so extremely flatter yourself. I never yet truckl'd to a waiter, nor will Venus allow I shou'd imbrace a gibbet. You must address your self to ladies that kiss the ensigns of slavery; be assur'd that I, though a servant, have too fine a taste to converse with any below a knight." I was amaz'd at the relation of such unequal passions, and thought it miraculous to find a servant, with the scornful pride of a lady, and a lady with the humility of a servant.

A still more elaborate scene concerns the techniques of recovering the faculty of erotic consummation. Encolpius, the narrator of the *Satyricon*, is attached homosexually to the young Gito. He is in a state of incapacity. At this juncture he receives a note from Circe, the mistress of the maid Chrysis, commenting on his inadequacy:

Chrysis enter'd my chamber, and gave me a billet from her mistress, in which I found this written:

"Had I rais'd my expectation, I might deceiv'd complain; now I'm obliged to your impotence, that has made me sensible how much too long I have trifl'd with mistaken hopes of pleasure. Tell me, sir, how you design to bestow your self, and whether you dare rashly venture home on your own legs? for no physician ever allow'd it cou'd be done without strength. Let me advise your tender years to beware of a palsie: I never saw any body in such danger before. On my conscience you are just going! and shou'd the same rude chilliness seize your other parts, I might be soon, alas! put upon the severe trial of weeping at your funeral. But if you would not suspect me of not being sincere, tho' my resentment can't equal the injury, yet I shall not envy the cure of a weak unhappy wretch. If you wou'd recover your strength, ask Gito, or rather not ask him for't—I can assure a return of your vigor if you cou'd sleep three nights alone: As to myself I am not in the least apprehensive of appearing to another less charming than I have to you. I am told neither my glass nor report does flatter me. Farewell, if you can."

When Chrysis found I had read the reproach, "This is the custom, sir," said she, "and chiefly of this city, where the women are skill'd in magick-charms, enough to make the moon confess their power, therefore the recovery of any useful instrument of love becomes their care; 'tis only writing some soft tender things to my lady, and you make her happy in a kind return. For 'tis confest, since her disappointment, she has not been her self."

I readily consented, and calling for paper, thus addrest myself:

"'Tis confest, madam, I have often sinned, for I'm not only a man, but a very young one, yet never left the field so dishonorably before. You have at your feet a confessing criminal, that deserves whatever you inflict: I have cut a throat, betray'd my country, committed sacrilege; if a punishment for any of these will serve, I am ready to receive sentence. If you fancy my death, I wait you with my sword; but if a beating will content you, I fly naked to your arms. Only remember, that 'twas not the workman, but his instruments that fail'd: I was ready to engage, but wanted arms. Who rob'd me of them I know not; perhaps my eager mind outrun my body; or while with an unhappy haste I aim'd at all; I was cheated with abortive joys. I only know I don't know what I've done: You bid me fear a palsie, as if the disease you'd do greater that has already rob'd me of that, by which I shou'd have purchas'd you. All I have to say for my self, is this, that I will certainly pay with interest the arrears of love, if you allow me time to repair my misfortune."

Having sent back Chrysis with this answer, to encourage my jaded body, after the bath and strengthening oyles had a little rais'd me, I apply'd my self to strong meats, such as strong broths and eggs, using wine very moderately; upon which to settle my self, I took a little walk, and returning to my chamber, slept that night without Gito; so great was my care to acquit my self honorably with my mistress, that I was afraid he might have tempted my constancy, by tickling my side.

The next day rising without prejudice, either to my body or spirits, I went, tho' I fear'd the place was ominous, to the same walk, and expected Chrysis to conduct me to her mistress; I had not been long there, e're she came to me, and with her a little old woman. After she had saluted me, "What, my nice Sir Courtly," said she, "does your stomach begin to come to you?"

At what time, the old woman, drawing from her bosom, a wreath of many colors, bound my neck; and having mixed spittle and dust, she dipt her finger in't, and markt my forehead, whether I wou'd or not.

When this part of the charm was over, she made me spit thrice, and as often prest to my bosom enchanted stones, that she had wrapt in purple; Admotisque manibus temptare coepit inguinum vives. Dicto citius nervi paruerunt imperio manusque aniculae ingenti motu repleverunt. At ilia gaudio exsultans, "Vides," inquit, "Chrysis mea, vides quod aliis leporem excitavi?"

Never despair; Priapus I invoke

To help the parts that make his altars smoke.

After this, the old woman presented me to Chrysis; who was very glad she had recover'd her mistress's treasure; and therefore hastening to her, she conducted me to a most pleasant retreat, deckt with all that nature cou'd produce to please the sight.

Where lofty plains o're-spread a summer shade,

And well-trimm'd pines their shaking tops display'd,

Where Daphne 'midst the Cyprus crown'd her head.

Near these, a circling river gently flows,

And rolls the pebbles as it murmuring goes.

A place design'd for love, the nightingale

And other wing'd inhabitants can tell.

That on each bush salute the coming day,

And in their orgies sing its hours away.

She was in an undress, reclining on a flowry bank, and diverting her self with a myrtle branch; as soon as I appear'd, she blusht, as mindful of her disappointment: Chrysis, very prudently withdrew, and when we were left together, I approacht the temptation; at what time she skreen'd my face with the myrtle, and as if there had been a wall between us, becoming more bold; "what, my chill'd spark," began she, "have you brought all your self today?"

"Do you ask, madam," I return'd, "rather than try?" And throwing myself to her, that with open arms was eager to receive me, we last a little age away; when giving the signal to prepare for other joys, she drew me to a more close imbrace; and now, our murmuring kisses their sweet fury tell; now, our twining limbs, try'd each fold of love; now, lockt in each others arms, our bodies and our souls are join'd; but even here, alas! even amidst these sweet beginnings, a sudden chilliness prest upon my joys, and made me leave 'em not compleat.

Circe, enrag'd to be so affronted, had recourse to revenge, and calling the grooms that belong'd to the house, made them give me a warming; nor was she satisfi'd with this, but calling all the servant-wenches, and meanest of the house, she made 'em spit upon me. I hid my head as well as I cou'd, and, without begging pardon, for I knew what I had deserv'd, am turn'd out of doors, with a large retinue of kicks and spittle: Proselenos, the old woman was turn'd out too, and Chrysis beaten; and the whole family wondering with themselves, enquir'd the cause of their lady's disorder.

I hid my bruises as well as I cou'd, lest my rival Eumolpus might sport with my shame, or Gito be concern'd at it; therefore as the only way to disguise my misfortune, I began to dissemble sickness, and having got in bed, to revenge my self of that part of me, that had been the cause of all my misfortunes; when taking hold of it,

With dreadful steel, the part I wou'd have lopt,

Thrice from my trembling hand the razor dropt.

Now, what I might before, I could not do,

For cold as ice the fearful thing withdrew;

And shrunk behind a wrinkled canopy,

Hiding his head from my revenge and me.

Thus, by his fear, I'm baulkt of my design,

When I in words more killing vent my spleen.

At what time, raising myself on the bed, in this or like manner, I reproacht the sullen impotent: With what face can you look up, thou shame of heaven and man? that can'st not be seriously mention'd. Have I deserv'd from you, when rais'd within sight of heavens of joys, to be struck down to the lowest hell? To have a scandal fixt on the very prime and vigor of my years, and to be reduc'd to the weakness of an old man? I beseech you, sir, give me an epitaph on my departed vigor; tho' in a great heat I had thus said:

He still continu'd looking on the ground,

Nor more, at this had rais'd his guilty head

Than th' drooping poppy on its tender stalk.

Nor when I had done, did I less repent of my ridiculous passion, and with a conscious blush, began to think, how unaccountable it was, that forgetting all shame, I shou'd contend with that part of me, that all men of sense, reckon not worth their thoughts. A little after, relapsing to my former humor: But what's the crime, began I, if by a natural complaint I was eas'd of my grief? or how is it, that we blame our stomachs or bellies, when 'tis our heads, that are distemper'd? Did not Ulysses beat his breast, as if that had disturb'd him? And don't we see the actors punish their eyes, as if they heard the tragic scene? Those that have the gout in their legs, swear at them; Those that have it in their fingers, do so by them: Those that have sore eyes, are angry with their eyes.

Why do the strickt-liv'd Cato's of the age,

At my familiar lines so gravely rage?

In measures loosely plain, blunt satyr flows,

And all the people so sincerely shows.

For whose a stranger to the joys of love?

Who, can't the thoughts of such lost pleasures move?

Such Epicurus own'd the chiefest bliss,

And such fives the gods themselves possess.

There's nothing more deceitful than a ridiculous opinion, nor more ridiculous, than an affected gravity. After this, I call'd Gito to me; and "tell me," said I, "but sincerely, whether Ascyltos, when he took you from me, pursu'd the injury that night, or was chastly content to lye alone?" The boy with his finger at his eyes, took a solemn oath, that he had no incivility offer'd him by Ascyltos.

This drove me to my wits end, nor did I well know what to say: For why, I consider'd, shou'd I think of the twice mischievous accident that lately befell me? At last, I did what I cou'd to recover my vigor: and willing to invoke the assistance of the gods, I went out to pay my devotions to Priapus, and as wretched as I was, did not despair, but kneeling at the entry of the chamber, thus beseecht the god:

Bacchus and Nymphs delight, O mighty God!

Whom Cynthia gave to rule the blooming wood.

Lesbos and verdant Thasos thee adore,

And Lydians, in loose flowing dress implore,

And raise devoted temples to thy power.

Thou Dryad's joy, and Bacchus's guardian, hear

My conscious prayer, with an attentive ear.

My hands with guiltless blood I never stain'd,

Or sacrilegiously the gods prophan'd.

To feeble me, restoring blessings send,

I did not thee, with my whole self offend.

Who sins thro' weakness is less guilty thought,

Be pacify'd, and spare a venial fault.

On me, when smiling fate shall smiling gifts bestow,

I'll not ungrateful to thy godhead go.

A destined goat shall on thy altar lye,

And the horn'd parent of my flock shall dye.

A sucking pig appease thy injur'd shrine,

And hallow'd bowls o're-flow with generous wine.

Then thrice thy frantick votaries shall round

Thy temple dance, with youth and garlands crown'd,

In holy drunkenness thy orgies sound.

While I was thus at prayers, an old woman, with her hair about her eyes, and disfigur'd with a mournful habit, coming in, disturb'd my devotions; when taking hold of me, she drew all fear out of the entry; and "what hag," said she, "has devour'd your manhood? Or what ominous carcase have you stumbl'd over in your nightly walks? You have not acquitted your self above a boy; but faint, weak, and like a horse o're-charg'd in a steep, tyr'd have lost your toyl and sweat; nor content to sin alone, but have unreveng'd against me, provokt the offended gods?"

When leading me, obedient to all her commands, a second time to the cell of a neighboring priestess of Priapus, she threw me upon the bed, and taking up a stick that fastened the door, reveng'd her self on me, that very patiently receiv'd her fury: and at the first stroak, if the breaking of the stick had not lessened its force, she might have broke my head and arm.

I groan'd, and hiding with my arm my head, in a flood of tears lean'd on the pillow: Nor did she then, less troubled, sit on the bed, and began in a shrill voice, to blame her age, till the priestess came in upon us; and "what," said she, "do you do in my chappel, as if some funeral had lately been, rather than a holy-day, in which, even the mournful are merry?"

"Alas, my Enothea!" said she, "this youth was born under an ill star; for neither boy nor maid can raise him to a perfect appetite; you ne're beheld a more unhappy man: In his garden the weak willow, not the lusty cedar grows; in short, you may guess what he is, that cou'd rise unblest from Circe's bed."

Upon this, Enothea fixt her self between us, and moving her head a while; "I," said she, "am the only one that can give remedy for that disease; and not to delay it, let him sleep with me to-night; and next morning, examine how vigorous I shall have made him:

"All Nature's work my magick powers obey,

The blooming earth shall wither and decay,

And when I please, agen be fresh and gay.

From rugged rocks, I make sweet waters flow,

And raging billows to me humbly bow.

With rivers, winds, when I command, obey,

And at my feet, their fans contracted lay,

Tygers and dragons too, my will obey,

But these are small, when of my magick verse,

Descending Cynthia does the power confess.

When my commands, make trembling Phoebus reign,

His fiery steeds, their journey back again.

Such power have charms, by whose prevailing aid

The fury of the raging bulls was laid.

The Heaven-born Circe, with her magic song,

Ulysses's men, did unto monsters turn.

Proteus, with this assum'd, what shape he wou'd.

I, who this art so long have understood,

Can send proud Ida's top into the main,

And make the billows bear it up again."

I shook with fear at such a romantick promise, and began more intensively to view the old woman; Upon which, she cry'd out, "O Enothea, be as good as your word"; when, carefully wiping her hands, she lay down on the bed, and half smother'd me with kisses.

Enothea, in the middle of the altar, plac'd a turf-table, which she heapt with burning coals, and her old crack cup (for sacrifice) repair'd with temper'd pitch; when she had fixt it to the smoaking-wall from which she took it; putting on her habit, she plac'd a kettle by the fire, and took down a bag that hung near her, in which, a bean was kept for that use, and a very aged piece of a hog's forehead, with the print of a hundred cuts out; when opening the bag, she threw me a part of the bean, and bid me carefully strip it. I obey her command, and try, without daubing my fingers, to deliver the grain from its nasty coverings; but she, blaming my dullness, snatcht it from me, and skilfully tearing its shells with her teeth, spit the black morsels from her, that lay like dead flies on the ground. How ingenious is poverty, and what strange arts will hunger teach? The priestess seemed so great a lover of this sort of life, that her humor appear'd in every thing about her, and her hut might be truly term'd, sacred to poverty:

Here shines no glittering ivory set with gold,

No marble covers the deluded mold,

By its own wealth deluded; but the shrine

With simple natural ornaments does shine.

Round Cere's bower, but homely willows grow.

Earthen are all the sacred bowls they know.

Osier the dish, sacred to use divine:

Both course and stain'd, the jug that holds the wine.

Mud mixt with straw, make a defending fort,

The temple's brazen studs, are knobs of dirt.

With rush and reed, is thatcht the hut it self,

Where, besides what is on a smoaky shelf,

Ripe service-berries into garlands bound,

And savory-bunches with dry'd grapes are found.

Such a low cottage Hecale confin'd,

Low was her cottage, but sublime her mind.

Her bounteous heart, a grateful praise shall crown,

And muses make immortal her renown.

After which, she tasted of the flesh, and hanging the rest, old as her self, on the hook again; the rotten stool on which she was mounted breaking, threw her into the fire, her fall spilt the kettle, and what it held put out the fire; she burnt her elbow, and all her face was hid with the ashes that her fall had rais'd.

Thus disturb'd, I arose, and laughing, took her up; immediately, lest any thing shou'd hinder the offering, she ran for new fire to the neighborhood, and had hardly got to the door, e're I was set upon by three sacred geese, that daily, I believe, about that time were fed by the old woman; they made an hideous noise, and, surrounding me, one tears my coat, another my shoes, while their furious captain made nothing of doing so by my legs; till seeing my self in danger, I began to be in earnest, and snatching up one of the feet of our little table, made the valiant animal feel my arm'd hand; nor content with a slight blow or two, but reveng'd my self with its death:

Such were the birds Alcides did subdue,

That from his conquering arm t'ward Heaven flew:

Such sure the harpyes were which poyson strow'd,

On cheated Phineus's false deluding food.

Loud lamentations shake the trembling air,

The powers above the wild confusion share,

Horrors disturb the orders of the sky,

And frighted stars beyond their courses fly.

By this time the other two had eat up the pieces of the bean that lay scatter'd on the floor, and having lost their leader, return'd to the temple. When glad of the booty and my revenge, I heal'd the slight old woman's anger, I design'd to make off; and taking up my cloaths, began my march; nor had I reach'd the door, e're I saw Enothea bringing in her hand an earthen pot fill'd with fire; upon which I retreated, and throwing down my cloaths, fixt my self in the entry, as if I were impatiently expecting her coming.

Enothea, entring, plac'd the fire, that with broken sticks she had got together, and having heapt more wood upon those, began to excuse her stay, that her friend wou'd not let her go before she had, against the laws of drinking, taken off three healths together. When looking about her, "What," said she, "have you been doing in my absence? Where's the bean?"

I, who thought I had behav'd my self very honorably, told her the whole fight; and to end her grief for the loss of her bean, presented the goose: when I shew'd the goose, the old woman set up such an outcry, that you wou'd have thought the geese were re-entering the place.

In confusion and amaz'd at so strange a humor, I askt the meaning of her passion? or why she pity'd the goose rather than me.

But wringing her hands, "you wicked wretch," said she, "d'ye speak too? D'ye know what you've done? You've killed the gods delight, a goose the pleasure of all matrons: And, lest you shou'd think your self innocent, if a magistrate shou'd hear of it, you'd be hang'd. You have defil'd with blood my cell, that to this day had been inviolate. You have done that, for which, if any's so malicious, he may expel me my office."

She said, and trembling, rends her aged hairs,

And both her cheeks with wilder fury tears:

Sad murmurs from her troubl'd breast arise,

A shower of tears there issu'd from her eyes.

And down her face a rapid deluge run,

Such as is seen, when a hills frosty crown,

By warm Favonius is melted down.

Upon which, "I beseech you," said I, "don't grieve, I'll recompence the loss of your goose with an ostrich."

While amaz'd I spoke, she sat down on the bed, lamented her loss; at what time Proselenos came in with the sacrifice, and viewing the murder'd goose, and enquiring the cause, began very earnestly to cry and pity me, as it had been a father, not a goose I had slain. But tired with this stuff, "I beseech you," said I, "tell me, tho' it had been a man I kill'd, won't gold wipe off the guilt? See here are two pieces of gold: with these you may purchase gods as well as geese."

Which, when Enothea beheld, "Pardon me, young man," said she, "I am only concern'd for your safety, which is an argument of love, not hatred; therefore we'll take what care we can to prevent a discovery: You have nothing to do, but intreat the gods to forgive the sin."

Who e're has money may securely sail,

On all things with all-mighty gold prevail.

May Danae wed, or rival amo'rous Jove,

And make her father pandar to his love.

May be a poet, preacher, lawyer, too:

And bawling win the cause he does not know:

And up to Cato's fame for wisdom grow.

Wealth without law will gain at bar renown,

How e're the case appears, the cause is won,

Every rich lawyer is a Littleton.

In short of all you wish you are possest,

All things prevent the wealthy mans' request,

For Jove himself's the treasure of his chest.

While my thoughts were thus engag'd, she plac'd a cup of wine under my hands, and having cleans'd my prophane extended fingers with sacred leeks and parsley, threw into the wine, with some ejaculations, hazel-nuts, and as they sunk or swam gave her judgment; but I well knew the empty rotten ones wou'd swim, and those of entire kernels go to the bottom.

When applying herself to the goose, from its breast she drew a lusty liver, and then told me my future fortune. But that no mark of the murder might be left, she fixt the rent goose to a spit, which, as she said, she had fatten'd a little before, as sensible it was to die.

In the mean time the wine went briskly round, and now the old women gladly devour the goose, they so lately lamented; when they had pickt its bones, Enothea, half drunk, turn'd to me; "and now," said she, "I'll finish the charm that recovers your strength": When drawing out a leathern ensign of Priapus, she dipt it in a medley of oyl, small pepper, and the bruis'd seed of nettles, paulatim coepit inserere ano meo. Hoc crudelissima anus spurgit subinde umore femina mea. Nasturcii sucum cum abrotano miscet perfusisque inguinibus meis viridis urticae fascem comprehendit, omniaque infra umbilicum coepit lenta manu caedere. Upon which jumping from her, to avoid the sting, I made off. The old woman in a great rage pursu'd me, and tho' drunk with wine, and their more hot desires, took the right way; and follow'd me through two or three villages, crying stop thief; but with my hands all bloody, in the hasty flight, I got off.

National Gallery of Art

THE KISS

by Rodin

Metropolitan Museum of Art

BESIDE THE SEA

by Rodin

Love manifestations and the passion for promoting weakened or inadequate functional activity are familiar themes in the most remote areas of the world. In the Arctic circle as well as in the Marshall Islands. Among the Eskimo of uttermost Greenland and among the Jibaro Indians of Equador. The Orang Kubau of Sumatra and the Semang and Senoi of Malacca are knowledgeable in this regard. The natives of these disparate territories are familiar with the plant and animal life of their regions, the nuts and fruits, the herbs and leaves, and their properties and specific virtues. They have tested them in food and drink, and in other functional directions: and by long, groping, deductive sequences they have come to definite practical conclusions. They have managed to extract or to use certain essences and elements in these roots and plants that they found conducive to specific purposes, particularly to the primary function of life, the erotic motif, the functional performance.

Oral traditions, the ways of the tribal society, derive, pre-historically, from a matriarchal hierarchy. And to the women of the tribe the obscure secrets of amorous practices and devices are all-important. Because they are the conditions of procreation, the source of fertility, the depositories of life and continuity. The love mystique, then, is the primary and virtually exclusive sacrosanct knowledge confined to the female of the tribe. Hence, after the ages of oral transmission, when we enter upon the centuries of writing, verbal transcription, and recording, then the sagas and chronicles, the legends and folk consciousness, invariably dwell on the female, the wise old woman, the witch, the adept, who possesses the arcana of erotic functions.

In the course of undetermined time, as literary mastery grows and develops culturally to the degree attained by Greece in the fifth century B.C., the witch, as guardian of Aphrodite's mysteries, is paramount. She is known to the peasant and the hoplite, to the cobbler and the young athlete, to the stroller in the agora, to the serious dramatist, even to the philosophers, to Socrates, to Plato.

In classical legend, Phaon, a ferryman of Lesbos, was given a potent periapt by Aphrodite, that made him remarkably handsome. The poetess Sappho consequently fell passionately in love with him. According to the Roman encyclopedist Pliny the Elder, author of the *Historia Naturalis*, Phaon had found a mandrake root that resembled the male genitalia. This root was an assurance of feminine love. Sappho, however, is said, in the version of Ovid's *Heroides*, to have flung herself from the Leucadian rock on his account.

Xenophon, the Greek historian who belongs in the fourth century B.C., recounts, in his *Memorabilia*, a dialogue between the philosopher Socrates and a hetaira named Theodote. The subject is the art of finding and retaining lovers.

Socrates: There are my lady friends, who will never let me leave them, night or day. They would always be having me teach them love-charms and incantations.

Theodote: Are you really acquainted with such things, Socrates?

Socrates: Of course I am. What else is the reason, think you, that Apollodorus and Antisthenes never leave my side? Why have Cebes and Simmias come all the way from Thebes to stay with me? You may be quite sure that not without love-charms and incantations and magic-wheels can this be brought about.

Theodote: Lend me your wheel, then, that I may use it on you.

Socrates: Nay, I do not want to be drawn to you. I want you to come to me.

Theodote: Well, I will come. But be sure to be at home.

Socrates: I will be at home to you, unless there be some lady with me who is dearer than yourself.

A speech attributed to the Greek orator Antiphon, who dates in the fifth century B.C., involves a belief that love could be secured by the administration of a potion.

The Attic orator is addressing the court:

The girl began to consider how she should administer the potion to them, before or after dinner, and, on reflection, she decided it would be better to give it after the meal. I will endeavor to give you a brief account of how the potion was actually administered. The two friends partook of a good dinner, as you can imagine, the host having a sacrifice to offer to the god of his household and the guest being on the eve of a sea voyage. When they had finished, they made a libation and added thereto some grains of incense. But while they were murmuring their prayer, the concubine slipped the poison into the wine she was pouring out for them: and furthermore, thinking that she was doing something clever, she gave Philoneos an extra dose, supposing that the more she gave the warmer would be his love for her.

The important deduction that follows as a corollary from the above passage is that the love-potion, mentioned without elaborate comment, was already, in the fifth century B.C., a matter of common knowledge and common use.

The plant called anciently telephilon was used by the Greeks for amatory purposes. Botanically, it has been identified with the poppy: and by some, with a kind of pepper tree. Theocritus, the Greek bucolic poet, refers to its use in the third Idyll. A goatherd goes to the cave of his sweet-heart Amaryllis. He tries to re-awaken her former love:

I learned my fate but lately, when upon my bethinking me whether you loved me, not even did the poppy leaf coming in contact make a sound, but withered away just so upon my soft arm.

Lovers were accustomed to guess by the poppy leaf placed between forefinger and thumb of the left hand, and then struck by the right, whether their love was reciprocated. If a loud crack was produced, it was a propitious amatory omen.

Among the ancient authorities the virtues of plants and herbs and spices and their medicinal curative powers and also their amatory impacts were frequently enumerated, described, and classified. In this group belongs Dioscorides, a Greek army surgeon who flourished in the first century A.D. His comprehensive treatise on the subject, *De Materia Medica Libri Quinque*, was for centuries consulted and used as a standard text. In the Middle Ages the famous Portuguese Marrano physician Amatus Lusitanus produced an excellent edition of Dioscorides. It was published, with numerous woodcut illustrations, at Leyden in Holland, in 1558.

According to the *Enquiry into Plants* by Theophrastus, and equally to the *Materia Medica* of the Greek army surgeon Dioscorides, cyclamen, which is sowbread, had erotic properties. The root of the plant was used as an ingredient in love-potions.

The plant itself produces colorful flowers, while the fleshy roots are favored by swine: hence the old name of sowbread.

The Greek physician Dioscorides, who served as a surgeon in the army of the Roman Emperor Nero, mentions, in his *Materia Medica*, mandrake as being anciently considered efficacious in love philtres. He also alludes to the practice in his own days, when a concoction of the root of mandrake steeped in wine was judged to be a favorable love-potion.

In the furious and unceasing search for some product of the earth, some fabricated distillation, some suddenly and miraculously discovered triumphant panacea that would efficaciously induce virile activity, the ancients grasped at any object that, by its mere outward and physical conformation, might conceivably have some cryptic, symbolic association with genital resemblances, and hence with amatory functions.

Such a resemblance was readily and gratefully found in the mandrake. The mandrake, even in Biblical times, was credited with unique properties, not least, with amatory stimulation.

Mandrake, or mandragore, which is botanically mandragora, mandragora officinarum, is a tuber with purple flowers, dark-leaved. It is native to Palestine, and hence has a Hebrew name, mentioned in Biblical literature. It is called there dudaim, an expression associated etymologically with *love*.

The peculiarity of mandrake is that it often assumes a human shape, the limbs in particular being formed like human extremities.

From the earliest literary eras mandrake was a customary ingredient in love-potions. Circe, the sorceress who appears in Homer's *Odyssey*, was traditionally an adept in concocting brews with mandrake infusions. So intimately was her name linked with this man-shaped plant, that it became known as *Circe's plant*.

As later Biblical confirmation of the significance of mandrake, the strange and moving episode of Jacob and Rachel and the employment of the very effective mandrake may be mentioned.

There is a further suggestion of its use in the Song of Songs.

The Greeks and the Romans likewise were acquainted with mandrake and its virtues. The Greeks considered the root an amatory excitant, and, by association, called Aphrodite, who presided over amatory functions, Mandragoritis, She of the Mandrake. Plutarch, the Greek philosopher and biographer, alludes to the plant and its resemblance to human genitalia. In his monumental encyclopedia, the *Natural History*, the Roman Pliny the Elder similarly dwells on this likeness, and adds that when a mandrake root that has grown into male genital form is found, it will unquestionably secure feminine love.

Without interruption the tradition of the mandrake lingered through the centuries. Old chroniclers allude to it. Woodcuts and illustrations in medieval vellum-bound folios present readers with the horrifyingly semi-human form of the plant. Sinister and abhorrent legends have grown up around the plant, many of them associated with death, gibbets, hangings, thieves.

Medieval folklore trusted to the consumption of the root as a reliable help in conception. This belief is also confirmed by a seventeenth century traveler. Sorcerers and alchemists and other occult practitioners concocted their elixirs with the aid of mandrake.

The seventeenth century English herbalist, John Gerarde, refers to mandrake in his *Herball or General Historie of Plantes*, and to its use in conception, particularly in the case of barrenness. He merely touches on its employment in amatory practices, but he is repulsed by the prurient and salacious nature of these devices.

In these days, too, mandrake evidently has not been neglected as a possible invigorating agent. In Greece and in Italy, folk beliefs in the plant still survive, and are put into active practice.

Sexual and procreative capacity was such a primal, essential factor in the old religious cults that, in classical mythology, Greek and Roman, and in Egyptian and Asian cults as well, the bull, the most potent among animals, was the ceremonial and pictorial symbol of this cosmic power. The bull, in fact, was equated with divinity. The processional sacrifice among the Romans, the taurobolium, highlighted the preeminence and the reverence due to the bull. In Egypt, he appears as Apis, the bull-god. He is also present in the Mithraic cult, and Mithra himself is sculpturally represented as holding a bull and cutting its throat. The bull was an expiatory sacrifice among the Germanic tribes, and also among the Northmen. In the Orient, too, the bull is sacred among the Japanese. Cows, also, have been no less venerated among the Greeks, the Hebrews, and the Hindus.

An ancient Egyptian record, the Doulaq Papyrus, reveals, in the translation by the famous Egyptologist Sir William Flinders Petrie, how even in antiquity sexual passion was channeled, promoted, and controlled: and how the cult of money and the phallic cult often went hand in hand and were intimately linked together. So that religious prostitution, the sacred erotic rites of pagan worship, transcended the common activities of the public prostitute and assumed a hieratic, reverential status.

This status is stressed and confirmed in the story of the sacred prostitute or hierodule Thubui, who was approached by Setna-Khamois, son of the Egyptian Pharaoh Usimares. In the papyrus the lavish richness of the hierodule's apartment is described, and the bloody conditions she exacts from her passionate prospective lover.

In the barber shops and the perfumers', in the furtive taverns and the baths and eating places, in Greece and later on in Rome, the lower types of prostitute plied their trade. They might ostensibly be musicians and singers of a sort, but these qualifications were mere preliminaries to their more intimate ministrations. The ways of these harlots, their outlook, their training, their future, are described vividly in Lucian's Dialogues of the Courtesans and in Alciphron's fictional letters. The poets, too, have their say about this institution, and many of their pieces, sensuous and sensual, erotic, scatological and lewd, are preserved in the Greek Anthology and the Palatine Anthology. In the collection known as The Girdle of Aphrodite, one of the pieces deals with the theme of Lolita. Another describes the operations of a masseuse. Others deal with amorous performances and reflect on love and its price.

The ancient cult of Bacchus, the god of wine and fertility, was marked by highly erotic rites and orgies and phallic manifestations. Bacchus himself was equated with the Greek god Dionysus, whose characteristics and functions were identical. Dionysus himself was associated with certain animals that were reputedly extremely lascivious by nature or erotically exceptionally dominant. Among these animals were: the bull, the ass, the panther, and the goat. The right testis of the ass, for instance, worn in a bracelet, was, according to the testimony of Pliny the Elder, who produced an encyclopedic Natural History, and the Greek physician Dioscorides, considered an effective sexual stimulant.

In many regions of ancient Greece, both on the mainland but particularly in the islands of the Aegean Sea, the Dionysiac cult was prevalent and passionately celebrated.

Euripides, the Greek tragic poet, presents a detailed and authoritative picture of Bacchic ceremonies and beliefs in his drama The Bacchae.

Among the priests of ancient Chaldea, noted for its thaumaturgic practices and esoteric cults, there was a tradition that the secretions of the liver of young boys would be a restorative of physiological vigor.

Among professional Greek and Roman courtesans, there were special devices for provoking male interest. During entertainments, for instance, drinking cups, made of earthenware, emitted a perfumed aura, while the contents themselves, containing myrrh and pepper, were direct stimulants.

In Asia Minor, some four millennia ago, the Sumerians flourished and produced a high literary culture. There is still extant a love song, chanted annually by the Sumerians, that is in the manner of the Biblical *Song of Songs*. It is an exultant amatory paean, dedicated to Inanna, the Sumerian goddess of love and procreation, who may be equated with the Babylonian Astarte and the Greek Aphrodite.

Storgethron, a plant used in ancient Greece as an amatory medicine, has been identified as the leek.

The root called surag was, in antiquity, held to have a stimulative virtue.

The aromatic leaves of tarragon, which grows in South East Europe, is considered, in addition to its use as a flavoring agent, as an amatory aid.

The oil extracted from the fresh leaves of the ruta graveolens plant produces an amatory excitation.

Both in ancient and in medieval days amatory virtues were attributed to the plant known botanically as radix Chinae.

The juice of the plant spurge, in composition with other items such as ginger, nettle seed, pellitory, cinnamon, and cardamom, is considered, among Arabs, as highly provocative.

The aromatic leaves of sage had an amatory repute. So with tulip bulbs and savory which the Romans knew as satureia.

Hierobota, or pisteriona, an herb mentioned by the medieval philosopher Albertus Magnus, was credited with such potency that its mere possession was said to act as a stimulant.

Pimpinella anisum, which is the botanical designation of anise, is native to the Eastern Mediterranean region. The ancients knew anise, and it was equally familiar to the Middle Ages, as a love attribute.

The testes of animals have always been popular in amatory preparations, both for their symbolic implications and also for their genesiac value. This was the case with the testes of lamb, deer, ram, and ass.

The head of the perch contains a number of small stones. These were included in the amatory preparations devised by sorceresses.

A French physician, Mery, in a treatise entitled *Traité Universel des Drogues Simples*, stated that the partes genitales of a rooster served as a potent stimulus.

Partridge was, according to the old writer Platina, in his *De Valetudine Tuenda*, believed, apart from its gastronomic relish, to 'arouse the half-extinct desire for venereal pleasures.'

In antiquity, snails were consumed for amatory purposes. The Roman poets refer to this practice. Even in modern times a concoction of snails, boiled in parsley, garlic, and onions, and fried in oil and again in red wine, is reputed to serve as a rejuvenating factor.

An ancient Egyptian device for achieving amatory efficiency involves a magic procedure:

Take a band of linen, of sixteen threads. Four of them white. Four, green. Four, blue. Four, red. Fasten all strands into one band, and strain with hoopoe blood. Bind with scarab posed as the sun-god wrapped in byssus. Bind to the body of the boy attendant who holds the sacred vessel.

The worship of the phallus in antiquity was not originally the worship of the human generative organs, but of the divine procreative faculty symbolized by the genitalia of the sacred bull and the sacred goat: in Egyptian religious terminology, by Apis and Priapis or Priapus respectively.

In Greece, the phallus, originally symbolic of the goat or bull, was attached, disproportionately and *a posteriori*, to a human figure: so that the phallus, in the course of time, became erroneously associated with human capacity.

The Athenian orator Isocrates postulated a maxim: What is improper to do is improper to say. Yet a rigid adherence to this view would mean a cessation of investigations of all kinds, of many historical records and archives, mores, and often matter that would give enlightenment on human traditions and the more intimate details of communal, tribal, or national life, of ethnic distinctions, of cultural progression.

Hence it might be more advisable to adapt the postulate of Isocrates and to introduce the proviso that whatever has been done or said or written by men should normally and regularly be transmitted to later generations or to wider circles, provided that this transmission is intended as a contribution to a knowledge of the past, or of contiguous races, or of disparate mores, and as a revealing exposition of what man performed in earlier ages, and not as a prurient and lewd inducement to wallow in scatological or libidinous depths for mere light or indifferent or transitory entertainment.

The anthropologist, the archaeologist, the professional scholar, the historian are, by virtue of their interests and training and their occupations, constantly dealing with subjects that have either been taboo in a general sense, or that involve the most secretive physiological and emotional human situations.

The ancient cult of the stars merged with religious ceremonials and religious beliefs, emerging in the zodiacal bull. This bull was anciently equated with the sun in its most auspicious phase, in spring time. The sun bull later became the actual bull itself, as in the Minoan and the Mithraic cults, and also among the Egyptians. For the bull was now definitely the symbol of creative potency, of cosmic fecundity and perpetuation.

The energized, salient phallus was the supreme symbol of being and fertility. In antiquity it had divine significance. It was carried in religious processions in ancient Egypt, in Greece, in the Greek islands, in Phoenicia, Assyria, and in Chaldea and Ethiopia. In Egypt, phalli, made of porcelain, were worn on the person as periapts.

In their fulminations against pagan mores and the sexual and erotic licentiousness and aberrations that were so prevalent in antiquity both socially and religiously, the ancient writers themselves were so descriptively forthright and detailed in their denunciations, that these very assaults and condemnatory attacks constitute in themselves, cumulatively, a vast corpus of circumstantial knowledge of ancient salaciousness, prurience, perversions, and total abandonment of amatory and sexual restraints. Among such witnesses and authorities were the Church Fathers Tertullian, Arnobius, and Clement of Alexandria.

The religious practice of women submitting or rather offering themselves to the priapic symbol, the phallus or lingam, dates back to millennia before this era. Herodotus, the Greek historian, mentions it; also Strabo the geographer, and the Church Father Clement of Alexandria.

Among the ancient Moabites, the god Baal-Peor, that was at one time worshipped by the Israelites and then execrated, was an idol equated with the Greek and Roman phallic Priapus.

The consciousness that in Nature, in the totality of the cosmic scheme, and in human beings the love motif conditions all existence and the continuance of being is manifest in the images, the religious rituals, symbols, ceremonials, and sacrificial offerings of all peoples, in every age, ancient and modern, in Greece and among the Romans, in pre-conquered Mexico and in India, throughout the East and in the Pacific Islands, and among the early tribal and racial denominations of Europe—the Germani and the Suevi, the Galli and the Normanni.

On the banks of the Euphrates, in Syria, there was anciently a vast, elaborate, richly decorated and endowed temple. At the entrance rose two gigantic phalli, dedicated, as the inscription ran, by Bacchus to the goddess Juno. Offerings were made to the phalli by the thronging suppliants, while within the building numerous wooden phalli were dispersed throughout the spacious interior. Similar images and rituals were manifest in contiguous countries, in Phoenicia, Persia, and Phrygia.

Throughout every polis and colony and settlement of ancient Greece, and also in the regions of the Mediterranean littoral, in Egypt and the Middle East, the phallus was a symbol of veneration always associated with religious ritual, with hieratic traditions, and temple worship on a wide and enthusiastic scale.

In Greece, there were the phallic hermae, enormous phalli attached to pedestals, tree-trunks, boundary-markers. They were protective and apotropaic, and where the phalli appeared, there would credibly be fecundity and erotic consummation, generation and abundance, in man and beast and throughout the cosmic design.

The phallus was variously named Priapus and Tutunus and Mutunus and Fascinum and, in Hindu religious mythology, the lingam. Among the esoteric Gnostics, Jao, the sun-god, equipped with ithyphallic force, had properties akin to those of Priapus. Thus the generative, energizing organs of virility, of the cosmic erotic impulse and of its purpose, are, despite variations of name and epichorial traits and accretions, basically comprehended under one concept, in all proto-history, in verifiable history, and, by traditional progression, in later ages.

Antiquity, free from the modern attitude that makes demarcations between what is obscene and what is not so, venerated the sexual act, and its symbolic representation of the phallus, as significant of the universal sense of generation and procreation. As a consequence, all sexual, all amatory performances, references, allusions were accepted as an integral element in human life, and involved no intrusive image of salaciousness, prurience, lewdness.

This phallic reverence, in its widest and most sweeping sense, was especially prevalent among the ancient Greeks. But it was not confined to this people. It was prevalent in Asia Minor, among the Hittites and the Sumerians, the Accadians and the Parthians, the Medes and the Babylonians and the Phoenicians. It was prevalent in Egypt and the North African littoral, and it was equally prevalent along the Mediterranean coastal regions. In the Far East, particularly but not exclusively in India, the cult of the phallus was a devout religious experience, equated with the dominant cults of the cosmic deities.

In later ages, when the human body became as it were dichotomous in function, the merely physiological acts began to be held in lesser esteem, and even became condemnatory in status, open to reproach and disdain, and even violent abuse and ill-treatment. The body, in fact, became obscene, invested with evil forces, compounded of malefic and defiled factors. The body was to be crushed and tortured and disfigured, in order to release the spiritual complements of the human being. The amatory acts were now turned into licentious and mephitic obscenities, into bestial defilements, into unspeakable carnal and animal manifestations of the lower nature. As a consequence, phallic worship, the glorification of the creative principle embodied in the male and female, went underground. And by the mere fact of going underground, it persisted, with qualifications, acquiring through the course of time veneers of secrecy, accretions of furtiveness, elements of ribaldry as a kind of protective coat.

Essentially, the phallic symbol was anciently viewed as an amatory agent, a generative stimulant, in as much as the phallus was cosmically the source of all being. Therefore offerings were made to the phallus in sacrificial rituals, just as to any other potent deity from whom privileges and favors were sought. Libations of milk were a normal form of offering to Priapus. Women, anxious to become mothers, stood reverently and suppliantly in puris naturalibus before the all-potent phalli, and in a further urgent procedure, performed the act of erotic consummation with the aid of the lingam figure itself. For the phallus, in a pose of lubricity, was the final appeal, the ultimate resort, of the pleading, awed, reverential mortal.

Among cities where the generative force symbolized by the phallus was held in deep veneration, were Orneae, Cyllene, and Colophon. Under the later impact of Christianity, however, the phallic cult diminished in its influence and extent, or was re-directed into other channels. In one specific direction, the cult merged into the Orphic mysteries.

Erotic awareness never went further than in the case of a city in Troas named Priapus, on account of its consecration to the cult of the phallus. There were other cities too, according to the testimony of Pliny the Elder, that were named Priapus for identical reasons. In the Ceramic Gulf there was an island named Priaponese: and an island in the Aegean Sea called Priapus.

A notorious incident in Greek history involved the nocturnal mutilation of hermae, in 415 B.C. Hermae were bronze or marble pillars surmounted by a head and a phallus. These marble figures appeared in the streets and squares of Athens and other Greek cities.

Suspicion for the defilement and desecration of the hermae fell upon the brilliant but wayward Athenian general and statesman Alcibiades and his companions. As a result, Alcibiades was condemned to banishment.

The cult of Priapus and his obscene association with the genitalia of the ass, the symbol of unbridled lust, were expounded in ancient fable and legend. Other commentaries and explanations were added later by Hyginus, who flourished in the first century A.D. Hyginus wrote on religious subjects and mystic cults. Pausanias, the Greek traveler and geographer, who belongs in the second century A.D., and Lactantius, the fourth century Church Father, also dwelt on the subject.

Of all cities of ancient Greece, Lampsacus, situated on the banks of the Hellespont, was most dedicated to the veneration of Priapus. In a legendary fable it was demonstrated that the origin of the priapic cult was Lampsacus itself.

In the Greek festival called Thargelia, celebrated in May, the rites were dedicated to Apollo, the sun god, and to Diana, the moon goddess. At the ceremonial there was a procession of youths who carried olive branches hung with food, fruit, and images of phalli.

The genesiac theme, in its most lustful implication, was so prevalent in early history that there was a sect, known as the Baptae, dedicated to Cotytto, an obscene and lewd goddess. They celebrated their nocturnal abominations at Athens, Corinth, in Thrace, and on the island of Chios.

One of the peculiar features of the Baptae was their custom of drinking from glass vessels shaped like a phallus. Juvenal, the Roman satirist, in describing the Baptae and their mystic and symbolic rites, refers to one participant who drinks from a glass Priapus: vitreo bibit ille Priapo.

According to the testimony of the Greek historian Herodotus, a certain Melampus brought the cult of Bacchus, the worship of the generative capacity, to Greece, approximately in the thirteenth century B.C. He expounded the features of the Egyptian cult and established processional rites and ceremonies adapted from Egyptian usage.

In ancient Greece Bacchus, the phallic divinity, was equated with Dionysus. In the cities the Greater Dionysia, or the Urban Dionysia, were celebrated in his honor for three days. The locale was at Limnae in Attica, and the season was the middle of the month of March.

In very early times, the Greek biographer and philosopher Plutarch declares, the rites were of a simple but joyous nature. But in his own time the celebration had reached a lavish, extravagant splendor.

Women, devotees of the Bacchic symbol and known as Bacchantes, introduced the ritualistic procession. Chaste maidens, impeccable in morality and of distinguished birth, followed. These were the Canephoroi, the Basket-bearers who bore on their heads baskets containing the sacred utensils used at the celebration: together with mystic objects, flowers, salt, sesame, and a flower-bedecked phallus. A detachment came next to the Canephoroi: these were the Phallophoroi. The Phallophoroi were the Phallus-bearers, carrying, attached to long staffs, the phallic emblem.

Musicians were also in the march, chanting and accompanying the choral odes with twanging strings, and at brief intervals emitting loud exclamations in glorification of the god.

There were other strange participants. The Ithyphalli, men dressed in women's garments, who chanted salacious phallic songs. Scandalous satyrs led goats for sacrifice, while Bacchantes performed obscene dance movements. There was, over the entire celebration, an atmosphere of debauchery and libidinous license consonant with the phallic context of the cult.

In Carthage, a spot outside the city was consecrated to Astarte, the goddess of generation, and called Sicca Veneria. Among the Phoenicians a similar spot, intended for the same purpose, that is religious fornication, was known as Siccoth Venoth.

In Biblical antiquity, the primary concept was for man to be fruitful and multiply, and replenish the earth. To this end, concubinage was consequently not frowned upon and was practiced *pari passu* with marriage. Maid servants were commonly taken by their masters as concubines, as in the case of Hagar, and also in that of Reumah. Lot even gave his maiden daughters for the satisfaction of the lustful inhabitants of Sodom. Later, he committed incest with these daughters.

The servant women of Jacob, Bilhah and Zilpah, became his concubines. These are instances, among many others, that illustrate cases of adultery and fornication that do not appear to have had a condemnatory stigma or reproach attached to them. For the object in these circumstances was procreation and propagation and that was the primal function enjoined upon man.

The corollary is that sterility is a personal reproach in Biblical times, a social defect that is looked upon with opprobrium, particularly in Oriental countries.

In Spain, the phallic cult was practiced under the name of Hortanes. This cult is mentioned by the Roman epic poet, Silius Italicus, in his *Punica*. He describes the orgiastic revels of Satyrs and Maenads in nocturnal rites in honor of the Hispanic fascinum.

In the South of France, also, and in Belgium, excavations unearthed relics, monuments, amulets and other artifacts, bas-reliefs and antiquities of various kinds, all testifying to the ancient cult of Priapus and his functions and the deep and wide reverence for his omnipotence. In Germany, Priapus lost the somewhat indulgent character of a phallic and generative deity responsive to supplication and promise, and became a violent, blood-lusting monstrosity. In parts of Eastern Europe, again, Priapus became Pripe-Gala, sanguinary and destructive.

Ancient Armenia had a deity analogous to Priapus or Aphrodite or Astarte. She was known as Diana Anaïtis, and her cult involved temple prostitution. The same practice, on the testimony of the Greek historian Herodotus, was in vogue in Lydia. Another writer, the Roman geographer Pomponius Mela, who belongs in the first century A.D., has similar references in the case of an African people called the Augilae.

Again, the practice was prevalent at Naucratis, in Egypt.

***

The phallic cult, that was originally consecrated to the propagation of all things, in as much as the fascinum itself symbolized the sacred regeneration of all Nature, in time degenerated so that only the phallus as such became the symbol of lust and passion and debauchery. It became the emblem of excesses in erotic encounters, the sign of the prostitute. Priapus actually became an object of some contempt, a humble scarecrow of the fields, chthonic guardian of the orchards, a subject of coarse ribaldry, as is testified in the Latin corpus of poems known under the name of Priapeia.

***

The lascivious mores of the Egyptians under the guise of veneration of the priapic bull Apis, and their obscene dances, rituals, and similar performances are described and commented on in great detail by Herodotus in his History of the Persian Wars.

***

The genitalia and all references to the phallic image were in very ancient times held in such sacred esteem and reverence that in Biblical literature the inviolable sanctity of an oath was ratified by touching the area of the genitalia, or the thigh, to use the Biblical euphemism. The Hebrews especially held the generative organs in the greatest respect, socially, ethnically, and religiously: and nudity as a consequence was a matter of shameful stigma and opprobrium.

Among the Moslems too the most binding oath was taken with respect to the sanctity of the genitalia.

***

In Egypt, in the temple of Isis, sacred prostitution was a regular religious practice. Reference to this circumstance is made by the Roman satirist, Juvenal, who calls Isis a procuress and her shrine a rendez-vous for adulterous and libidinous practices.

***

Among symbolic emblems that represented, in combination, the male and female principles of generation and fecundity, were the Egyptian crux ansata and the seal of Solomon.

***

The phallic symbol was so pervasive, so potent, in the lives of the ancients, that the priapic function and the erotic variations of the generative performance were pictorially represented in every conceivable form of reproduction: scenes on vases representing perverted consummations: baskets filled with phalli that were offered for sale to yearning women: ithyphallic figures: monuments, lamps and other objects depicting orgiastic lubricities.

In Ezekiel 16.17 there is a reference to the phallic figure: Fecisti tibi imagines masculinas et fornicata es in eis.

In one of the bucolic Idyls of the Greek poet Theocritus (c. 310–c. 250 B.C.) the maiden Simaetha, in love with Delphis, who has abandoned her, attempts to regain his love by performing certain magic rites and making invocations to Selene, Aphrodite, and the horrendous Hecate.

She fashions a wax image of Delphis and by sympathetic magic anticipates the melting of his heart in correspondence with the melting of the image.

In addition, she makes use of the magic wheel, and her refrain throughout the performance is:

My magic wheel, draw home to me

The man I love!

Intertwined with these rituals is the further refrain, addressed to Selene, the moon goddess:

Bethink thee of my love,

And whence it came,

My Lady Moon!

In his *De Sanitate Tuenda Praecepta*, Advice on keeping Well, Plutarch, the Greek philosopher and biographer, comments on lust and potions:

While we loathe and detest women who contrive philtres and magic to use upon their husbands, we entrust our food and provisions to hirelings and slaves to be all but bewitched and drugged. If the saying of Arcesilaus, addressed to the adulterous and licentious, appears too bitter, to the effect that 'it makes no difference whether a man practices lewdness in the front parlor or in the back hall,' yet it is not without its application to our subject. For in very truth, what difference does it make whether a man employ aphrodisiacs to stir and excite licentiousness for the purpose of pleasure or whether he stimulate his taste by odors and sauces to require, like the itch, continual scratchings and ticklings.

(Loeb)

In Greek mythology, Andromache, the wife of the Trojan warrior Hector, was accused by Hermione, wife of Neoptolemus, of gaining his love by means of love-potions. Euripides, the tragic poet (c. 485–406 B.C.), refers to the situation in his drama *Andromache*:

Not of my philtres thy lord hateth thee,

But that thy nature is no mate for his.

That is the love-charm: woman, 'tis not beauty

That witcheth bridegrooms, nay, but nobleness.

Philtres were in actual use beyond mythological times. Xenophon (c. 430–354 B.C.), the Greek historian, author of *Memorabilia*, alludes to the practice:

"They say," replied Socrates, "that there are certain incantations which those who know them chant to whomsoever they please, and thus make them their friends; and that there are also love potions which those who know them administer to whomso they will; and are in consequence loved by them."

Propertius, however, the Roman elegiac poet (c. 48 B.C.–16 B.C.), refers to the futility of love potions:

Here herbs are of no avail,

nor nocturnal Cytaeis,

nor grasses brewed by the

hand of Perimede.

Cytaeis is the witch Medea: while Perimede is another witch, called by Homer Agamede.

The Bacchic cult in Egypt is described by the Greek historian Herodotus in Book 2 of his *History of the Persian Wars*:

To Bacchus, on the eve of his feast, every Egyptian sacrifices a hog before the door of his house, which is then given back to the swineherd by whom it was furnished, and by him carried away. In other respects the festival is celebrated almost exactly as Bacchic festivals are in Greece, excepting that the Egyptians have no choral dances. They also use instead of phalli another invention, consisting of images a cubit high, pulled by strings, which the women carry round to the villages. A piper goes in front, and the women follow, singing hymns in honor of Bacchus. They give a religious reason for the peculiarities of the image.

In Book 5 of *The History of the Persian Wars*, Herodotus describes some of the marital customs of the Thracians:

The Thracians who live above the Crestonaeans observe the following customs. Each man among them has several wives; and no sooner does a man die than a sharp contest ensues among the wives upon the question, which of them all the husband loved most tenderly; the friends of each eagerly plead on her behalf, and she to whom the honor is adjudged, after receiving the praises both of men and women, is slain over the grave by the hand of her next of kin, and then buried with her husband. The others are sorely grieved, for nothing is considered such a disgrace.

The Thracians who do not belong to these tribes have the customs which follow. They sell their children to traders. On their maidens they keep no watch, but leave them altogether free, while on the conduct of their wives they keep a most strict watch. Brides are purchased of their parents for large sums of money.... The gods which they worship are but three, Mars, Bacchus, and Dian.

An ancient Hittite text contains invocations and rituals intended to remedy conditions of incapacity or lack of erotic desire.

A sacrifice is performed to Uliliyassis, continuing for three days. Food is prepared: sacrificial loaves, grain, a pitcher of wine. The shirt of the male suppliant is brought forth.

The suppliant bathes. He twines cords of red and of white wool. A sheep is sacrificed. An invocation is made, beseeching help and favor: Come to this man, the cry arises. Come down to this man. Make his wife conceive and let him beget sons and daughters.

An Egyptian love song, belonging in the second millennium B.C., is still extant. The love song was usually chanted to a musical accompaniment. The lover is addressed as sister, or brother.

The heart is sick from love, laments the victim, and no physician, no magician can heal this disease, except the appearance of the sister. There is abundant reference to spices, to myrrh and incense, and the tone of the amatory supplications and yearnings is the tone of the Song of Songs. Listlessness on the part of the love-sick suppliant is banished, as soon as he beholds his beloved, as soon as her arms open in embrace.

In ancient orgiastic cults, particularly those dedicated to Dionysus and to the Syrian Baal, religious frenzies were accompanied or stimulated by drugs, fermented drink, by rhythmic dance movements, by tambourine, drum, and flute music that culminated in ecstatic self-mutilation followed by wild sexual debaucheries.

Passion, lust, incest, fornication, adultery, as well as concubinage and polygamy, most of the sexual perversions and aberrations that are now included under medico-psychiatric categories, occur in the Bible, in both Testaments.

King David married eight women. On his flight from Absalom he left ten concubines behind him. Jacob had two wives. King Solomon had seven hundred wives and three hundred concubines.

There are instances of enduring affection too, as in the case of Jacob, who labored for Rachel for fourteen years.

There is sudden, rapturous love at first sight, at all costs:

It happened, late one afternoon, when David arose from his couch and was walking upon the roof of the king's house, that he saw from the roof a woman bathing, and the woman was very beautiful. And David sent and inquired about the woman. And one said, "Is not this Bathsheba, the daughter of Eliam, the wife of Uriah the Hittite?"

So David sent messengers and took her, and he lay with her.

Amnon is overwhelmed by a passionate infatuation for his half sister Tamar. He was so tormented that he made himself sick because of his sister. He is advised by his friend Jonadab to go to bed and claim illness. Tamar brings him food and at this point Amnon attempts seduction. When she suggests an approach to the king, for permission to marry Amnon, his lust overpowers him, and he consummates his passion. After which, in a frenzy of hate, he banishes her.

The Song of Solomon is a paean to sexual love, an erotic exultation, the apogee of amatory sensuality.

In the New Testament, too, there is frequent reference to harlots and debauchees and to a variety of 'sinners.'

Babylonian customs, in addition to the rites of temple prostitution, included both male and female sacred concubines. There was considerable pre-marital sexual freedom. But there was also monogamous marriage involving rigid fidelity. Trial marriage was acknowledged. Adultery was punished by drowning the guilty wife. In the degenerative days of Babylon, morality broke down. Male prostitutes rouged their cheeks and bedecked themselves with jewelry, while the poor exposed their daughters to prostitution. Sensuality and erotic libertinage became dominant and pervasive.

Among the Canaanites the most potent deities—Baal and El and Asherah—were the symbols of procreation and sexuality. Hence, all acts, all objects, all rituals associated with copulation, with the phallus, with fecundity were divinely inspired and inherently sacred. Ceremonials dedicated to the deities invariably included sexual activity, sacred and ecstatic orgies. The voluptuous and sensual character of the dedicatory rites was evidently so appealing that they lured the Israelites into acceptance and imitation, for the deity of the Israelites was one, supreme, without kin, without consort, without sexuality.

The New Testament attacks pagans, particularly Roman paganism, for unnatural sexual practices, lusts, and corrupt and degenerate mores.

In primitive Greek society, under a primal matriarchy, the male functioned as a kind of passive sexual partner, and virtually thereafter as a domestic drudge.

But in the course of the centuries the male acquired dominance, in the divine pantheon, and equally on a mortal and earthly plane, politically, socially, and domestically.

But the concept of the inter-relationship of the sexes grew into a concept of one primary harmonious principle of aesthetics, of essential perfection of beauty, irrespective of sex and hence irrespective of any compulsive admiration and appreciation of such beauty by one sex or the other. Beauty became an entity in itself, a sexless trait. In the Platonic dialogue, in fact, in the *Symposium*, the theory is postulated that man was at one time androgynous.

The Greek hetaira or male companion was virtually a prostitute. Sometimes she acquired a more permanent status, when she was bought by a master and became a *pallakis* or concubine.

Homosexuality, on the other hand, brought no stigma to the boys or young men involved in the practice. Because homosexuality was a corollary, applied in practice, of the primary concept of aesthetic beauty irrespective of sex.

In the case of women, there was the corresponding though possibly not so widespread cult of tribadism.

The Romans cultivated sexuality, particularly in a heterosexual direction, with great vigor and lustfulness. It was largely through the growing consciousness of Rome as an imperial power, and through the increase in industry and commerce, in wealth and consequent luxury and idleness, that perversions of all kinds increased and multiplied to such an abnormal extent that in the first century A.D. the Romans themselves, through their own poets, commented on the situation and contrasted it, with some sense of nostalgia, with the severe and rigid and essentially stabilized moral code that prevailed in the old pre-imperial days.

During the Roman Empire, with the increase of childless families, women were able to give more scope to their femininity, their sexual appeal, and their erotic allurements. As a consequence, there was an upsurge of marital license, on the part of both husband and wife, but notoriously so in the case of the women. This situation reached the most shameless depths, as the poet Juvenal testifies: and as the Church Fathers later on asserted, in their wholesale condemnations of pagan practices.

Early in the first century A.D. the insidious decline of domestic morality became so manifest that imperial decrees required marriage in the case of men under sixty and of women under fifty: and these ordinances also restricted the freedoms of bachelorhood.

Marriage was thus officially encouraged, and large families were granted special privileges and monetary awards from the imperial treasury. But these and similar measures were abortive in their primary purpose. For prostitution flourished and grew and became so flagrant and yet so characteristically identified with later Roman society that there were at least a score of designations for the public harlot, according to her social status, her price, and her locale. Thus lust and eros were rampantly triumphant.

Harlotry was manifestly rife in Old Testament days, for there is repeated allusion to the practice: in the symbolism of Oholah and Oholibah, in the Psalms and in the prophets, particularly Isaiah and Jeremiah, in the Book of Judges, and in Samuel.

In addition, there is mention of the allurements of the harlot: her chamber fragrant and enticing with spices and perfumes, aloes and myrrh and cinnamon.

There is reference to the personal seductive persuasiveness of the harlot's coaxing words, the urgency of her erotic devices.

———

The Old Testament mentions and illustrates the morality involved in sexual impulses resulting in physiological consummations. Under certain circumstances, stoning the guilty pair was enjoined. In some cases, the man only was punished, by death. In other situations the man who spurned the woman after carnally knowing her was whipped and fined one hundred shekels of silver. For fornication, the death penalty was normally enforced. Sacred prostitution in the temple, too, whether affecting male or female, was prohibited.

———

Homosexuality and sacred male prostitution are both known to the Bible. In Deuteronomy there is an injunction against the sons of Israel becoming sacred prostitutes. The abominations of Sodom receive ample treatment. Even transvestism is prohibited, for it suggests sexual dubiety, physiological ambiguity, and a possible merging of the sexes, a potential elimination of the sexual demarcations. Other amatory abnormalities also appear in Biblical contexts, among them: rape, voyeurism, and bestiality.

———

With the onset of the Hellenistic Age, concurrent with Alexander the Great's death in 323 B.C., the Mysteries, the exclusive secretive cults, advanced in importance and in the extent of their influence. Many of these cults came from the East and merged, with adaptations and various amplifications or modifications, into the Greek and Roman religious sphere. The cult of Cybele, Magna Mater Deorum, the Mighty Mother of the gods, was most dominant, transcending all other cults and to some degree absorbing them. In addition, there were the cults of Sabazios, of Mithras, of Isis and Osiris. These cults bound the initiates to close secrecy: and thus only occasional fragments, hints, references from various sources can present any degree of coherence and design in the cults. It is known that there were dramatic presentations involving communion with the deities, dark rites and ceremonials, even vague adumbrations of the concept of immortality, as well as castigation and castration, fertility symbolisms and seasonal fructifying cycles. There were, further, the Gnostics, searchers for divine knowledge. Some of these speculative cosmologists were scrupulously ascetic in every sense, while others orgiastically indulged, toward the attainment of the same end, in fleshly passions.

At the Greek celebration of the Phallophoria, leather or wooden representations of the phallus were carried processionally through the public streets of the polis. It was the thematic manifestation of all-embracing fertility, on land, among the beasts of the fields, and in human relationships. It was a kind of visual paean, in fact, to the primal sexual impulse, to the basic erotic conflict.

One of the earliest instances of multiple incest occurs in Book 10 of Homer's *Odyssey*, in which Odysseus describes his visit to Aeolus. Aeolus has a family of six daughters and six sons, and he has given his daughters in marriage to his own sons.

In Greece the Aphrodision, and in Rome the Venereum, were the private bordellos that were not used by the general indiscriminate public.

Both in antiquity and in later ages the public baths, with both sexes in nude contacts in the *balnea mixta*, were a direct amatory stimulant. As further provocatives, there was, in particular cases, bathing in asses' milk, in essences of myrtle and lavender, in rose water, in almond paste and in honey water, and also in champagne.

In Greece, the phallus was so pervasive as a genesiac symbol in every phase of daily life, that there were loaves baked in phallic form. These loaves were known, for another erotic reason, as olisbokolices.

Drillopotae were glass vessels in phallic form. They were used, in ancient Rome, as drinking cups: and thus were an added erotic reminder at banquets and similar gatherings.

In Roman antiquity the color yellow was associated with prostitutes, and was a symbol of their profession. Yellow still retained this significance in the Central European countries in later ages. In Tsarist Russia, the yellow ticket was the official prostitute's occupational token. Alexander Kuprin's *Yama the Pit* describes the situation in a vivid and grim narrative.

Figurae Veneris is a Latin expression meaning *positions of Venus*. This phrase refers to the range of sexual positions. The Greeks were familiar with some seventy such permutations and manipulations. There were the symplegma and the catena, which involved more than two partners, and the dodekamechanon. Hesychius the Greek lexicographer, Philaenis, and, among the Romans, the poet Martial mention these contortions. In the Middle Ages, the licentious poet Pietro Aretino produced a poetic commentary on the entire extent of erotic possibilities.

Among periapts and amulets that were credited with promoting erotic activity were charms in the shape of an extended hand, a wild boar, the head of a bull, astrological signs; magic formulas too, inscribed on various objects; the crux ansata, and genitalia.

Among erotic pieces that are no longer extant are certain elegiac poems, of an amatory type, attributed formerly to Plato the philosopher. An ancient Roman poet named Laevius wrote an erotopaegnion. Apuleius, the Roman philosopher and novelist, produced a number of amatory epigrams. These references, together with others that include Vergil's *Aeneid* and the *Georgics*, are made by the Roman poet Ausonius himself.

He adds, also, that, like Martial and other poets, his life is unblemished though his verses may be dubious:

Igitur cui hic ludus noster non placet, ne legerit: aut cum legerit, obliviscatur: aut non oblitus, ignoscat.

Phallic priests were called phallobatai. Not only Priapus, but other deities as well in ancient Greece, were worshipped with erotic fervor. Among these were Phanes, Lordon, and Orthanes.

Metropolitan Museum of Art

LOVE AND PSYCHE

by Rodin

Philadelphia Museum of Art

THE ABDUCTOR

by Rodin

Philodemus of Gadara, who flourished in the first century B.C., was a Greek poet who settled in Rome. He became an intimate of powerful political forces, and also gathered around him a coterie of Romans interested in philosophy and literature. Among other works, mostly of a philosophical nature, Philodemus produced erotic pieces marked by extreme lewdness. Some twenty-five of these epigrams are still extant, collected in the corpus known as the *Anthologia Palatina.* These poems became popular in Rome and were imitated by both Horace and Ovid.

As an erotic stimulus, Greek women wore diaphanous thin-spun robes made of silk from the island of Cos. In Rome, similarly, prostitutes sometimes wore a toga vitrea—a glassy or transparent toga. There were, too, vestes sericae—silk dresses, in feminine use.

All such robes, of course, were of a purposely revealing and tantalizing nature, acting upon the viewer in a marked amatory direction. Seneca, the Roman Stoic philosopher, makes blunt and condemnatory remarks on the custom.

In Athens, there was an old quarter of the city dedicated to prostitution of the lowest type. This area was known as the Ceramicus.

The agents who acted as intermediaries, as panders and procurers and enticers in the furtive sexual commerce, in the seamy undercurrents of ancient life, were known under various descriptive designations. In Greece, there were the maulis and the draxon, the karbis and the proagogos, the mastropos, the prokyklis and the nymphagogos and the pornoboscos. Romans had their own counterparts: the professional procurer, the leno, the mercator meretricius, the admissarius and the institor, the lenonum minister, the perductor and the conductor: and, among the female operatives, the agaga and the stimulatrix, the conciliatrix and the stupri sequestra.

Phallic symbols enter into the Biblical context in I Kings, where Judah is described as building high places and pillars on every high hill. These pillars were actually phallic symbols, in the style of the abominations of the Canaanite cults.

In antiquity, in Biblical and post-Biblical times, the woman, in the widest sense, was the amatory slave of man. But with the woman's increase of knowledge in erotic skills and practices, in the secrets of her potent physiological attractions, in the use of unguents and cosmetics, potions and concoctions, in corporeal and mechanistic allurements and seductions, the woman's status gradually rose and extended and became all-embracing. Slowly, by virtue of these very artifices and techniques, by means of gyrations and gestures, provocative dances and tantalizing dress, silent invitations and ocular speech, she began to dominate man, to render him subservient and even obsequious, to control his habits and inclinations and tendencies in social and political directions: until woman, reaching the apogee of her power, based primarily on her erotic compulsiveness, became the woman behind the throne. She had attained her highest end, her ultimate destiny, as the implicit director of human activities. She usurped man's status, and assumed the regal baton. She manipulated kings and sultans, and her endearments were bought at the price of nations. She decided the fate of empires by her mere brusque whims, or personal resentment, her unpredictable likes. Man exchanged realms and justice for her amatory acquiescence, her erotic beneficence.

In a formal religious-ceremonial sense, antiquity acknowledged participation of women in the sacred temples. In Asia Minor, in the cults of Baal-Peor, in the Egyptian cults of Isis and Osiris, in the Mediterranean

Hellenic islands where the cult of Aphrodite in various forms and of analogous deities of passion and lust and procreation was prevalent, in the case of the Vestal guardians of the Roman state religion, priestesses took part in the hieratic rituals, in festive ceremonials, in sacrificial and processional rites.

Even with the advent of Christianity the Greek church in the East had its female votaries, while deaconesses were normally attached to the Church in the West. In the course of time, however, this acquiescence in a female priesthood turned into resentment, into hate, and finally into bitter and continuous official condemnation. Woman became the evil daemon, the essence of every malefic, licentious, forbidden, obscene practice, the sink of turpitude, the scourge of men, the destruction of humanity. Thus many early Fathers of the Church, Tertullian and Arnobius and Clement of Alexandria, inveigh against the serpentine machinations of woman. Hence this view and these attitudes were transmitted into the Middle Ages. In these middle centuries woman is depicted as the ally of Satanic forces, powerful on account of her very femininity, her presumed innocent frailty. She is essentially guileful and treacherous, amoral and immoral, and bent on the spiritual subjugation and desecration of perplexed man. Woman became the symbol of all sin, the prototype of every sacrilegious concept. She was stripped of a soul. She was in league with the demoniac tenebrous forces, the Satanic legions that furtively and thaumaturgically work their evil spells on man. She became, in short, the Anti-Christ incarnate, the Abominable Witch, consort of horned and hoofed Satan. And her attractions, her feminine beauty, were merely distorted and insidious forms of her fundamental iniquities.

Woman was conceived as attaining her sanguinary or lustful purposes by means of feminine stratagems or conspiratorial schemes, by personal ruthlessness that swept aside all frustrations, all moralities, and stopped neither at poisoning nor at murder. The roster of such women, in the stream of universal history, is long and challenging. It includes, among many others equally notorious, equally branded, Lilith and Cleopatra, Claudia and Messalina, Antonina and Theodora, Catherine of Russia and Elizabeth Bathory, Madame de Montespan and Lady Kyteler, the Borgias and Isobel Gowdie, Jeannette Biscar: and, in goetic contexts, Sagana, Canidia, and Oenothea.

Aphrodite had many forms, multiple aspects of her functions and her patronage, numberless descriptive designations, both in Greece itself and in the cults of Asia Minor where her attributes were equated with the properties of analogous and indigenous divinities. But basically she was one, the universal, the cosmic force that dominates all amatory contacts, that drives men, intent votaries of the goddess and bent on adherent dedication to her offices, to the realization of her injunctions at all costs, resorting to charms and mystic recipes, to fantastic interpretations of precious stones and flowers, to talismans and amatory manuals, grimoires, exotic herbs and insidious preparations.

For centuries man and woman have displayed mutual hostilities and resentments in a number of directions: personally and socially, politically and spiritually. Yet there appears a strange dichotomy in this human pair of male and female. They have despised each other and have sought each other, as Plato suggests in one of his more fanciful moments. The mutual act of racial procreation merged and was subsequently largely lost in the erotic consummations itself. So that, as the complexities of life grew, and as its manifestations multiplied and offered man a variety of experiences, motifs, recreational facilities and diversions, the woman as such came into her own, and Aphrodite established her sacred and profane sanctuaries at the crossroads, in sundered islands of the Aegean Sea, on the highways, in luxurious retreats, and in rural fastnesses. And, casting aside all spiritualities in man's search for a teleological significance to existence, made Eros the alpha and omega, the final purpose, of cosmic being.

Initiation into the cult of Aphrodite was known by the Greek expression mysterion: the mystery. The participants, the mystai, after bathing in the sea—and the sea itself was symbolic, for it was the source of Aphrodite's own birth—, they assembled in the evening in the Mystery Hall. Torches were lit, casting flitting shadows and tenebrous shapes through the chamber.

Then the ritual began. There were recitals by the initiates. Sacred objects were shown to the awed gathering, as well as certain phenomena about which too little knowledge has been transmitted. Then some kinds of performances were presented, all associated with the portentous relation between mortals, striving toward passionate intimacy with the divinity, and the puissant deity herself.

Three degrees of initiation were in force: the first initiate approach: the preliminary stage: and the highest rites. This final ritual, it is believed, brought into communion the adept and the deity. Erotic and sexual symbols were dominant factors in this ceremonial.

In this mystic cult of the goddess, the hierodule, the courtesan, is the intermediary between the suppliant and the divinity. She is the sexual passport, so to speak, that leads to the more secretive ritual of the Aphroditic temple.

There is, in the course of this rite, the necessity for a purgation, a purification by water. There is a reference to such an initiation in the Roman poet Juvenal's second satire. He speaks of a mystic sect called the Baptae. This expression derives from the Greek baptizo, dipping in water. The Baptae drank, as an element in their ritual, powerful liquids from phallus-shaped vessels. These Baptae were devotees of Cotytto, an obscene and salacious goddess.

Women were not admitted to the Aphroditic rites: but, strangely, the men came robed as women, painted and powdered and reeking in exotic perfumes. Subsequently, they dedicated themselves to every form of sexual subtlety.

In another more advanced stage of initiation, where physical love became sublimated, Aphrodite was in this phase the Syrian goddess Derceto or Atargatis: the half woman, half fish deity. Basically she was a fertility goddess, sometimes called Dea Syria, the Syrian goddess, the universal divinity. Her cult is described by the Greek writer Lucian: and Apuleius, the Roman philosopher and novelist, speaks about her priests, the wandering Galli:

How the Priests of the Goddesse Siria Were Taken and Put in Prison.

After that we had tarried there a few dayes at the cost and charges of the whole Village, and had gotten much mony by our divination and prognostication of things to come: The priests of the goddesse Siria invented a new meanes to picke mens purses, for they had certaine lofts, whereon were written: Coniuncti terram proscindunt boves ut in futurum laeta germinent sata: that is to say. The Oxen tied and yoked together, doe till the ground to the intent it may bring forth his increase: and by these kind of lottes they deceive many of the simple sort, for if one had demanded whether he should have a good wife or no, they would say that his lot did testifie the same, that he should be tyed and yoked to a good woman and have increase of children. If one demanded whether he should buy lands and possession, they said that he should have much ground that should yeeld his increase. If one demanded whether he should have a good and prosperous voyage, they said he should have good successe, and it should be for the increase of his profit. If one demanded whether hee should vanquish his enemies, and prevaile in pursuite of theeves, they said that this enemy should be tyed and yoked to him: and his pursuite after theeves should be prosperous. Thus by the telling of fortunes, they gathered a great quantity of money, but when they were weary with giving of answers, they drave me away before them next night, through a lane which was more dangerous and stony then the way which we went the night before, for on the one side were quagmires and foggy marshes, on the other side were falling trenches and ditches, whereby my legges failed me, in such sort that I could scarce come to the plaine field pathes. And behold by and by a great company of inhabitants of the towne armed with weapons and on horseback overtooke us, and incontinently arresting Philebus and his Priests, tied them by the necks and beate them cruelly, calling them theeves and robbers, and after they had manacled their hands: Shew us (quoth they) the cup of gold, which (under the colour of your solemne religion) ye have taken away, and now ye thinke to escape in the night without punishment for your fact. By and by one came towards me, and thrusting his hand into the bosome of the goddesse Siria, brought out the cup which they had stole. Howbeit for all they appeared evident and plaine they would not be confounded nor abashed, but jesting and laughing out the matter, gan say: Is it reason masters that you should thus rigorously intreat us, and threaten for a small trifling cup, which the mother of the Goddesse determined to give to her sister for a present? Howbeit for all their lyes and cavellations, they were carryed back unto the towne, and put in prison by the Inhabitants, who taking the cup of gold, and the goddesse which I bare, did put and consecrate them amongst the treasure of the temple.

Aphrodite exacted from her devotees certain prescribed ceremonies, testimonies to their communion with the goddess, palpable evidences of their total mystic and spiritual absorption in the sacraments she demanded of her votaries.

The ritual followed an established design. At sunset the catechumen is conducted to the temple. Then, facing the East, the priest raises his left hand skyward and with his right he seizes a bronze knife, plunges it into boiling water, and then performs the ritual sexual rite with respect to the catechumen.

Then followed solemn and hieratic instruction in the amatory procedures, including the methods of arousing erotic sensibilities, provocative postures and gestures, words and formulas, osculation and its pervasive corporeal significance. There were, furthermore, illustrative consummations, considered without lewdness, but accepted as formal elements in the grave cosmic scheme. There was a musical accompaniment that softly intertwined in the sequence of the various rituals and presentations, a kind of amatory, seductive litany, enfolding the entire ceremonial in a sacred aura of mysticism. In the concluding phase of these rites, there appeared the phallic procession, the symbolic glorification of the creative urge, and the actual illustration of this potency culminated in an abandoned sexual orgy, indiscriminate and incestuous, exultant and fleshly, carnal and spiritual in one fervid syncretism. A concomitant of this vast sensual exhibition, this release of the physical carapace, was prostitution itself, which for long retained a ritualistic character.

The next step in this genesiac process was sacred prostitution, whereby the woman symbolized the solemnity and the compulsiveness of the Aphroditic cult, while the man was the visitant, a suppliant for the favor of the divinity. And the hierodule thus was a kind of prototype, associated with wise skills, a vestal of the goddess, initiating men into secret amatory and sacred rituals: an adept too in concocting love philtres to further genesiac exultation, to induce total participation in a sort of Aphroditic gnosticism.

The Aphroditic injunction embraced, in a sense, the entire cosmos. It involved primarily self-love, love of being, awareness of the significant entity, the ego itself, marked by dignity, by esteem. Then followed the love of the social milieu of which one formed part, and of the impulse to maintain its equilibrium by contributing one's own efforts, one's personal function, to the totality of the social frame. Lastly, there was a kind of all-embracing, comprehensive cosmic love, directed to a synthesis of corporeal love that mystically rose to a sublimated spiritual-amatory zone.

In the mystic cults, it was postulated that the amatory embrace partakes of both a human and a cosmic form of attraction, and becomes, in a sublimated degree, an act of prayer, an erotic supplication.

The priapic cult was the male counterpart of the Aphroditic cult. Just as the hierodule was the official priestess of the goddess, mentor in the feminine erotic and reverential mysteries, so the priapic cult had for its primary objective the exaltation of the male generative principle. In remote antiquity, and particularly in Egyptian mysticism, the phallus was the representative symbol of Osiris, the ultimate creative potency. Gradually, in the course of the centuries, the phallic symbol acquired a pejorative and degrading and exclusively and narrowly functional nature associated with the mere physical act. And Priapus, equated at one time with Osiris, degenerated into a secondary and minor figure, a mere rustic threat. Yet Priapus retained some semblance of his former repute. He still had his temple and his priestly ministrants. He still received favors and offerings. He still made promises to his devotees and listened to their urgent amatory pleas. He still maintained his sexual rituals, however much they had lost their spiritual and cosmic values. He still presided, in the actuality of performance, over marriage initiations, over nuptial consummations. But with time he disappeared as a member of the mystery cults. And only in vestiges of legend, in old rites transmitted into the Middle Ages, in sculptural presentations, in phallic symbolisms, did his former magnificence and his primary rank retain any fragmentary reminiscence of his vanished glories.

In the smaller towns of Italy festive occasions in honor of Priapus were perpetuated until far into the Middle Ages; and Priapus, in some instances, particularly in Brittany, in Belgium, and in France, merged with Christian saints, who appropriated, in their turn, the genesiac properties of their prototype.

In rural districts, shrines dedicated to Priapus defied the spread of Christianity, while phallic forms, in marble and stone, adorned public buildings, baths, columns, churches. Priapus, to some extent, thus went underground. He became a furtive and then an obsolescent and forgotten figure: but in Switzerland and in Sweden, in Provence and in Germany, Priapus clung tenaciously, if only in an etymological sense. For Friday, Friga's day, is merely a Teutonic or Anglo-Saxon form of the Day of Priapus.

Strange how the antique charms and periapts, the old Roman fascina, were still suspended from the necks of children and women: often without any awareness of the actual significance of the talisman, but just as frequently, until late into the fourteenth century at least, ecclesiastical ordinances and prohibitions made it evident that there was official knowledge of the priapic survival.

Among the ancient Chaldeans, Assyrians, and Babylonians, the erotic cult was dedicated to the fertility deities Ishtar and Bel and Sin. Ishtar was the Mesopotamian Aphrodite: a goddess of love and at the same time a warrior deity. Bel is Baal-Peor, the phallic deity, while Sin is the moon divinity.

Aphrodite, as a universal goddess, with universal erotic functions that embrace all humanity, all elements of the cosmos, appears in different regions and centuries under a variety of names. She is Aphrodite Callipygos and she is Aphrodite Anosia: Aphrodite Peribaso and Aphrodite Anadyomene and Aphrodite Hetaira. Sometimes she is designated with reference to her beauty, or to her amatory functions, or to her epichorial association with temple worship dedicated to her person, or to the suppliants whom she intimately protects. She is thus Aphrodite Pandemos and Aphrodite Porne. She is Aphrodite Trymalitis and Aphrodite Stratonikis. She is Aphrodite Pontia and Aphrodite Urania.

Then she becomes, retaining her essential character but merely transferring her rituals, Venus Fisica and Venus Caelesiis and Venus Erycian. She is the Cytherean and the Paphian, she is the Cyprian divinity.

She is known, again, as Anaïtis and as Astoreth. She is Allat and Argimpasa and Atargatis. In later ages she is Milda in Eastern Europe and Merta and Freya in the North.

But under whatever designation she appears, in Arabia or Scythia, in the Greek Islands or in Carthage, she is fertility incarnate and love. She is the alma Venus genetrix that the Roman poet Lucretius reverently invokes.

Through the ages the concept of generation has undergone progressively definitive changes. In proto-historical times, when legend and myth, mingling with supernatural fantasies, conceived imaginative unrealities in relation to the medical and physiological facts, the ancient Hindu epics assumed man as sprung from the forests, from aspen and ash trees, sylvan creatures, in some sense, corresponding to the half-human form of the ancient Hellenic satyrs. In some regions of India there was a belief that the produce of certain trees was human beings, male and female, and that the mortals fell upon the earth like ripe fruit. Among the Persians and contiguous races of antiquity, pregnant women were given soma juice to drink, to ensure handsome children. Soma is an intoxicating brew that is often mentioned in Vedic religious rituals. According to Pliny the Elder's testimony, water in which mistletoe has been steeped encourages procreation in women and animals.

The oak tree and the chestnut also have been reputed to aid in procreation. So with plants too, that have at all times been treated as potential and actual amatory aids. An African legend makes a girl, after drinking the juice of a certain plant, give birth to a mighty warrior.

The chewing of lilies was considered conducive to fertility, in medieval folklore. So, in still earlier times, with the pomegranate and the almond. In many cases, the belief arose from the similarity of the plant or flower or herb, in certain respects, to the genitalia or the pudenda. This was so in the case of the bean. So with mandrake, and cress, and certain species of berries.

Another legendary mode of conception, prevalent in ancient classical and Oriental mythology, was theriomorphic theogamy: that is, generation by a divinity who assumes animal form.

Instances are multiple. Zeus, in the shape of a bull, pursues Europa in cow form. In Egypt, Apis the bull has a similar function. The seductive serpent, again, is Zeus once more, exercising his protean capacity. On occasion, he becomes a swan, and associates with Leda. Or he becomes a variety of creatures: an ant, or a dove, or a goat, or an ass. Once, Neptune, for a similar purpose, turned into a ram.

Sometimes, also, the divine serpent, sinuous and wily and knowledgeable, is actually devoured by the woman, as in Arab regions.

Not only animals and plants were associated with generative capacities, but natural phenomena as well: the winds and storms, hail and the sun and the rain. Some primitive tribes attributed their origin to snow: some to lightning, or to thunder, to the rainbow, to clouds, to the morning star. A warm breeze, or a cyclone might equally well have been their source. Greek, Roman, and Chinese myths contain numberless illustrations of astral or phenomenal association with mortal generation.

There is a wry anecdote on this phase in Flavius Josephus, the historian. An ingenious suitor performs the function of the deity Anubis with complete faithful acceptance.

This type of mortal substitution in place of the divinity was common in the priestly rituals of Egypt, and was not unknown in Asia Minor, in India, and in China.

Periapts or talismans as an erotic provocation were anciently devised in phallic form. They were carried on the person, by both men and women, or were used to decorate temples and shrines and public buildings.

In later ages, amatory talismans assumed a great variety of forms, in the shape of rings, necklaces, plaques engraved with formulas or astrological figures and signs of the Zodiac or possibly a bull, a dove, a number or a series of mystic numbers. A piece of parchment might be inscribed with names, or the alphabetical sign of Venus. Precious stones were talismans, each possessing an esoteric virtue or property according to color or substance. A periapt might be set in some strategic spot: buried underground, placed under a pillow: or even ground into a powder.

The all-powerful goddess herself, Venus, had her own minerals. Copper, associated with the love goddess, was known to the Greeks as aphrodon. Tin also was of Aphroditic significance: while sulphur springs were also, in a legendary sense, related to Venus.

It has even been credited that floral nomenclature contains amatory significance, and that certain plants have their erotic symbolisms.

Flowers in antiquity as well as in modern times had their erotic implications. To the Greeks and Romans, the essence of *areté*, of beauty and perfection, was the rose, while the Egyptians too revered the rose as the prototype of perfection.

To Aphrodite were consecrated the mistletoe and myrtle, the lily, satyrion, the iris, celandine, sengreen, mallow, and verbena.

CHAPTER II
GREEK

Plato

Plato (c. 429–347 B.C.), the Greek philosopher who developed his metaphysical and cosmological theories through a series of some twenty-five dialogues and the *Apology*, has a great deal to say on the erotic theme.

In the *Timaeus*, he says of sexual excess:

He who has the seed about the spinal marrow too plentiful and overflowing, like a tree overladen with fruit, has many throes, and also obtains many pleasures in his desires and their offspring, and is for the most part of his life deranged because his pleasures and pains are so very great; his soul is rendered foolish and disordered by his body; yet he is regarded not as one diseased, but as one who is voluntarily bad, which is a mistake. The truth is that sexual intemperance is a disease of the soul due chiefly to the moisture and fluidity which is produced in one of the elements by the loose consistency of the bones. And in general, all that which is termed the incontinence of pleasure and is deemed a reproach under the idea that the wicked voluntarily do wrong is not justly a matter for reproach. For no man is voluntarily bad, but the bad become bad by reason of an ill disposition of the body and bad education—things which are hateful to every man and happen to him against his will.

Again, of sexual love, Plato says, in the *Timaeus*:

On the subject of animals, then, the following remarks may be offered. Of the men who came into the world, those who were cowards or led unrighteous lives may with reason be supposed to have changed into the nature of women in the second generation. And this was the reason why at that time the gods created in us the desire of sexual intercourse, contriving in man one animated substance, and in woman another, which they formed, respectively, in the following manner. The outlet for drink by which liquids pass through the lung under the kidneys and into the bladder, which receives and then by the pressure of the air emits them, was so fashioned by them as to penetrate also into the body of the marrow, which passes from the head along the neck and through the back, and which in the preceding discourse we have named the seed. And the seed, having life and becoming endowed with respiration, produces in that part in which it respires a lively desire of emission, and thus creates in us the love of procreation. Wherefore also in men the organ of generation becoming rebellious and masterful, like an animal disobedient to reason, and maddened with the sting of lust, seeks to gain absolute sway, and the same is the case with the so-called womb or matrix of women. The animal within them is desirous of procreating children, and when remaining unfruitful long beyond its proper time, gets discontented and angry, and wandering in every direction through the body, closes up the passages of the breath, and, by obstructing respiration, drives them to extremity, causing all varieties of disease, until at length the desire and love of the man and the woman, bringing them together and as it were plucking the fruit from the tree, sow in the womb, as in a field, animals unseen by reason of their smallness and without form; these again are separated and matured within; they are then finally brought out into the light, and thus the generation of animals is completed.

In the *Symposium*, Plato postulates a philosophy of love:

Love is the love of beauty and not of deformity?

He assented.

And the admission has been already made that love is of that

which a man wants and has not?

True, he said.

Then love wants and has not beauty?

Certainly, he replied.

And would you call that beautiful which wants and does not possess beauty?

Certainly not.

Then would you still say that love is beautiful?

Agathon replied: I fear that I did not understand what I was saying.

Nay, Agathon, replied Socrates; but I should like to

ask you one more question:—is not the good also the

beautiful?

Yes.

Then in wanting the beautiful love wants also the

good? I can not refute you, Socrates, said Agathon.

And let us suppose that what you say is true.

Say rather, dear Agathon, that you can not refute the

truth; for Socrates is easily refuted.

And now I will take my leave of you, and rehearse the tale of love which I heard once upon a time from Diotima of Mantineia, who was a wise woman in this and many other branches of knowledge. She was the same who deferred the plague of Athens ten years by a sacrifice, and was my instructress in the art of love. In the attempt which I am about to make I shall pursue Agathon's method, and begin with his admissions, which are nearly if not quite the same which I made to the wise woman when she questioned me: this will be the easiest way, and I shall take both parts myself as well as I can. For, like Agathon, she spoke first of the being and nature of love, and then of his works. And I said to her in nearly the same words which he

"As in the former instance, he is neither mortal fair; and she proved to me as I proved to him that, in my way of speaking about him, love was neither fair nor good. "What do you mean, Diotima," I said, "is love then evil and foul?"

"Hush," she cried; "is that to be deemed foul which is not fair?"

"Certainly," I said.

"And is that which is not wise, ignorant? do you not see that there is a mean between wisdom and ignorance?"

"And what is this?" I said.

"Right opinion," she replied; "which, as you know, being incapable of giving a reason, is not knowledge (for how could knowledge be devoid of reason? nor again, ignorance, for neither can ignorance attain the truth), but is clearly something which is a mean between ignorance and wisdom."

"Quite true," I replied.

"Do not then insist," she said, "that what is not fair is of necessity foul, or what is not good evil; or infer that because love is not fair and good he is therefore foul and evil; for he is in a mean between them."

"Well," I said, "love is surely admitted by all to be a great god."

"By those who know or by those who don't know?"

"By all."

"And how, Socrates," she said with a smile, "can love be acknowledged to be a great god by those who say that he is not a god at all?"

"And who are they?" I said.

"You and I are two of them," she replied.

"How can that be?" I said.

"That is very intelligible," she replied; "as you yourself would acknowledge that the gods are happy and fair—of course you would—would you dare to say that any god was not?"

"Certainly not," I replied.

"And you mean by the happy, those who are the possessors of things good and fair?"

"Yes."

"And you admitted that love, because he was in want, desires those good and fair things of which he is in want?"

"Yes, I admitted that."

"But how can he be a god who has no share in the good or the fair?"

"That is not to be supposed."

"Then you see that you also deny the deity of love."

"What then is love?" I asked; "Is he mortal?"

"No."

"What then?"

"As in the former instance, he is neither mortal nor immortal, but in a mean between them."

"What is he then, Diotima?"

"He is a great spirit, and like all that is spiritual he is intermediate between the divine and the mortal."

"And what is the nature of this spiritual power?" I said.

"This is the power," she said, "which interprets and conveys to the gods the prayers and sacrifices of men, and to men the commands and rewards of the gods; and this power spans the chasm which divides them, and in this all is bound together, and through this the arts of the prophet and the priest, their sacrifices and mysteries and charms, and all prophecy and incantation, find their way. For God mingles not with man; and through this power all the intercourse and speech of God with man, whether awake or asleep, is carried on. The wisdom which understands this is spiritual; all other wisdom, such as that of arts or handicrafts, is mean and vulgar. Now these spirits or intermediate powers are many and divine, and one of them is love."

"And who," I said, "was his father and who his mother?"

"The tale," she said, "will take time; nevertheless I will tell you. On the birthday of Aphrodite there was a feast of the gods, at which the god Poros or Plenty, who is the son of Metis or Discretion, was one of the guests. When the feast was over, Penia or Poverty, as the manner was, came about the doors to beg. Now Plenty, who was the worse for nectar (there was no wine in those days), came into the garden of Zeus and fell into a heavy sleep; and Poverty considering her own straitened circumstances, plotted to have him for a husband, and accordingly she lay down at his side and conceived love, who partly because he is naturally a lover of the beautiful, and because Aphrodite is herself beautiful, and also because he was born on Aphrodite's birthday is her follower and attendant."

(B. Jowett)

In Book 8 of *The Laws*, too, Plato discusses a variety of subjects, among them festivals and contests in which men and women meet together. This topic introduces the question of the sexes, and Plato makes definitive statements in this respect. Licentiousness, he declares, is abominable. Men ought to live under controlled moderation. That is what nature herself enjoins. Man otherwise would fall below the level of beasts. Here the laws should be restrictive. But if that is not possible, there must at least be some adherence to decent mores.

Lust and desire are discussed in Book 6 of *The Laws* and in the *Greater Hippias*. The three universal appetites are food, drink, and lust of procreation, which is linked with the imperious sexual frenzy and its concomitant excitements. Sexual desire, the necessities of love, overflowing into excesses, may be harmful to the welfare of the state. Excesses must therefore be stemmed and controlled by laws. In this manner evil may be diminished and the good of the state as a whole will be promoted.

With regard to exhausted capacity and the loss of passion as a corollary to old age, Plato says, in Book I of *The Republic*:

I will tell you, Socrates, he said, what my own feeling is. Men of my age flock together; we are birds of a feather, as the old proverb says; and at our meetings the tale of my acquaintance commonly is—I can not eat, I can not drink; the pleasures of youth and love are fled away; there was a good time once, but now that is gone, and life is no longer life. Some complain of the slights which are put upon them by relations, and they will tell you sadly of how many evils their old age is the cause. But to me, Socrates, these complainers seem to blame that which is not really at fault. For if old age were the cause, I too being old, and every other old man, would have felt as they do. But this is not my own experience, nor that of others whom I have known. How well I remember the aged poet Sophocles, when in answer to the question, How does love suit with age, Sophocles,—are you still the man you were? Peace, he replied; most gladly have I escaped from a mad and furious master. His words have often occurred to my mind since, and they seem as good to me now as at the time when he uttered them. For certainly old age has a great sense of calm and freedom; when the passions relax their hold, then, as Sophocles says, we are freed from the grasp not of one mad master only, but of many. The truth is, Socrates, that these regrets, and also the complaints about relations, are to be attributed to the same cause, which is not old age, but men's characters and tempers; for he who is of a calm and happy nature will hardly feel the pressure of age, but to him who is of an opposite disposition youth and age are equally a burden.

Of sexual appetite Plato declares, in Book 8 of *The Republic*:

Are not necessary pleasures those of which we can not get rid, and of which the satisfaction is a benefit to us? And they are rightly called so, because we are framed by nature to desire both what is beneficial and what is necessary, and can not help it.

True.

We are not wrong therefore in calling them necessary?

We are not.

And the desires of which a man may get rid, if he takes pains from his youth upwards—of which the presence, moreover, does no good, and in some cases the reverse of good—shall we not be right in saying that all these are unnecessary?

Yes, certainly.

Suppose we select an example of either kind, in order that we may have a general notion of them?

Very good.

Will not the desire of eating, that is, of simple food and condiments, in so far as they are required for health and strength, be of the necessary class?

That is what I should suppose.

The pleasure of eating is necessary in two ways; it does us good and it is essential to the continuance of life?

Yes.

But the condiments are only necessary in so far as they are good for health?

Certainly.

And the desire which goes beyond this, of more delicate food, or other luxuries, which might generally be got rid of, if controlled and trained in youth, and is hurtful to the body, and hurtful to the soul in the pursuit of wisdom and virtue, may be rightly called unnecessary?

Very true.

May we not say that these desires spend, and that the others make money because they conduce to production?

Certainly.

And of the pleasures of love, and all other pleasures, the same holds good?

True.

And the drone of whom we spoke was he who was surfeited in pleasures and desires of this sort, and was the slave of the unnecessary desires, whereas he who was subject to the necessary only was miserly and oligarchical?

Very true.

(B. Jowett)

Nakedness, both of boys and girls, was not an obscenity in ancient Greece. The statesman Lycurgus, for example, established exercises in Sparta in which boys and girls, in puris naturalibus, took part.

To the Greek philosopher Plato, too, nudity involved no indecency. He actually advocated, in *The Laws*, naked dances by boys and girls, for the purpose of mutual acquaintance.

Dioscorides

Pedanius Dioscorides, who flourished in the first century A.D., was born in Anazarbus. He became an army physician: but, in addition, he was deeply interested and versed in pharmacological subjects. With the purpose of compiling a kind of encyclopedic work in this field, Dioscorides traveled widely throughout Greece, Asia Minor, and the Mediterranean countries, collecting information, legends, and prescriptions.

Dioscorides is the author of a systematic Materia Medica, written with clarity and precision and with an informative rather than a stylistic purpose. His work includes plants and herbs, animals, minerals: all arranged in exact subdivisions, and emphasizing the medicinal and pharmacological virtues of all the items included. The text is arranged in five books, and covers some thousand drugs. An English translation, under the title of the Greek Herbal of Dioscorides, was produced by John Goodyer in 1655, and was edited by Robert T. Gunther and first printed by the Oxford University Press in 1934.

Apart from the fascination of the work in itself, Dioscorides lists a number of herbs and roots that are of amatory interest as philtres. Goodyer's text, for the relevant items, follows:

Greek Cyclamen: It is sayd also that the root is taken amongst love-procuring medicines being beaten, and soe made into Trochiscks. Trochiscks are pastilles.

Brassica Rapa: Turnip: Also called Gongule. The Romans call it Rapum. The roote of it being sod is nourishing, yet very windie, and breeding moist and loose flesh, and provoking to Venerie.

(As an infusion) being dranck it is good against deadly medicines, and doth provoke to Venerie.

Kuprinon: Oil of Cuperos. An invigorating oil.

Lolium Temulentum: Darnel: Being suffumigated with polenta, or Myrrh, or Saffron, or Franckincense, it doth help conceptions.

Cardamom Lepidium Sativum: Cress: Some call it Cynocardamom. The best is found in Babylon. The seed is effectual in inciting to copulation.

Orchis Rubra: Orchis Papilionacea: And of this root it is said that if the greater roote is eaten by men, it makes them beget males, and the lesser, being eaten by women, to conceive females. It is further storied that ye women in Thessalia do give to drink with goates milk ye tenderer root to provoke Venerie, and the dry root for ye suppressing, dissolving of Venerie. And that it being drank ye one is dissolved by the other.

Satyrion: Also called Trifolium, because 'it bears leaves in three's, as it were,' bending down to ye earth like to Rumex or Lilium, yet lesser, and reddish. But a naked stalk, long, as of a cubit, a flower like a Lilly, white; a bulbous root, as bigg as an apple, redd, but within white, like an egg, to ye taster sweet and pleasant to ye mouth. This one ought to drink in black hard wine for ye Opisthotonon, and use it, if he will lie with a woman. For they say that this also doth stirr up courage in ye conjunction.

Saturion Eruthronion: Called by the Romans Morticulum Veneris. It hath a seed like to flax seed. It is said that it doth stirr up conjunctions, like ye Scincus doth. It is storied that the root being taken into ye hand doth provoke to Venerie, but much more, being drank with wine.

Salvia Horminum: The Romans call it Geminales. It is an herb like to Marrubium. In the wild it is found round swart, but in the other somewhat long, and black, of which there is use, and this also is thought being drank with wine to provoke conjunction.

Galium Verum: Gallion. But ye root doth provoke to conjunction.

Katananke: The Romans call it Herba Filicula. The roots are of two kinds. 'But some report that both kinds are good for Philters, and they say that the Thessalian women do use them.'

Phuteuma: Also called Silene spurium. Phuteuma hath leaves like to Radicula, but smaller, much seed, bored through, little root, thin, close to the earth, which some relate to be good for a love medicine.

Nonnus

Nonnus was a Greek epic poet of Panopolis, in Egypt. He flourished in the fifth century A.D., and is the author of *Dionysiaca*. This is a long epic poem describing, in abundant detail, with picturesque imagery, the triumphal progression of Dionysus, god of wine and fertility, to India.

The poem is packed with quaint geographical lore, with a miscellaneous mass of information on astrology and plants and other subjects intertwined into the primary theme, and it also contains many erotic incidents of a mythological nature.

The Corybantes take a prominent place in the worship of Dionysus. They are the frantic, orgiastic priests of Cybele, the Mighty Mother of the Gods, and their passionate ceremonials touch the erotic field.

The handsome, effeminate Cadmus appears—the cheeks of his love-begetting face are red as roses, chants the poet: and the sight of Cadmus is itself an amatory urge.

It is effective, too, in the case of Harmonia, destined to be Cadmus' mate. Aphrodite addresses the prospective bride:

I will teach those grace-breathing kisses to women unhappy in love.

There was, evidently, knowledge of potions and similar excitants, for one character pleads:

Tell me what varied store of balsams can I apply in my heart to cure the wound of love.

And again:

I shrink before a woman, for she shoots bright shafts from her lovesmit countenance and pierces me with her beauty.

In the sixth century A.D., Theodora, a public courtesan whose name was a byword in Byzantium, became first the mistress and then the wife of the Roman Emperor Justinian. Even as an Empress she did not abandon her profligate ways. She had experienced and invited every possible variety of erotic practice. She went out with bands of youths and spent the night in their riotous company. Her erotic frenzies drove her to public exhibitionism. Often she had appeared in the theatre in puris naturalibus. Yet her personal beauty made the Emperor her blind slave, while her lusts extended in every direction.

The Greek chronicler Procopius describes the court of the Roman Emperor Justinian and his consort Theodora. The Imperial general attached to the court was Belisarius. He had a wife, named Antonina, who was so passionate that she consummated her erotic impulses, in relation to a youth named Theodosius, in the full presence of her servants and attendant maids.

The Byzantine general Belisarius, attached to the court of the Emperor Justinian, in the sixth century A.D., was again and again the victim of his wife's flagrant infidelities. Again and again, however, he forgave her. He permitted himself self-deception, in spite, at times, of the evidence of his own eyes. He was so deeply infatuated with her that he preferred to retain her at all costs.

The Greek orator Demosthenes, in one of his famous legal speeches, successfully pleaded for the death penalty in the case of one of the mistresses of the dramatist Sophocles. She was associated with a secret club, and was initiated in the preparation of philtres and magic potions.

Among the Greeks, the concept of love in the modern sense was rare. Nor was the medieval attitude to amatory sensibilities, embodied in courtly love, any more prevalent. Love, in a general sense, was treated as an aberration from normal life, a kind of sickness, a lack of balance in the elements of the entity. Yet there was, of course, as the Greek Anthology and other poetic testimony indicate, lust and passion and erotic intimacy. There was, too, a greater freedom in this relationship between men and public women, nor did this association affect in a negative sense the marriage relationship.

There were these professional public hetairae, female companions who often had marked intellectual endowments, whose association with poets and dramatists, statesmen and philosophers brought not the slightest stigma on such men in their artistic or public career. Aspasia of Miletus was one of the most outstanding of this group. She was the mistress of the statesman Pericles. Gnathaena and Lais were equally known. It was said that Plato was in love with the hetaira Archeanassa of Colophon. The comic poet Menander was associated with Glycera. Phryne, the priestess of Aphrodite, as she was termed, was the most beautiful of them all, the model for the sculptor Praxiteles' Aphrodite.

The seductive equipment of the hetaira was as various as in modern times, and as effective. It included diaphanous robes, of Coan silk, veils and scarves, mirrors and unguents and rouge, jewelry for neck and ears and arms. And the hetaira replenished her armory and refurbished her memory of her techniques: for there were at hand, for her constant use, manuals that contained guidance, amatory and financial and social, specific instructions in a multiplicity of hypothetical but more than probable cases, and ominous warnings as well.

CHAPTER III
ROMANS

In the first century B.C. the licentiousness of the Roman matron was already a subject for grim condemnation. Horace, who was virtually the Poet Laureate of the Augustan Age, laments the degeneration of morality. The temples are abandoned, he bewails, and lie in ruins. The sacred marriage vows are broken. The uprightness of the old domestic life is gone. Our own generation is plunging headlong into destruction. Against the women in particular he inveighs as follows:

The matron, when bidden, arises and goes forth publicly, not without the knowledge of her husband, whether some pedlar invites her, or the captain of a Spanish sailing vessel, who buys her shame at a high price.

A notorious, unsavory district in ancient Rome was known as the Subura. It was a valley lying between the Esquiline and the Viminal Hills of the city. This area was clamorous with brothels, with the dregs of Romans, foreigners, slavers, pimps, and harlots. Loads of marble passed through the narrow alleys. The lanes were cluttered with mules, dogs, goats, and sheep.

There were also shops of various kinds, practically nothing but openings in the wall spaces, where provisions were sold and various delicacies. Barbers and tailors plied their occupations, while minor trades, according to epigraphical evidence, were also conducted here. Julius Caesar himself resided in the Subura. There was also a Jewish synagogue in this district. The Subura is mentioned frequently in Roman literature, in a derogatory and contemptuous sense, particularly by the poets Juvenal, Persius, and Martial.

In the Subura all kinds of amatory contrivances, concoctions and aids were offered to an eager clientele: amulets, incantations, spells, philtres, drugs; and a flourishing market in these commodities prevailed, at first furtively and warily: then with more determined and acknowledged public awareness.

The Roman satirist Juvenal, who dates in the first century A.D., mentions potions and philtres used by women; frequently, however, for purposes of torture or poisoning their husbands. Again, describing the immoralities and licentiousness of the frantic Roman matrons of his own days, Juvenal thunders:

From one person she secures magic incantations. From another, she buys Thessalian love-potions to destroy her husband's mind.

The Roman poet Lucan produced an epic poem entitled *Pharsalia*. Book 6 contains a vivid, elaborate description of magic scenes and practices. The capacities of the witch are enumerated with a feeling of mounting horror. Her skills come in for horrendous comment: brewing concoctions for malefic purposes: pronouncing incantations that inspire strange passions by virtue of their goetic potency. These spells, the poet awesomely declares, are more effective than even love goblets.

The implication is that love philtres were manifestly in common use for amatory purposes and in common knowledge.

Certain deities were anciently associated with particular sexual practices. Volupia, an old Roman goddess mentioned by St. Augustine, encouraged voluptuous pleasures. Strenia bestowed vigor on the male. Stimula aroused the erotic desires of husbands.

The practice of amatory aids, among the Romans, reached as far as the Imperial court. The Emperor Julian, known as the Apostate, for instance, mentions, in a letter to his friend Callixenes, mandrake as a love agent.

In antiquity, both Greek and Roman, Medea is the arch sorceress, the supreme exemplar of witchcraft, the most powerful adept in the Black Arts of Colchis.

Seneca, the Stoic philosopher and dramatist, who was also the tutor of the Roman Emperor Nero, is the author of a drama entitled *Medea*, in which he depicts the protagonist herself in frenzied action.

Medea's nurse appears upon the scene, speaking of her mistress.

She describes Medea gathering potent herbs with her magic sickle, by the light of the moon. Medea sprinkles the herbs with venom extracted from serpents. Into this compound she thrusts the entrails and organs of unclean birds: the heart of the screech owl, vampire's vitals, torn from the living flesh. Over the entire foul brew she murmurs her magic incantations, concocting her philtres.

In spite of the frenzied commerce in philtres and other means of stimulation, both in ancient and in modern times, Ovid himself, the Roman poet who produced the superlative amatory guides in poetic form, asserts categorically that invocations and formulas, enchantments and sorcery, secretive recipes and exotic philtres are ultimately of no avail in their purpose. Even witches and enchantresses such as Medea and Circe, for all their skill in the goetic arts, could not circumvent man's own personal perversities, or prevent Jason, for instance, or Ulysses, from amatory unfaithfulness.

In the contest of love, then, concludes the poet, philtres achieve nothing but imbalanced minds, wrecked health, and, sometimes, death itself.

Love philtres were not infrequently fatal in their effects. Such veneficia amatoria were forbidden by imperial decree. But there were furtive ways of circumventing these prohibitions.

Ingredients, apart from their poisonous nature, might be nauseating and repulsive to administer. As an instance, the milk of an ass mixed with the blood of a bat was considered a genesiac encouragement. The ingredients, again, might induce sickness, madness, and even death.

Among known ingredients that went to form the final, putatively effective brew were herbs, organs of birds, insects, blood, and genitalia.

With the ages, the range of ingredients and recipes was extended. In Mediterranean regions old traditional amatory philtres remained in folk use. In other areas, particularly in the South American continent, the natives used concoctions that were often virtual poisons. For they ceaselessly ransacked the forests and jungles for amatory aids.

Among the Romans, the sepia octopus had a wide reputation for its amatory potential. It is mentioned by the Roman comedy writer Plautus. In a scene depicting an exhausted elder, an octopus is bought by him at the market, as a rejuvenating aid.

In his *De Re Coquinaria*, a cookery book produced by Apicius, a Roman of the first century A.D., there are many recipes for the preparation of gourmet dishes as well as less luxurious fare: fish and game, meats, vegetables, fruit, dessert, cereals.

Among the herbs that Apicius includes as ingredients in stews, roasts, pottages, soups, and sauces, there are many that had and still have reputedly, an amatory reaction, as: cumin and dill, aniseed, bay-berry, celery-seed, capers and caraway, sesame, mustard, shallots, nard, thyme, ginger and musk, wormwood, basil, parsley, origanum, pennyroyal, rocket, safflower, rue-berry, flowers of mallow, rue-seed, lovage, hyssop and garlic and capers.

Many vegetables, too, that are credited with genesiac virtue are included in Apicius' book, as: artichokes and beans, asparagus, turnips, truffles, parsnips and leeks, beets and bryony, cabbage, chicory, cucumbers, fenugreek, radishes, and lettuce.

Apicius' culinary directions and preparations include a variety of fish that had, in Rome times and also in later ages, provocative amatory properties. Among such piscatory agents are: Grilled red mullet, young tunny, sea-bream, murena, horse-mackerel, gold-bream. And, among sea food: octopus and mussels, sea-urchin, oysters, cuttlefish, squid, sea-crayfish, electric ray.

In some of the fragments and extant verses of the Roman philosopher Seneca, there are illustrations of the erotic theme. In one poem the partly obliterated verses run:

Love, my darling, and be loved in turn always,

So that at no instant may our mutual love cease ...

From sunrise to sunset,

And may the Evening Star gaze

upon our love

And the Morning Star too.

An instance of abnormal lust also occurs:

Fortunate is she who caresses your neck.

Fortunate is the girl who presses close to you, body

To body,

And crushes her tongue against your soft lips.

Another fragment inveighs against a wealthy, beautiful, noble matron, lustful and incestuous.

In ancient Italy the cult of Liber or Bacchus was so widespread that festivals held in his honor and called Liberalia were continued for an entire month. During this period the phallus, carried in procession exultantly, to the accompaniment of lewd songs, lascivious talk, and obscene gestures, was decked with garlands, while erotic acts in their final consummation were freely performed in public view, as reverential testimony to the potency of the deity so symbolized.

The cult of Bacchus and of his symbol the phallus was introduced among the Romans by the priests of Cybele, the Mighty Mother of the Gods, who were known as Corybantes. Clement of Alexandria, the Church Father, also calls these priests Cabiri.

In the Imperial Age of Rome, a certain distinguished poet, Verginius Rufus, an elderly friend of Pliny the Younger, was known for his erotic poems. These, however, are no longer extant.

In Imperial Rome, the professors of grammar and of rhetoric, two of the basic subjects taught to young Romans, used many Greek and Roman authors in bowdlerized versions. In the case of the lyric poets in particular, the suggestive and erotic elements were minimized or excised.

During the Imperial Age of Rome, writers appeared at intervals who were cumulatively known as *scriptores erotici*—writers on love themes. Their tales, elaborately expanded and decked out with circumstantial details, were concerned with the amatory adventures of mythological personalities, among them, for instance, Acontius and Cydippe.

The Roman epigrammatist Martial (c. 40 A.D.–c. 104) claimed that, despite his obscene verses, his own personal life was unstained. He produced a large body of epigrams and occasional poems dealing, to a very considerable extent, with erotic and sexual topics: perversions, sodomy and incest, adultery and pederasty. His pieces mention actual contemporary figures, and thus present a realistic and intimate picture of Roman salacious aberrations at all levels of society, as well as the erotic degeneration of the age.

The Emperor Nero, with all his inhuman and vicious traits and bloody crimes, was a versatile poet. He was the author of sportive and also erotic pieces, none of which, however, are now extant.

Among the rites practiced by the Romans with respect to the cult of Priapus, there was the custom of the bride who, seated before the phallic image, made at least a symbolic contact, and most commonly an actual one, with a view to encourage later marital fecundity. It was at the same time an apotropaic measure as well. Married women were included in this ritual, and participated in similar practices. These rites, described in violently condemnatory terms, are mentioned by St. Augustine and Lactantius and Arnobius, who take occasion to point out the Roman pagan abominations in sexual matters.

With respect to the cult of Bacchus, the god himself had in his service women as priestesses. In the fanes dedicated to the phallic god, these priestesses celebrated nocturnal mystic rites. This practice is described in some detail by Petronius, the author of the remarkable Roman picaresque novel entitled the *Satyricon*:

We had resolv'd to keep out of the broad streets, and accordingly took our walk thro' that quarter of the city where we were likely to meet least company; when in a narrow winding lane that had not passage thro', we saw somewhat before us, two comely matron-like women, and followed them at a distance to a chappel, which they entred, whence we heard an odd humming kind of noise, as if it came from the hollow of a cave: Curiosity also made us go in after them, where we saw a number of women, as mad as they had been sacrificing to Bacchus, and each of them an amulet, the ensign of Bacchus, in her hand. More than that we could not get to see; for they no sooner perceived us, that they set up such a shout, that the roof of the temple shook agen, and withal endeavored to lay hands on us; but we scamper'd and made what haste we could to the inn.

Nor had we sooner stuff'd our selves with the supper Gito had got for us, when a more than ordinary bounce at the door, put us into another fright; and when we, pale as death, ask'd who was there, 'twas answered, "Open the door and you'll see." While we were yet talking, the bolt drop'd off, and the door flew open, on which, a woman with her head muffl'd came in upon us, but the same who a little before had stood by the country-man in the market: "And what," said she, "do you think to put a trick upon me? I am Quartilla's maid, whose sacred recess you so lately disturb'd: she is at the inn-gate, and desires to speak with ye: not that she either taxes your inadvertency, or has a mind to so resent it, but rather wonders, what gods brought such civil gentlemen into her quarters."

We were silent as yet, and gave her the hearing, but inclin'd to neither part of what she had said, when in came Quartilla her self, attended with a young girl, and sitting down by me, fell a weeping: nor here also did we offer a word, but stood expecting what those tears at command meant. At last when the showre had emptied it self, she disdainfully turn'd up her hood, and clinching her fingers together, till the joints were ready to crack, "What impudence," said she, "is this? or where learnt ye those shamms, and that sleight of hand ye have so lately been beholding to? By my faith, young-men, I am sorry for ye; for no one beheld what was unlawful for him to see, and went off unpunisht: and verily our part of the town has so many deities, you'll sooner find a god than a man in't: And that you may not think I came hither to be revenged on ye, I am more concern'd for your youth, than the injury ye have done me: for unawares, as I yet think, ye have committed an unexpiable abomination."

Among the Romans the symbol of satisfied and contented love was the myrtle branch, offered in sacrifice, along with milk and honey, to the obscene deity Priapus.

As a fetish, an apotropaic periapt, protective against all kinds of mishaps, the Romans made use of an amulet in the form of a fascinum. It was fashioned of various materials, often in the shape of a phallic symbol in high relief, on a plaque or medallion. The object was hung round children's necks, on garden walls, on doors, or chariots, and on public buildings.

The Roman historian Julian Capitolinus, in his biography of the Emperor Pertinax, mentions glass vessels, phallic-shaped, that were used by the Romans for drinking. These vessels were known as phallovitroboli.

The ithyphallic concept as the source of creation was so deeply ingrained in the Roman consciousness, that they attached the ithyphallic device on all manner of objects: stones, seals, rings, medals, and lamps. As an extension of this concept, the Romans engraved on their drinking vessels phallic designs, as well as lewd scenes that would create in the drinker violent erotic provocations.

Sextus Pompeius Festus was a Roman lexicographer of the second century A.D., who describes a shrine in Rome dedicated to the obscene deities Mutunus and Tutunus. In this religious cult the suppliants were women. With head veiled, they came to offer sacrifice to the phallic powers.

The lewd rites of the phallic god Bacchus were celebrated by the Romans in a sacred wood near the River Tiber. Originally open to women only, the ceremonies were later on extended to men also, particularly to young men not over twenty years of age. At the nocturnal rituals there was clashing of cymbals, beating of drums. After an interval of excessive wine drinking, there ensued wild scenes of sexual promiscuity and perversions unlimited. Those initiates who seemed to have any scruples were sacrificed, and their bodies were thrown into the depths of a cavern. Men and women went frantic, shrieking their exultation to the deity, performing abandoned dance sequences. Sinister plots and furtive machinations also formed part of the aftermath of these tenebrous rites, malefic in their intentions, often fatal in their effects.

In addition to Priapus as the supreme generative deity, the Romans were dedicated to a number of other divinities endowed with analogous properties. Venus herself was worshipped at Rome in four temples.

A late Latin poem, entitled Pervigilium Veneris, *The Vigil of Venus*, the date and authorship of which are unknown, is dedicated to Venus and her spring festival. The poem itself is full of vernal descriptions. The theme is a paean to erotic passion. Its amatory refrain, the sense of which pervades the entire poem, runs:

Cras amet qui numquam amavit,

Quique amavit cras amet.

He who has never loved will love tomorrow.

And he who has loved will love tomorrow.

A still older deity was Flora, associated with the blossoming of plants and hence with cosmic generation. At her festival, held during the month of April, lewd farces were performed, all implicitly generative and genesiac in intent.

One of the most mysterious and libidinous cults in Rome was that of the Bona Dea, the Good Goddess, to which women only had access. An annual ceremonial was held in her honor, when a sow was sacrificed to her.

Juvenal, the satiric poet, describes the excesses of the initiates. Frenzied with intoxication, overwhelmed with deafening and clamorous music, these women practiced the most salacious dances. In their lubricity they were athirst for erotic conflict, and were even willing, adds the poet, to submit to bestial caresses.

Among the Roman deities associated with marriage rites and connubial consummations were: Stimula, who aroused the male erotic urges: Strenia, who furnished vigor: Virginiensis, who detached the bride's zona or girdle: Volupia, who excited voluptuous sensations: Iugatinus, who united the marital partners. Also Domiducus, who conducted the bride to her new home: Munturnae, who presided over her settlement in her new position: and, more intimately involved in the physiological performance, Liber and Libera, Pertunda, Prema, and Subigus.

The Romans represented the male and female genitalia in the shapes of their wheaten-flour loaves. The epigrammatist Martial, in Book 9, 2, alludes to this priapic custom:

Illa siligineis pinguescit adultera cunnis.

The Roman poet Ovid (32 B.C.–17 A.D.) presents the ancient witch Medea in action. She invokes aid in concocting a potion to refurbish old age and induce youthful vigor:

Ye spells and arts that the wise men use; and thou, O Earth, who dost provide the wise men with thy potent herbs; ye breezes and winds, ye mountains and streams and pools; all ye gods of the groves, all ye gods of the night; be with me now. With your help I stir up the calm seas by my spell; I break the jaws of serpents with my incantations. I bid ghosts to come forth from their tombs. Now I have need of juices by whose aid old age may be renewed and may turn back to the bloom of youth and regain its earthly years.

The Roman elegiac poet Tibullus (c. 48 B.C.–19 B.C.) addresses Delia, the girl who scorned him. He has employed magic means to regain her love:

Thrice I with Sulphur purified you round,

And thrice the Rite, with Songs th'Enchantress bound:

The Cake, by me thrice sprinkled, put to flight

The death-denouncing Phantoms of the Night,

And I next have, in linen Garb array'd,

In silent Night, nine Times to Trivia pray'd.

In one of the Eclogues of the Roman poet Nemesianus, who flourished in the third century A.D., there is a dialogue between two shepherds who discuss their amatory affairs and love spells:

Mopsus: What does it benefit me that the mother of rustic Amyntas has purified me thrice with fillets, thrice with a sacred bough, thrice with the vapour of frankincense, burning the crackling laurels with live sulphur, and pours the ashes out into the stream with averted face, when thus wretched I am every way inflamed for Meroë?

Lycidas: These same things the many-colored threads have done for me, and Mycale has carried round me a thousand unknown herbs. She has chanted the charm, by which the moon swells, by which the snake is burst, the rocks run and standing corn removes, and a tree is plucked up. Lo! My handsome Iollas is nevertheless more, is more to me.

Horace, the Roman poet (65 B.C.–8 B.C.) depicts, in his *Satires*, a scene in which a love philtre is prepared.

As thus the boy in wild distress

Bewail'd, of bulla stripp'd and dress,

So fair, that ruthless breasts of Thrace

Had melted to behold his face,

Canidia, with dishevell'd hair

And short crisp vipers coiling there,

Beside a fire of Colchos stands,

And her attendant hag commands

To feed the flames with fig-trees torn

From dead men's sepulchres forlorn,

With dismal cypress, eggs rubb'd o'er

With filthy toads' unvenom'd gore,

With screech-owl's plumes, and herbs of bane,

From far Iolchos fetch'd and Spain,

And fleshless bones by beldam witch

Snatch'd from the jaws of famish'd bitch.

And Sagana, the while, with gown

Tucked to the knees, stalks up and down,

Sprinkling in room and hall and stair

Her magic hell-drops, with her hair

Bristling on end, like furious boar,

Or some sea-urchins wash'd on shore;

Whilst Veia, by remorse unstay'd,

Groans at her toil, as she with spade

That flags not digs a pit, wherein

The boy imbedded to his chin,

With nothing seen save head and throat,

Like those who in the water float,

Shall dainties see before him set,

A maddening appetite to whet,

Then snatch'd away before his eyes,

Till famish'd in despair he dies;

That when his glazing eyeballs should

Have closed on the untasted food,

His sapless marrow and dry spleen

May drug a philtre-draught obscene.

Nor were these all the hideous crew,

But Ariminian Folia, too,

Who with unsatiate lewdness swells,

And drags by her Thessalian spells

The moon and stars down from the sky,

Ease-loving Naples' vows, was by;

And every hamlet round about

Declares she was, beyond a doubt.

Now forth the fierce Canidia sprang,

And still she gnawed with rotten fang

Her long sharp unpared thumb-nail. What

Then said she? Yea, what said she not?

"O Night and Dian, who with true

And friendly eyes my purpose view,

And guardian silence keep, whilst I

My secret orgies safely ply,

Assist me now, now on my foes

With all your wrath celestial close!

Whilst, stretch'd in soothing sleep, amid

Their forests grim the beasts lie hid,

May all Suburra's mongrels bark

At yon old wretch, who through the dark

Doth to his lewd encounters crawl,

And on him draw the jeers of all!

He's with an ointment smear'd, that is

My masterpiece. But what is this?

Why, why should poisons brew'd by me

Less potent than Medea's be,

By which, for love betray'd, beguiled,

On mighty Creon's haughty child

She wreaked her vengeance sure and swift,

And vanish'd, when the robe, her gift,
In deadliest venom steep'd and dyed,
Swept off in flames the new-made bride?
No herb there is, nor root in spot
However wild, that I have not;
Yet every common harlot's bed
Seems with some rare Nepenthe spread,
For there he lives in swinish drowse,
Of me oblivious, and his vows!
He is, aha! protected well
By some more skilful witch's spell!
But, Varus, thou (doom'd soon to know
The rack of many a pain and woe!)
By potions never used before
Shalt to my feet be brought once more.
And 'tis no Marsian charm shall be
The spell that brings thee back to me!
A draught I'll brew more strong, more sure,
Thy wandering appetite to cure;
And sooner 'neath the sea the sky
Shall sink, and earth upon them lie,
Than thou not burn with fierce desire
For me, like pitch in sooty fire!"

On this the boy by gentle tones
No more essay'd to move the crones,
But wildly forth with frenzied tongue
These curses Thyestean flung.
"Your sorceries, and spells, and charms
To man may compass deadly harms,

But heaven's great law of Wrong and Right

Will never bend before their might.

My curse shall haunt you, and my hate

No victim's blood shall expiate.

But when at your behests I die,

Like the Fury of the Night will I

From Hades come, a phantom sprite—

Such is the Manes' awful might."

The Roman poet Vergil (70 B.C.–19 B.C.) depicts, in one of his pastoral Eclogues, a love episode that involves magic rites for the purpose of winning the love of Daphnis:

Scarce had night's cold shade parted from the sky, just at the time that the dew on the tender grass is sweetest to the cattle, when leaning on his smooth olive wand Damon thus began:

Rise, Lucifer, and usher in the sky, the genial sky, while I, deluded by a bridegroom's unworthy passion for my Nisa, make my complaint, and turning myself to the gods, little as their witness has stood me in stead, address them nevertheless, a dying man, at this very last hour. Take up with me, my pipe, the song of Maenalus.

Maenalus it is whose forests are ever tuneful, and his pines ever vocal; he is ever listening to the loves of shepherds, and to Pan, the first who would not have the reeds left unemployed. Take up with me, my pipe, the song of Maenalus.

Mopsus has Nisa given him; what may not we lovers expect to see? Matches will be made by this between griffins and horses, and in the age to come hounds will accompany timid does to their draught. Mopsus, cut fresh brands for to-night; it is to you they are bringing home a wife. Fling about nuts as a bridegroom should; it is for you that Hesperus is leaving his rest on Oeta. Take up with me, my pipe, the song of Maenalus.

O worthy mate of a worthy lord! There as you look down on all the world, and are disgusted at my pipe and my goats, and my shaggy brow, and this beard that I let grow, and do not believe that any god cares aught for the things of men. Take up with me, my pipe, the song of Maenalus.

It was in our enclosure I saw you gathering apples with the dew on them. I myself showed you the way, in company with my mother—my twelfth year had just bidden me enter on it. I could just reach from the ground to the boughs that snapped so easily. What a sight! what ruin to me! what a fatal frenzy swept me away! Take up with me, my pipe, the song of Maenalus.

Now know I what love is; it is among savage rocks that he is produced by Tmarus or Rhodope, or the Garamantes at earth's end; no child of lineage or blood like ours. Take up with me, my pipe, the song of Maenalus.

Love, the cruel one, taught the mother to embrue her hands in her children's blood; hard too was thy heart, mother. Was the mother's heart harder, or the boy god's malice more wanton? Wanton was the boy god's malice; hard too thy heart, mother. Take up with me, my pipe, the song of Maenalus.

Aye, now let the wolf even run away from the sheep; let golden apples grow out of the tough heart of oak; let narcissus blossom on the alder; let the tamarisk's bark sweat rich drops of amber; rivalry let there be between swans and screech-owls; let Tityrus become Orpheus—Orpheus in the woodland, Arion among the dolphins. Take up with me, my pipe, the song of Maenalus.

Nay, let all be changed to the deep sea. Farewell, ye woods! Headlong from the airy mountain's watchtower I will plunge into the waves; let this come to her as the last gift of the dying. Cease, my pipe, cease at length the song of Maenalus.

Thus far Damon; for the reply of Alphesiboeus, do ye recite it, Pierian maids; it is not for all of us to have command of all.

Bring out water and bind the altars here with a soft woolen fillet, and burn twigs full of sap and male frankincense, that I may try the effect of magic rites in turning my husband's mind from its soberness; there is nothing but charms wanting here. Bring me home from the town, my charms, bring me my Daphnis.

Charms have power even to draw the moon down from heaven; by charms Circe transformed the companions of Ulysses; the cold snake as he lies in the fields is burst asunder by chanting charms. Bring me home from the town, my charms, bring me my Daphnis.

These three threads distinct with three colours I wind round the first, and thrice draw the image round the altar thus; heaven delights in an uneven number. Twine in three knots, Amaryllis, the three colours; twine them, Amaryllis, do, and say, 'I am twining the bonds of Love.' Bring me home from the town, my charms, bring me my Daphnis.

Just as this clay is hardened, and this wax melted, by one and the same fire, so may my love act doubly on Daphnis. Crumble the salt cake, and kindle the crackling bay leaves with bitumen. Daphnis, the wretch, is setting me on fire; I am setting this bay on fire about Daphnis. Bring me home from the town, my charms, bring me my Daphnis.

May such be Daphnis' passion, like a heifer's, when, weary of looking for her mate through groves and tall forests, she throws herself down by a stream of water on the green sedge, all undone, and forgets to rise and make way for the fargone night—may such be his enthralling passion, nor let me have a mind to relieve it. Bring me home from the town, my charms, bring me my Daphnis.

These cast-off relics that faithless one left me days ago, precious pledges for himself, them I now entrust to thee, Earth, burying them even on the threshold; they are bound as pledges to give me back Daphnis. Bring me home from the town, my charms, bring me my Daphnis.

These plants and these poisons culled from Pontus I had from Moeris' own hand. They grow in plenty at Pontus. By the strength of these often I have seen Moeris turn to a wolf and plunge into the forest, often call up spirits from the bottom of the tomb, and remove standing crops from one field to another. Bring me home from the town, my charms, bring me my Daphnis.

Carry the embers out of doors, Amaryllis, and fling them into the running stream over your head, and do not look behind you. This shall be my device against Daphnis. As for gods or charms, he cares for none of them. Bring me home from the town, my charms, bring me my Daphnis.

Look, look! the flickering flame has caught the altar of its own accord, shot up from the embers, before I have had time to take them up, all of themselves. Good luck, I trust! Can I trust myself? Or is it that lovers make their own dreams? Stop, he is coming from town; stop now, charms, my Daphnis!

A renewal of vigor by magic means is described in Ovid's *Metamorphoses*. The scene involves the witch Medea, her lover Jason, and Jason's aged father, Aeson:

Unaccompanied, she stepped uncertainly through the still silence of midnight. Deep slumber had relaxed men and birds and wild beasts. Without a sound, the hedges, the motionless branches lay still. The dewy air was still. Lonely, the stars glimmered. Thrice extending her arms, she turned toward them. Thrice, taking some water, she copiously bedewed her locks. Thrice she uttered howls from her lips. Then, on bent knee, touching the hard ground, she said:

"O night, most propitious for mysteries, and you, golden stars, that, along with the moon, follow the fiery day, and you, triple Hecate, who, aware of our undertaking come forth to help in incantation and magic art, and you, Earth, who teach magicians the potency of herbs, and you, zephyrs and winds and hills and streams and lakes, and all you gods of the groves, be my aid. By your aid, when I so willed, the streams returned to their springs to the astonishment of the river banks, and by your aid I stay the upturned waters and upheave the stagnant straits by spells, and I drive away the clouds and bring them back, and banish and summon the winds and break the jaws of snakes with my words and spells, and move natural rocks and trees uprooted from the ground and forests and I bid the mountains tremble and the ground rumble, and the spirits of the dead arise from the tomb. You also, O Moon, I draw down, and Helios' chariot too pales at my incantation. The Dawn grows pale with my poisons. All of you have quenched the flames of the oxen for me and pressed their necks, reluctant for the task, under the crooked plough. You brought wars upon the serpent-born warriors and sleep upon the grim guardian.

Now there is need of juices whereby old age revived may bloom once more, and regain its former years. And you deities will grant this request—for not in vain is the chariot at hand, drawn by winged dragons."

There was the chariot, sent from high heaven. No sooner had she mounted and soothed the frenzied necks of the dragons and shaken the reins lightly with her hands than she was whisked off aloft, and beheld the herbs growing on Mount Ossa and lofty Pelion and Othrys and Pindus and Olympus greater than Pindus. She plucked out suitable herbs by the root, and some she cut away with the curved blade of a bronze sickle. The herbs that grew thick on the banks of the Apidanus caught her fancy too and those on the banks of the Amphrysus. Nor were you overlooked, Enipeus: and the Peneus and the waters of the Spercheus contributed their quota, and the reedy banks of the Boebeis. Medea gathered too the sturdy grasses in Euboean Anthedon. And now when the ninth day had seen her traversing all the fields in her winged-dragon chariot, she returned.

As she advanced, she halted at the threshold and the gate, and stood under the sky. And she shunned contacts with men: and set up two altars of turf, on the right of Hecate, on the left of Youth. After she had wreathed them with vervain and wild foliage, close by she made a sanctuary by means of two ditches, and pierced the throat of a black ram with the sacrificial knife, and soaked the wide ditches in the blood.

Then she poured over it a beaker of flowing wine and a bronze beaker of warm milk and at the same time murmured words over it, and called upon the divinities of the earth, and begged the King of the Lower Regions and his stolen wife not to hasten to rob the limbs of the aged soul.

When she had propitiated them with prayer and many a chant, she bade that the exhausted body of Aeson be carried out of doors, and on the strewn herbs she extended the lifeless shape, relaxed by incantation in deep slumber. She bade Aeson's son stand clear away, and the attendants too, and she admonished them to withdraw their profane sight from the mysteries. So bidden, they scattered in different directions. With disheveled hair, like a Bacchante, Medea encircled the blazing altars. She dipped finely split torches in the dark pool of gore, and lighted the bloody brands on the two altars. Thrice she encircled the aged body with fire, thrice with water, thrice with sulphur.

Meanwhile the potent drug boiled in the bronze kettle and leapt and whitened in the swelling froth. She threw in roots cut in Thessalian valley and seeds and blossoms and pungent spices. She added pebbles secured from the remote East and sands washed by the refluent Ocean stream. She added too the frost caught in the full moon and the baleful wings of a screech-owl together with the flesh itself, and the entrails of a werewolf wont to change its animal form into a man. Nor was there lacking the scaly skin of a water-serpent, the liver of a living stag. In addition, she threw in the head of a crow nine centuries old. By these and a thousand other unspeakable means she planned to delay the destined function of Tartarus. With a dry twig of long softened olive she stirred all the ingredients together, turning them over from top to bottom.

Behold now the old twig stirring in the boiling kettle first turned green, and presently put forth leaves, and suddenly became loaded with heavy olives. But wherever the fire belched out foam from the hollow kettle and the drops fell hot on the ground, the soil grew fresh, and flowers and soft grass sprang up.

As soon as she beheld this sight, with drawn sword Medea pierced the aged man's throat and, allowing the old blood to exude, filled the spot with juices. After Aeson had drunk them, either with his lips or through his wound, his beard and hair, shedding their greyness, quickly assumed a dark color. The emaciation vanished, and the pallor and decay disappeared, and the hollow wrinkles were filled up in the fresh body, and the limbs grew rapidly.

Aeson stood amazed, recalling that this was how he was forty years back.

Petronius, who belongs in the first century A.D., produced a remarkable novel entitled *The Satyricon*, in which he describes an instance of renewed virility by means of witchcraft:

"This is the custom, Sir," said she, "and chiefly of this City, where the women are skill'd in Magick-charms, enough to make the Moon confess their power, therefore the recovery of any useful Instrument of Love becomes their care; 'tis only writing some soft tender things to my Lady, and you make her happy in a kind return. For 'tis confest, since her Disappointment, she has not been her self."

I readily consented, and calling for Paper, thus addrest myself:

"'Tis confest, Madam, I have often sinned, for I'm not only a Man, but a very young one, yet never left the Field so dishonorably before. You have at your Feet a confessing Criminal, that deserves whatever you inflict: I have cut a Throat, betray'd my Country, committed Sacrilege; if a punishment for any of these will serve, I am ready to receive sentence. If you fancy my death, I wait you with my Sword; but if a beating will content you, I fly naked to your Arms. Only remember, that 'twas not the Workman, but his Instruments that fail'd: I was ready to engage, but wanted Arms. Who rob'd me of them I know not; perhaps my eager mind outrun my body; or while with an unhappy haste I aim'd at all; I was cheated with Abortive joys. I only know I don't know what I've done: You bid me fear a Palsie, as if the Disease cou'd do greater that has already rob'd me of that, by which I shou'd have purchas'd you. All I have to say for my self, is this, that I will certainly pay with interest the Arrears of Love, if you allow me time to repair my misfortune."

Having sent back Chrysis with this Answer, to encourage my jaded Body, after the Bath and Strengthening Oyles, had a little rais'd me, I apply'd my self to strong meats, such as strong Broths and Eggs, using Wine very moderately; upon which to settle my self, I took a little Walk, and returning to my Chamber, slept that night without Gito; so great was my care to acquit my self honourably with my Mistress, that I was afraid he might have tempted my constancy, by tickling my Side.

The next day rising without prejudice, either to my body or spirits, I went, tho' I fear'd the place was ominous, to the same Walk, and expected Chrysis to conduct me to her Mistress; I had not been long there, e're she came to me, and with her a little Old Woman. After she had saluted me, "What, my nice Sir Courtly," said she, "does your Stomach begin to come to you?"

At what time, the Old Woman, drawing from her bosome, a wreath of many colours, bound my Neck; and having mixt spittle and dust, she dipt her finger in't, and markt my Fore-head, whether I wou'd or not.

In Rome the inns—the tabernae, the popinae, and the ganea—were virtually, in addition to their primary purpose in serving drink, houses of prostitution and assignation.

In wedding celebrations among the Romans, ribald and licentious songs played no mean part. These songs were known as Fescennini Versus, and were believed to have apotropaic significance, while they also recalled the primary purpose of the nuptial union.

At harvest festivals similar lewd verses were exchanged between masked performers.

As visual guides to the lupanaria in ancient Rome, there were lighted lamps, of phallic shape, near the doors. Seneca the philosopher refers to this custom. Also the poet Juvenal in the sixth satire:

fumoque lucernae

Foeda lupanaris

An old commentator adds: Prostabant autem meretrices ad lucernas.

Acca Larentia was a Roman goddess whose festival—the Larentalia or Larentinalia—fell on December 23. The tradition was that she herself had been a prostitute. Her festival was a fertility ritual, as in the case of Lupa and Flora.

There was a tradition that the Emperor Heliogabalus sponsored a brothel in Rome called Senatulus Mulierum: The Little Senate of Women.

Nonariae were public prostitutes in Rome who were not allowed to appear before the ninth hour. The satirist Persius refers to this custom:

Si Cynico barbam petulans Nonaria vellat.

The ancients believed that the feminine lips had some relation to the genitalia: and likewise that a prominent nose indicated a corresponding membrum virile. There is evidence of this view in a short epigram by the Roman poet Martial:

Mentula tam magna est quantus tibi, Papyle,

nasus, ut possis, quotiens arrigis, olfacere.

Ovid

One of the richest sources of eroticism is the Roman poet Publius Ovidius Naso, commonly called in English Ovid. Born in 43 B.C., he reached the greatest literary and social heights of his time, but, falling under imperial disfavor, he ended his life in bleak and desolate banishment.

At Rome he acquired a deep knowledge of rhetoric, both academic and applied, and then continued his studies in Athens. As was then usual, he subsequently made the grand tour of the East. Although he was destined, by his family's wishes, for a career in law, Ovid dedicated himself to his supreme and exclusive love, the poetic Muse.

His output was tremendous. He addressed a certain Corinna in a series of love elegies. He wrote fictional poetic letters of enamoured women. His *Metamorphoses* describes strange changes undergone by mortals and divinities in pursuit of love. His Love Letters of Heroines, Directions for a Lady's Cosmetic Preparations, the Art of Love, and the Remedies for Love belong in a common category.

The principal climactic situation in his life was his banishment, by the imperial mandate of the Emperor Augustus, to the desolation of Tomis, on the Black Sea. He had to abandon his wife and home—he had been married three times—, his literary friends, and his social circle. It was a kind of living death, a spiritual and intellectual cataclysm. At Tomis, a wild, barbaric, inhospitable spot, Ovid spent the remaining years of his life, in regret and supplications fruitlessly addressed to the Emperor, and in writing, particularly his *Tristia*, Sad Themes.

The reason for the banishment is still obscure, although Ovid himself hints at a 'poem and a blunder.' The poem was his Art of Love, which was frowned upon imperially and excluded from the public libraries in the Roman capital. The blunder of which Ovid was apparently guilty was associated, as he declares, with his possession of eyes—that is, he may have been a spectator or observer of some adulterous act involving the imperial family. Whatever the factual reason, the Emperor remained obdurate to the poet's pleas, and Ovid died in exile.

In the voluminous corpus of poetic accomplishment, Ovid produced many major contributions to erotic literature. His *Ars Amatoria* is a universal handbook to love and its manifestations. His *Amores* is a sequence of amorous vignettes. His *Remedia Amoris*, Remedies for Love, constitutes a body of amatory expiations that in spite of their negative tone are as voluptuously and cynically libidinous as his forthright prescriptions. In all, here is a body of themes, views, techniques that expound the most intimate secrets of the boudoir and the salon, of the entire range of erotic manifestations. Among his known contemporaries Ovid became a kind of arch-consultant in love, the ultimate arbiter of dalliance, the poetic confessor of sensual delights. And continuously through the ages his poetic presentations, descriptions, enumerations, his almost legalized counsel in debauchery, translated into most European languages, have served as a final, authoritative, cynical and libidinous source book.

Ovid probes into both normal and perverted forms of amatory experience, and reveals in vivid and not infrequently lurid detail, the sophisticated gallantries, the urbane wantonness, the suave and polished salaciousness, and the cultivated prurience of the Roman capital during the first century before the Christian era.

In respect of the means of inspiring and promoting amatory activity, both in men and women, Ovid has many pointed things to say about potions. In Latin, the *poculum amatorium* is the common expression used to designate the potion, that is, the love-goblet.

Ovid's primary theme, in these exciting productions of his, is: Love is a campaign, long and ruthless. It requires skill, training, equipment, strategy, vision. So, in his pleas to Corinna his poetic offerings are in the nature of addresses to Woman, tantalizing, shameless, an epitome of feminine wiles and graces.

As stimuli toward erotic diversions, Ovid generously and without resentment recommends, in addition to his own poetic manuals, his Roman contemporaries Propertius and Tibullus, the elegiac poets, as well as Vergil: and, among the Greeks, the erotic lyrics and occasional pieces of Callimachus and Philetas, Anacreon and Sappho.

In Book 3 of the *Metamorphoses* we have the story of Narcissus, enamoured aphrodisiacally by his own image reflected in a pool. The image of himself is so clearly defined, the lips move so appealingly in response to his own pleas, that he is ready to succumb amorously. Then he realizes the truth, that he and his reflection are one, his own self, his very identity. And he longs to free himself from himself, to escape the duplication. By this imaginative and symbolical mythological design, Ovid is unquestionably stressing the erotic passion itself, the frenzied ecstasy to detach oneself from one's own being, the clamor of man against his fettered self and his erotic agonies.

A potion may appear in various guises. A vision of beauty can itself act like an enriched, stimulating philtre. The enraptured glance sends its erotic pronouncement to the enraptured heart, and the potion is virtually consummated. So, it seemed to Ovid, was the strange episode involving the sculptor Pygmalion:

Pygmalion loathing their lascivious life,

Abhorr'd all womanhood, but most a wife:

So single chose to live, and shunn'd to wed,

Well pleas'd to want a consort of his bed.

Yet fearing idleness, the nurse of ill,

In sculpture exercis'd his happy skill;

And carv'd in iv'ry such a maid, so fair,

As nature could not with his art compare,

Were she to work; but in her own defence,

Must take her patterns here, and copy hence.

Pleas'd with his idol, he commends, admires,

Adores; and last, the thing ador'd, desires.

A very virgin in her face was seen,

And had she mov'd, a living maid had been:

One wou'd have thought she could have stirr'd; but strove

With modesty, and was asham'd to move.

Art hid with art, so well perform'd the cheat,

It caught the carver with his own deceit:

He knows 'tis madness, yet he must adore,

And still the more he knows it, loves the more:

The flesh, or what so seems, he touches oft,

Which feels so smooth, that he believes it soft.

Fir'd with this thought, at once he strain'd the breast,

And on the lips a burning kiss impress'd.

'Tis true, the harden'd breast resists the gripe,

And the cold lips return a kiss unripe:

But when, retiring back, he look'd again,

To think it iv'ry, was a thought too mean:

So wou'd believe she kiss'd, and courting more,

Again embrac'd her naked body o'er;

And straining hard the statue, was afraid

His hands had made a dint, and hurt his maid:

Explor'd her, limb by limb, and fear'd to find

So rude a gripe had left a livid mark behind:

With flatt'ry now he seeks her mind to move,

And now with gifts, (the pow'rful bribes of love:)

He furnishes her closet first; and fills

The crowded shelves with rarities of shells;

Adds orient pearls, which from the conch he drew,

And all the sparkling stones of various hue:

And parrots, imitating human tongue,

And singing-birds in silver cages hung;

And ev'ry fragrant flow'r, and od'rous green,

Were sorted well, with lumps of amber laid between:

Rich, fashionable robes her person deck:

Pendants her ears, and pearls adorn her neck:

Her taper'd fingers too with rings are grac'd,

And an embroider'd zone surrounds her slender waist.

Thus like a queen array'd, so richly dress'd,

Beauteous she shew'd, but naked shew'd the best.

Then, from the floor, he rais'd a royal bed,

With cov'rings of Sidonian purple spread:
The solemn rites perform'd, he calls her bride,
With blandishments invites her to his side,
And as she were with vital sense possess'd,
Her head did on a plumy pillow rest.
The feast of Venus came, a solemn day,
To which the Cypriots due devotion pay;
With gilded horns the milk-white heifers led,
Slaughter'd before the sacred altars, bled:
Pygmalion off'ring, first approach'd the shrine,
And then with pray'rs implor'd the pow'rs divine:
"Almighty gods, if all we mortals want,
If all we can require, be yours to grant;
Make this fair statue mine," he would have said,
But chang'd his words for shame; and only pray'd,
"Give me the likeness of my iv'ry maid."
The golden goddess, present at the pray'r,
Well knew he meant th'inanimated fair,
And gave the sign of granting his desire;
For thrice in cheerful flames ascends the fire.
The youth, returning to his mistress, hies,
And, impudent in hope, with ardent eyes,
And beating breast, by the dear statue lies.
He kisses her white lips, renews the bliss,
And looks and thinks they redden at the kiss:
He thought them warm before: nor longer stays,
But next his hand on her hard bosom lays:
Hard as it was, beginning to relent,
It seem'd, the breast beneath his fingers bent;

He felt again, his fingers made a print,

'Twas flesh, but flesh so firm, it rose against the dint:

The pleasing task he fails not to renew;

Soft, and more soft at ev'ry touch it grew;

Like pliant wax, when chafing hands reduce

The former mass to form, and frame for use

He would believe, but yet is still in pain,

And tries his argument of sense again,

Presses the pulse, and feels the leaping vein.

Convinc'd, o'erjoy'd, his studied thanks and praise,

To her who made the miracle, he pays:

Then lips to lips he join'd; now freed from fear,

He found the savor of the kiss sincere:

At this the waken'd image op'd her eyes,

And view'd at once the light and lover, with surprise.

The goddess present at the match she made,

So bless'd the bed, such fruitfulness convey'd,

That e'er ten moons had sharpen'd either horn,

To crown their bliss, a lovely boy was born;

Paphos his name, who, grown to manhood, wall'd

The city Paphos, from the founder call'd.

The realism of the sculptured figure, together with the aroused passion of the artist, produced a kind of symbiotic philtre, a flaming, kinetic periapt.

In Book 1 of the *Ars Amatoria* Ovid introduces his basic subject: love unrestrained, Aphrodite Pandemos, patroness of free love, of passion unconfined:

Far hence, ye Vestals, be, who bind your hair;

And wives, who gowns below your ankles wear.

I sing the brothels loose and unconfin'd,

Th'unpunishable pleasures of the kind;

Which all alike, for love, or money find.

And, in a brief preface, he offers an epitome of early Roman history, which is equated succinctly with military prowess and sexual prowess:

Thus Romulus became so popular;

This was the way to thrive in peace and war;

To pay his army, and fresh whores to bring:

Who wou'd not fight for such a gracious king!

Now Ovid dwells on wine as an amatory stimulant, a virtual flaming potion:

But thou, when flowing cups in triumph ride,

And the lov'd nymph is seated by thy side;

Invoke the God, and all the mighty pow'rs,

That wine may not defraud thy genial hours.

Then in ambiguous words thy suit prefer;

Which she may know were all addrest to her.

Practice all the variations conceivable in winning your designated conquest, Ovid advises recurrently. Your wit and suavity will prevail: far more, in fact, than artificial aids, such as philtres. Philtres, Ovid asserts from the richness of his erotic experience, are futile in the contests of love:

Pallid philtres given to girls were of no avail. Philtres harm the mind and produce an impact of madness.

He enumerates many items that were popularly reputed to possess aphrodisiac properties. But you should shun them, he reiterates, for their effect is minimal. Hippomanes, the excrescence on a new-born colt, is ineffectual: similarly with the traditional magic herbs purchased furtively from some wizened old hag. Reject, equally, formulas for exorcism and similar enchantments. The best love philtre, in short, is the lover's own passion. Even the ancient enchantress Circe, whom Homer describes so vividly, could not, by the aid of her occult devices, prevent the unfaithfulness of Ulysses: nor could the tumultuous Medea, practiced in the lore of the sorceress, combat the waywardness of Jason.

It is true, the poet acknowledges, that in the popular mind many objects, grasses, roots are associated with the virtues of the love potion: but erroneously so, he adds. He lists the items as follows:

Some teach that herbs will efficacious prove,

But in my judgment such things poison love.

Pepper with biting nettle-seed they bruise,

With yellow pellitory wine infuse.

Venus with such as this no love compels,

Who on the shady hill of Eryx dwells.

Eat the white shallots sent from Megara

Or garden herbs that aphrodisiac are,

Or eggs, or honey on Hymettus flowing,

Or nuts upon the sharp-leaved pine-trees growing.

Morality, especially sexual morality, descended to its most degenerative nadir in the period of the Roman Empire. The poets and satirists, the historians and the moralists all uniformly fulminate against the profligacies of Roman matrons, particularly in the upper social levels and in the court circles, and blast and condemn the utter licentiousness, lewdness, and abandonment of all restraints.

Seneca the philosopher asserts:

Anything assailed by countless desires is insecure. And the young and even more mature matrons, descendants of distinguished figures in the tumultuous sequence of Roman history, were exposed to every kind of inducement to laxity, every urgent temptation, domestically, publicly, and politically. There was a vogue of indiscriminate flirtation, highly skilled, ingeniously practiced, that led into violent passion and into adultery, into incest and multiple perversions. Lust became the primary satisfaction, and its consummation was the most common, the most clamant factor in the social frame.

Even the earlier days of the Roman Republic were, as the poet Horace declares—and he was the Augustan Poet Laureate—'rich in sin.' Propertius too confirms this view, and goes one step further. The sea, he suggests, will be dried up and the stars torn from heaven before women reform their immoral ways.

The entire nation, rich and prosperous, masters of the universe, overwhelmed and sated with exotic luxuries, attended, for their every whim, by hordes of slaves, had lost all human modesty, all human virtues. Yet all was not entirely lost, for voices cried out, however feebly and helplessly, in the midst of their successions of wantonness and orgies.

The poet Ovid wryly says:

Only those women are chaste who are unsolicited, and a man who is enraged at his wife's amours is merely a boor.

Seneca says again, in respect of married women: A woman who is content to have two lovers only is a paragon.

For adultery and divorce were the usual recreations of many Roman matrons in Imperial times. Marriage itself was often a mere formality, and it implied no loyalties, no honor. Some women, declares Seneca, counted the years not by the consuls, but by the number of husbands they had.

And the Church Father, Tertullian, added later, in the same vein: Women marry, only to divorce. Ovid himself, the archpoet of love, was married three times. Caesar had four wives in succession. Mark Antony also had four. Sulla the statesman and Pompey each had five wives. Pliny the Younger had three wives. Martial the epigrammatist mentions a certain Phileros who had seven wives.

Women were no better, no less restless. Tullia, Cicero's daughter, had three husbands. The Emperor Nero was the third husband of Poppaea, and the fifth of Messalina. The poet Martial refers to a woman who had eight husbands, and to another who was suspected of murdering her seven husbands, one after the other.

Every passion, every illicit amour, was a provocation to the Roman women. They had intrigues with their slaves, with actors and pantomimists, with jockeys, charioteers, gladiators, and flute-players.

Roman temples were rendez-vous, and prostitution and adultery were practiced among the altars and in the cells that were heavy with incense. In a striking passage, Tertullian personifies Idolatry, who confesses: My sacred groves of pilgrimage, my mountains and springs, my city temples, all know how I corrupt chastity.

Astrological and magic techniques contributed to the already degenerate Romans of the Empire. Old hags practiced procuring and other dubious trades. They prepared drugs and potions and salves for beauty and passion and poisoning. In time, these practices assumed a mysterious aura. They absorbed the secret cults of the Nile and the Ganges and the Euphrates. Some of the practitioners were actually reputable, dignified, eagerly sought after by women. Lucian describes a certain Alexander of Abonuteichos—stately, with well-trimmed beard, penetrating look, modulated voice. He wore a wig of flowing locks. He was dressed in a white and purple tunic, and a white cloak, and in his hand he carried a scythe.

CHAPTER IV
ORIENT

Ancient Hindu literature treats in startling detail every conceivable aspect of erotic manifestations. There are guides and manuals and elaborate treatises and monographs devoted to particular topics: to coital procedures, to male and female characteristics and tendencies, to strange stimuli, and to amatory potions and philtres. Of all these manuals possibly the Kama Sutra of Vatsyayana Malanaga, who is presumed to belong in the fourth century A.D., is the best known. It is, in fact, the most widely disseminated treatise on all phases of erotic practices.

The Kama Sutra furnishes specific information on the techniques of sexual relationships, the virtues and defects of women, the degrees of sensuality among both men and women, the criteria of beauty and attractiveness, the most effective devices in the matter of dress and hair arrangement, foods and cosmetics, perfumes, and the symbolic language of love.

It also stresses potions, their component elements, their preparation, and the type of philtres that are most favorable to the erotic sensibilities.

The Hindu manuals also make special classifications of women according to the degree and durability of their erotic sensations, their physical appearance, and the osphresiological conditions arising from the pudenda muliebria. Nothing is secretive, nothing is taboo. The primary and universal activity, it is assumed, necessitates wide and deep and exact and revelatory knowledge, so that the man or woman may function to the fullest and most complete extent.

The male is also subjected to analysis, in an amatory direction, according to physiological and erotic categories. The most personal, the most intimate, the most normally cryptic and unspoken matters are subjected to forthright description and comment. For example, one subject discussed with the utmost candor is the intensity of the male erotic potential and his general reactions to sexual conjugation.

Embraces and their varieties of erotic significance, postures and degrees of proximity and physiological contiguity come under observation and exposition. Especially the thirteen types of kissing, each in its own way symptomatic of the intensity of the passion. The art of kissing was itself so important in both ancient classical and Asiatic eroticism that, in the Middle Ages, it reached a literary climax. Johannes Secundus, a Dutch scholar, wrote a passionate amatory sequence of Latin poems entitled *Basia*, Kisses, in which he exceeded the lyrical surge and sway and the pulsating exultation of the Roman poet Catullus.

In the course of his surgical and medical experiences in various countries, notably in the Orient, Dr. Jacobus X, the French army surgeon who is the author of a voluminous corpus of anthropological matter entitled *Untrodden Fields of Anthropology* (2 volumes. Paris: Published by Charles Carrington: 2nd. edition, 1898), the author gathered a great deal of unique and miscellaneous and little known information on sexual practices. In discussing potions, he dwells on cubeb pepper, a popular item in the love philtres of the East.

A drink in which the leaves of cubeb pepper have been steeped, according to Dr. Jacobus, produces pronounced genital excitation.

The Arabs were astoundingly prolific in producing manuals on erotic themes, ranging over the entire field of sexual practices, normal and perverted, to which man is physiologically bound.

The attitude adopted in such handbooks, however, is free from the contrived prurient or lascivious tone that might possibly have been expected, particularly in relation to occidental erotic literature. There is apparent, on the contrary, a certain reverential humility, as of one who treats a sacred subject for which supreme gratitude is to be accorded to the ultimate and beneficent Maker. In this sense, therefore, erotic matters have inherently a sanctity that is acknowledged by the Arab writers again and again. As in the case of the Sheikh Nefzawi's *The Perfumed Garden*. Or in the amorous episodes that pervade the corpus of tales of the *Arabian Nights*. Or in the *Book of Exposition in the Science of Coition*, attributed to a certain theologian and historian named Jalal al-Din al-Siyuti. Many Arab erotic treatises actually introduce the subject with a devout invocation to Allah as the creator and dispenser of such beatific and voluptuous pleasures as are detailed in the text.

In one specific instance the Sheikh Nefzawi, after describing a preparation for correcting amatory impairment, adds: This preparation will make the weakness disappear and effect a cure, with the permission of God the Highest.

A Chinese amatory concoction, whose base was opium, was known as affion. Reputedly, it had decided erotic effects: which, however, were of an intensely violent nature accompanied by flagrant brutality. The fact of opium as a major ingredient, however, was evidently an inducement to its use.

Often small creatures, insects, reptiles, formed the base of amatory philtres. In Africa, for example, the amphibious animal that belonged to the lizard species and was named lacerta scincus was anciently ground into powder and taken as a beverage.

This concoction was considered an aphrodisiac of remarkable potency.

A cogently recommended prescription in the famous Hindu manual, the Ananga-Ranga, consists of the juice of the plant bhuya-Kokali, dried in the sun, and mixed with ghee or clarified butter, honey, and candied sugar. This potion, it is urged, is taken with great pleasurable anticipation.

In Arabia, a highly recommended beverage, designed to strengthen and maintain amatory energy, is camel's milk in which honey has been poured. The prescription requires consecutive and regular application.

Identical in intent, and somewhat similar in ingredients, is a kind of broth prescribed by the Sheikh Nefzawi, the erotologist. It consists of onion juices, together with purified honey. This mixture is heated until only the consistency of the honey remains. Then it is cooled, water is added, and finally pounded chick-peas. To be taken in a small dose, advises Nefzawi, during cold spells of weather, and before retiring to bed, and for one day only. The result, he promises, will be startlingly successful.

A Turkish recipe recommends olibanum, which is frankincense, mixed with rose water, along with camphor, myrrh, and musk, all pounded and fricated together. The resultant mixture is sealed hermetically in a glass. Then it is left for a day or two in the sun. Now the preparation is ready for use: as a spray over the hands in washing, or on the body, or on the clothing, with consequent impacts on the person and on the erotogenic areas.

In the Orient, honey normally and regularly takes the place occupied by sugar in Western countries. Hence honey is a common ingredient in many foods, pastries and drinks. Basically, it appears repeatedly in prescriptions designed as love-potions. It is, to take an instance, frequently mentioned by Avicenna, the eleventh century Arab philosopher, physician, and libertine, as well as by the erotologist the Sheikh Nefzawi. Honey, compounded with pepper, or with ginger, or with cubebs, in various proportions and variously formed into a consistent brew, is a standard recipe in the amatory pharmacopoeia of the East.

––––––––––––––

Indian manuals on erotology contain many directions, suggestions, and specific prescriptions relative to the increase of masculine potency. Some of these prescriptions advise rare or unobtainable herbs. Others are hazardous, and may occasion dangerous reactions. Some are merely humorously and naively fantastic and impossible or futile of realization: while occasional recommendations may be warranted and may have some amatory validity.

A drink consisting of milk, with sugar added and the root of the uchchata plant, piper chaba, which is a species of pepper, and liquorice reputedly has strong support as an energizing agent.

Another milk concoction contains seeds of long pepper, seeds of sanseviera roxburghiana, and the hedysarum gangeticum plant, pounded together.

Still another recipe advocates milk and sugar, in which the testes of a ram or goat have been boiled.

––––––––––––––

An Indian excitant, reputedly effective, is a kind of liquid paste consisting of roots of the trapa bispinosa plant, tuscan jasmine, the kasurika plant, liquorice, and kshirakapoli. All these ingredients, most of them indigenous to India, are crushed together and the conglomerate powder is put into a mixture of milk, sugar, and clarified butter, that is, ghee. The entire concoction is then slowly boiled. This is considered a potent amatory beverage, and is so recommended in the manuals.

––––––––––––––

Ghee is commonly used in Indian culinary practice. It is also a frequent ingredient in potions and compounds that are directed toward genital excitations. A reputedly forceful agent of this sort is the following recipe, in which ghee appears. Sesame seeds are soaked with sparrows' eggs: then boiled in milk, to which ghee and sugar, the fruit of the trapa bispinosa plant and the kasurika plant, as well as beans and wheat flour, have been added.

Sparrows' eggs and rice, boiled in milk with an admixture of honey and ghee, provide what is considered an effective amatory stimulant.

A concoction of milk, honey, ghee, liquorice, sugar, and the juice of the fennel plant is considered a provocative beverage.

Boiled ghee itself, taken as a morning drink in spring time, is believed, in Hindu erotology, to form a positive excitant for amorous practices.

Certain oriental plants that have special erotic virtues are mentioned frequently in Hindu amatory treatises. Among such plants are: the shvadaustra plant, asparagus racemosus, the guduchi plant, liquorice, long pepper, and the premna spinosa. These are often used in compounds to form a potion.

Among the diversified prescriptions, compounds, and philtres contained in the Ananga-Ranga or in similar erotic manuals mentioned in this survey, not a few are merely innocuous in action by virtue of their innocuous ingredients. Others are merely ineffective, while still others may be decidedly fraught with hazards and dangers in their reactions. All potions and amatory concoctions, therefore, either alluded to or described in greater detail in this present conspectus, are treated from an academic or historical or solely informative viewpoint, not as ad hoc specifics for any physiologically amatory condition whatever.

The Ananga-Ranga usually includes, among amatory items that form energizing concoctions, plants, roots, blossoms, flowers that are indigenous to India. Many of these plants have their modern botanical designations in Latin terminology, while others still remain unidentifiable or extremely rare.

Kuili powder, lechi, kanta-gokhru, kakri, and laghushatavari, compounded as a mixture in milk, will, it is asserted, create manifest physiological vigor.

An amatory drink concocted in the East is thus compounded: Pith of the moh tree, well pounded and mixed with cow's milk. It constitutes a highly strengthening potion.

Among wealthy Chinese, lavish dining includes a special broth or soup. This soup is particularly favored for its energizing and provocative excitation. The soup is prepared from the nests of sea-swallows, highly spiced. These nests are built from edible sea-weeds, to which cling fish—spawn particles rich in phosphorus. As an erotic beverage, the soup is reputed to be extremely efficacious.

Among Chinese in low economic levels, nuoc-man is used as a love stimulant. It is an extraction of decomposed fish, prepared like cod-liver oil.

The leaves of cubeb pepper, in an infusion, are considered in Chinese erotology to produce marked amatory tendencies.

A very popular pill, whose composition, however, is not revealed to the reader, appears again and again in the long picaresque, erotic Chinese novel entitled *Chin P'ing Mei*. One of the characters, a monk, recommends to the adventurous hero that a certain pill, to be taken in a drop of spirits, has remarkable potency, which is specified numerically and in the degree of its voluptuousness. The erotic effects, in fact, are described by the monk in verse. The pill, yellow in hue, and ovoid in shape, is of the utmost efficacy, over a long expanse of days, the masculine vigor, described generously and enticingly, increasing with each successive day and each amatory encounter.

From a genital gland of the musk-deer and also of a species of goat that thrives in Tartary, a bitter, volatile substance is extracted, that is termed musk. In the Orient, notably in Tibet and in Iran, musk has been in use, in culinary preparations, for its assumed erotic virtues.

Musk, in fact, is pervasively associated with amatory sensations. To the ideal woman, according to Hindu erotology, whose pulchritude and appeal are beyond criticism, clings the aroma of musk, elusive, tantalizing.

Musk has long been involved in erotic practices, and its virtue in this direction has been repeatedly emphasized in amatory manuals, particularly among the Arabs. Even in tales and legends, in poetry and in chronicles, the perfume of musk and its marked allure play no small part in the creation of romantic episodes.

The tradition of musk as an amatory agent, arousing mental and sensual erotic images and inclinations, lingers on into contemporary times. In a popular mystery tale, *The Return of Dr. Fu-Manchu*, by Sax Rohmer, the plot centres around a sinister, super-intelligent Oriental operator named Dr. Fu-Manchu. One of his hirelings is the woman called Kâramanèh. Her nearness is sensed by the narrator, a certain Dr. Petrie. He detects the perfume, which 'like a breath of musk, spoke of the Orient.' It seemed to intoxicate the narrator, disturbing his rational faculties, suggesting the beauty of the villainous Kâramanèh.

In the inexhaustible richness of world literature, in every country and in every century, there are texts, memoirs, guides, novels, dramas, poetry, sagas and legends that are devoted largely, occasionally exclusively, to the amatory theme: from the Dialogues of Luisa Sigea to Pietro Aretino's lascivious sonnets, from the amatory epistles of Alciphron to the lush and fantastic orgiastic extravagances of the Marquis de Sade.

Among all this heterogeneous variety of treatment, viewpoint, and exposition, there is the almost universally accepted standard text, originally produced in Sanskrit by Vatsyayana, of the Kama Sutra, the Apothegms on Love, the essence of amatory science, the distillations of erotic precepts.

A certain plant named Pellitory of Spain, and, in Latin terminology, Anacyclus Pyrethrum, has a traditionally credited amatory quality. The plant is so considered in Arab erotological literature.

The Orient, knowledgeable in the virtues and characteristics of numberless extracts and distillations, unguents and lotions, considered ambergris, as a perfume, to be endowed with restorative, life-preserving properties. Anciently, among the Persians, there was a tonic composed of precious stones—pearls, and rubies, and gold, and powdered ambergris, producing a pastille that was eaten with anticipatory amatory prospects.

In modern times, too, in the East, coffee is often drunk in which a touch of ambergris has been intruded.

Very anciently, ambergris had reputedly amazing qualities, that would produce, temporarily, a state of rejuvenescence in aged suppliants.

Almonds belong to the Orient. Their fragrance is entwined in Oriental poetry, in Oriental legend, and in Oriental modes of living. It is therefore not surprising that the almond, variously prepared, whether powdered, or reduced to an oil, is associated with invigorating tonics. *The Perfumed Garden,* the erotic handbook written by the Arab erotologist the Sheikh Nefzawi, describes a number of preparations in which the base is almond.

He recommends the eating of some twenty almonds, with a glassful of honey, and one hundred pine-tree grains, just before retiring to bed. As an alternate, there is chicken broth, with cream, yolk of eggs, and powdered almonds.

In Eastern Asia there has always been, for untold ages, an awareness of the stimulating effects of certain foods. So, among the Annamites, the chief food was fish, which, according to certain anthropological studies and investigations, gives an appreciably lascivious tendency to this people.

Among other foods, they are addicted to garlic, which they consume in large quantities, ginger, and onion, all of which have aphrodisiac properties.

There are other erotogenic means, contrivances and manipulative devices, mentioned in Hindu manuals, that are designed for ithyphallic inducements.

The Orient has always been a rich source for erotic material. Formal manuals, anthologies, poetry all stress amatory concepts, erotic situations, amorous encounters. In 1907 the Mercure de France published an Anthologie de L'Amour Asiatique, by a certain Thalasso. It ranges over many countries of the Asiatic continent, describing the traits and temperaments of the women of these countries from an amatory viewpoint. The author quotes a Georgian popular song, that contains the essence of the anthology. It is that the purpose of every man, every husband, should be to devise varying amatory pleasures. He should know how to renew the enjoyments of Aphrodite. He should be skilled in avoiding monotony and satiety. Every woman of every country has her own peculiarities, her own coyness, her own aggressiveness. The women of Egypt, he says, are promiscuous, though beautiful. All the coquettish arts are known to Persian women. The Abyssinians are slim and well-formed and appealing in looks. The women of the Hedjaz are apart; they maintain their honor and their modesty, and there are no harlots among them. In Constantinople all the women, in pulchritude, resemble Venus, but they are of varying degrees of chastity. Circassian women are like the moon. Georgian women are very tender-hearted, and persistent pleas will win the day with them.

The Orient is always prepared to experiment with strange objects, unique devices, complicated contraptions, protracted and difficult treatments, all for the ultimate purpose of recovering the libido, or protracting the amatory span, or maintaining full and effectual vigor.

Take, for instance, a man's molar tooth: and the bone of a lapwing's left wing. Place in a purse, under the woman's pillow. Tell her of your action. The result, presumably by means of the implied sympathetic magic, will be very favorable.

A plant belonging in the satyrion species, called Orchis Morio, that is native to the South East of Europe, particularly in the area near Istanbul, is used in Turkey as an excitant.

The juice of the roots of the mandayantaka plant, the clitoria ternateea, the anjanika plant, the shlakshnaparni plant and the yellow amaranth, compounded into a lotion, constituted an Oriental invigorating recipe.

Among the Japanese, a root highly esteemed for its amatory potential is ninjin, which has properties analogous to those of the mandrake.

The Chinese are fond of a sauce called nuoc-man. Spiced with garlic and pimento, this fish extract, similar to the Roman garum, is treated as a stimulant, containing, as it does, genesiac elements: salt and phosphorus.

As the West inherited and absorbed many cultural phases, views, concepts, practices, mores from the East, it likewise acquired some of the amatory and medicinal knowledge relating to electuaries and healing methods, herbs and plants that might be contributory to health and well-being, and, as an antique encyclopedic work suggests, an exciter to venery. Thus Zacutus Lusitanus, Zacutus the Portuguese, a medieval physician, author of a medical text entitled *Praxis Medica Admiranda*, enumerates the ingredients of an amatory preparation. The composition is as follows: Musk and ambergris, pterocarpus santalinus, both red and yellow, calamus aromaticus, cinnamon, bole Tuccinum, galanga, aloes-wood, rhubarb, absinthe, Indian myrobalon: all pounded together.

The most remarkable literary erotic production of China may reasonably be considered to be the picaresque novel Chin P'ing Mei, the adventurous history of Hsi Men and his six wives. It has been styled the Chinese Decameron, but it transcends the scope, the contents, the variousness of incident and characterization and sense of vivid reality manifested in Boccaccio's Decameron. The Chinese tale is full of a variety of scenes and episodes, in the manner of the European large-scaled, spacious novel. It is also permeated by a tone of ribaldry, a vein of salacious eroticism, and a large number of episodes describing amatory experiences. One particular scene deals with a species of pill, the composition of which is not revealed, that has unique functional effects.

In China erotic perversions were as numerous as in ancient Rome. The cinaedus, the Gito who is prominent in Petronius' *Satyricon*, is termed in China *amasi*. Dr. Jacobus X, the French anthropologist, has a great deal to say on this subject.

The Islamic concept of erotic practice is associated with devoutness. It implies the transmission to man of the divine creative force. Thus the erotic never becomes lewd or lascivious or prurient for the mere purpose of lubricity. The Koran counsels physiological intimacy as a sacred function, an ordained and enjoined rite. Omar Haleby ibn Othman, the Arab erotologist, likewise chants the erotic act as an expression, a manifestation derived from sacred sources. The erotic consummation has lost its fleshly, earthy connotation. It has assumed a venerable and venerated sanctity.

In the ancient Orient and even in much later ages, the phallus was an object of veneration not in a prurient or lustful sense, but as the source of procreation, the emblem of maternity. For sterility was the major, the primary curse. Hence any means might be exercised to counteract this catastrophic condition, this mark of divine disfavor, this racial blight. Hence too among certain ethnic communities as well as in Biblical literature the stranger, or the occasional traveler, or the concubine, was offered conjugal status, for the sole purpose of effecting generation.

Horror of sterility drove women to ceaseless supplications, to priapic invocations, to priapic contacts, to secret devices, and to magic aid. In the East, there was the belief that to walk over certain stones was a remedy for such sterility. In Madagascar a stone was held in reverence as promoting both agricultural and human fertility. In obscure regions of the Pyrenees Mountains, as well as in France, similar stones were believed conducive to amatory excitation and also to fertility. And these stones were merely worn and weather-beaten vestiges of the original phallic shapes or other analogous forms.

In India, too, the lingam and the yoni were pervasively revered throughout the continent. There were temples lined with hundreds of lingams, garlanded with flowers, anointed with ghee in continuous adoration.

A mixture of rose water, powdered almonds, and sugar is an old Arab drink that was commonly considered to correct incapacity. So too with a mixture, cooked together, of cloves, ginger, nuts, wild lavender, and nutmeg.

The Koran contains prescriptions that govern the daily life, material and spiritual, of Moslems. For amatory purposes, which in themselves imply a sacred function, certain perfumes are recommended as stimulants. Musk is most frequently mentioned and used. Also camphor, essence of rose, olibanum, and cascarilla.

The erotic theme in general is always associated, in Arab texts, with reverence and sanctity, never with prurience. The Arab erotologist Omar Haleby asserts that the Prophet himself advised recourse to invocations in the case of physiological incapacity.

The erotic consummation, repeats Omar Haleby, must be considered as an act inspired by the divinity. It is the why and the wherefore of the entire cosmos, the divine law of the conservation of the human species.

To promote physiological vigor, Moslem tradition recommends frequent cold ablutions. Nourishment also holds an important position, and specific suggestions of food are made. Fish caught in the sea are helpful. Also: lentils and truffles, mutton boiled in fennel, cumin, and anise: eggs, especially the yolk, and saffron. Dried dates have a value in this respect, as well as honey and pigeon's blood. Effective electuaries may be compounded with these ingredients.

An old Oriental manual, putatively basing many of its assertions on the secrets of the Kabbala, classifies various types of love: Lust and passion and the rarer, ultimate, absolute spiritual love. Amatory emotions are enumerated and guidance is offered in several directions. Women are placed in various categories, according to their physical traits, their personal attractions, their sensibilities.

As a general counsel of perfection, particularly for celibates, corporeal hygiene is enjoined at all times. The routine of Nature itself, it is suggested, is an exemplary mentor, involving alternations of rest and work in due moderation. In the matter of consumption of food, too, restraint is advised. Food should be taken in silence, slowly, and while facing the East. Adherence to such prescriptions, it is stressed, will produce a corporeal and spiritual balance free from violent entanglements.

In the case of the woman, there are thirty-two points that, in their totality, produce perfection and beauty for the allurement of men. These points include whiteness of skin, dark hair, pink tongue, small ears, and moderate height.

Other Oriental handbooks elaborate, on the other hand, on all the possible permutations conducive to amatory consummations. These almost exclusively follow Hindu, Arab, and Turkish tradition.

CHAPTER V
INDIA

India is a spacious land of astounding contrasts and variations. It is a land of mystery and mysticism, and at the same time it investigates reality with infinite patience. It is a land of diversified, age-old cultures, and its ancient university at Taxila in the Punjab ante-dated the Hellenic Academy and Aristotle's Lyceum by long centuries. Yet it has had and still has illiterate villages, where legends and sagas of antique doings are still transmitted orally. It is a continent of abundant wealth, and its maharajas and princelings and emperors have been resplendent in golden raiment, exultant in their treasure houses where lakhs of rupees lie heaped alongside rubies and emeralds, diamonds and pearls, and a dozen other varieties of precious stones, almost beyond human reckoning and evaluation. Yet, within this very century, children have stood at lonely wayside stations, from Bombay to Rawalpindi, in the Punjab and in Bengal, in the North West Frontier and in Madras Presidency, clamoring for roti and pani, bread and water. It is a land of lavish fertility, and a land of recurrent famine and devastation. A land of hieratic formalities and a land of innovation.

India is a country of artistic achievements of the highest order, of profound philosophical speculation, of monumental poetic and literary production. It is dedicated to things of the spirit, yet its Kali craves blood. It clings adhesively to remote traditions, to ethnic and religious mores, to indurated social ways. Yet it forges ahead, eager to maintain itself in the forefront of industrial expansion. It maintains old domestic and communal demarcations and rigidities, yet it welcomes the novelties, the mutations of this restless age. It is dedicated to intellectual, cosmological meditation, yet it probes into sexual manners, into the characteristics of lust and passion, and all the secretive unspoken intimacies of carnality. It has practically made a monopoly of texts and treatises on the subject of love and all its darker and more intricate and subtle manifestations. It is a country that has produced, in this field, six of the major manuals, poetic eulogies or expositions, dealing with the forms and practices of Aphrodite Pandemos.

The Ratirahasya, variously called the Koka Shastra, was the work of the poet Kukkoka. It consists of some eight hundred verses on love techniques.

The Ananga-Ranga, also called Kamaledhiplava, was written by the poet Kullianmull, and belongs in the fifteenth or sixteenth century A.D. The contents describe factually and realistically the physical characteristics of various types of women, their deportment, dress, facial and bodily traits, their amatory responsiveness, together with certain principles that establish objective amatory criteria.

The Rasmanjari was the work of the poet Bhanudatta. It classifies men and women according to personal behavior, age, physical type.

The Smara Pradipa, consisting of some four hundred verses, expounds amatory laws or tendencies. It was the work of the poet Gunakara.

The Ratimanjari is a brief poetic exposition on love, whose author was the poet Jayadeva.

The Panchasakya is considerably longer, and is divided into five Arrows. The author was Jyotirisha.

Woman, in these treatises and poetic elaborations and expositions, is the central theme, and her physical traits, ideally considered, and the elements that, cumulatively, constitute her dominant attraction, are minutely and imaginatively depicted: the texture of the skin, the shape of the moon face, the coloring of the hair, the brightness of eye are measured and defined in relation to cosmic phenomena, to flowers, to the lotus, to the mustard blossom, to the lily and the fawn, and, above all, her devoutness is stressed, and her impassioned worship of the Hindu pantheon, the totality of the deities.

The Kama Sutra is an extended exposition of love and its procedures and manipulations, in some 1200 verses divided into sections in which various aspects and techniques in amatory mores are treated.

And, like The Perfumed Garden and similar Oriental excursions into sexual activities, it diffuses an aura of religiosity, a solemn sense of reverence, a divine acknowledgment. The tone is frank without prurience: the elaborate classifications and injunctions are minute and lucid without introducing an undercurrent, however unobtrusive, of deliberate and gross scurrilities. It is not libidinous, then, in intent, for the author himself, a profoundly contemplative religious devotee, adumbrated his work, not as a salacious and lewd inducement to debauchery, but as an exposition of the physiological man who, while making concessions in conformity with certain established amatory principles, may yet transcend his carnal desires and, instead of being enslaved by his erotic lusts, may become master of them and use them under due control, but never without restraint and a kind of Hellenic and Aristotelian moderation, a physiological aurea mediocritas.

The floruit of the author of the Kama Sutra has not been determined definitively. It has been variously assigned between the first and the sixth century A.D.

The entire work is pervaded by the three Hindu concepts of Dharma, goodness or virtue, in the Greek sense, Artha, which is wealth, and Kama, sensual pleasure.

The range of topics covers normal and abnormal conditions and practices: wedded love and fellatio, public harlotry and transvestism, courtship and the frenzies of passion, the behavior of wives during a husband's absence, the artifices of feminine conquest, osculation and amatory permutations, the employment of an intermediary, the ways of the courtesan, and, finally, personal adornment, tonic medicines, methods of exciting desire.

In respect of the latter, there are various recipes involving oils, unguents, and juices. One unguent that has amatory appeal is composed of tabernamontana coronaria, costus speciosus, and flacourtia cataphracta.

Another aid is oil of hogweed, echites putrescens, the sarina plant, yellow amaranth, and leaf of nymphae. This salve is applied to the body.

Let the man eat the powder of the nelumbrium speciosum, the blue lotus, the mesna roxburghii, together with clarified butter, which is ghee, and honey.

The bone of a peacock, or of a hyena, covered with gold and fastened on the right hand, has an exciting effect.

Similarly with a bead made from the seed of the jujube or a conch shell, that is enchanted by magic spells and then fastened on the hand.

A mixture of powders of white thorn apple, black pepper, long pepper, and honey is reputedly a means of female subjugation.

So with an ointment made of the emblica myrabolens plant.

A drink of milk and sugar, the pipar chaba, liquorice, and the root of the uchchata plant is an invigorating agent.

A liquid consisting of milk mixed with juice of the kuili plant, the hedysarum gangeticum, and the kshirika plant is likewise a stimulant.

A drink of a paste consisting of asparagus racemosus, the guduchi plant, the shvadaushtra plant, long pepper, liquorice: boiled in milk, ghee, and honey, and taken in the spring time.

A man who plays on a reed pipe smeared with juices of the bahupadika plant the costus arabicus, the euphorbia antiquorum, the tabernamontana coronaria, the pinus deodora, the kantaka plant, and the vajfa plant will effect female subjugation.

A camel bone, dipped into the juice of the eclipta prostata, then burned, and pigment from the ashes placed in a box made of camel bone, and applied to the eyelashes with a camel bone pencil are also a means of subjugation.

A drink of boiled clarified butter, in the morning, in the spring time, is equally effective.

A drink of asparagus racemosus and the shvadaushtra plant, with pounded fruit of premna spinosa, in water.

A drink composed as follows: The covering of sesame seeds, soaked in sparrows' eggs: boiled in milk, with ghee and sugar, with fruit of the trapa bispinosa and the kasuriki plant: with the addition of flour of beans and wheat.

Vigor is increased by a brew consisting of rice, with sparrows' eggs: boiled in milk, together with honey and ghee.

The Kama Sutra suggests that the means of arousing vigor may also be learned from medicine, from the Vedas, and from adepts in Magic. Nothing that may be injurious in its effects, however, should be employed, only such means as are holy and recognized as good.

Other stimulants that are known to the Hindu manuals of erotology include the following:

The anvalli nut is stripped of its outer shell. The juice is then extracted. It is dried in the sun and subsequently mixed with powdered anvalli nut. The paste is eaten with ghee, honey, and candied sugar.

A compound of hog plum, eugenia jambreana, and flowers of the nauclia cadamba. These items are all indigenous to India, as are so many of the ingredients mentioned in the Indian treatises. In many cases, however, the plants and fruits, herbs and extracts are not unknown and are available in the Occident.

To gain amatory acquiescence and supremacy over the person desired, the following Hindu preparation is recommended: A few pieces of arris root are mixed with mango oil. They are then placed in an aperture in the trunk of the sisu tree. The pieces are left thus for some six months, at which time an ointment is compounded, reputedly effective in a genital sense.

The lotus, jasmine, and the asoka plant are in the opinion of Hindu erotologists provocative of venery. With respect to the lotus, this plant is associated with the ideal feminine personality, supreme pulchritude and perfection symbolized by the Lotus Woman.

Hemp contains elements productive of sexual stimuli. In Hindu erotology, the leaves and seeds of the plant are chewed in this expectation. On occasion, the seeds are mixed with other ingredients: ambergris, sugar, and musk: all of which are credibly of aphrodisiac quality.

An infusion of hemp leaves and seed capsules is drunk as a liquor.

An extract of hemp, much used in India, is charas, which is both smoked and eaten. Botanically, hemp is the plant Cannabis Indica, from which are produced over 150 drug preparations.

An Indian plant named bhuya—kokali and, in botanical terminology, solanum Jacquini, is credited with erotic properties. The juice is extracted and dried in the sun. This is then mixed with ghee, candied sugar, and honey, and taken as a potion.

Calamint, an aromatic herb, was used in India as an amatory excitant.

Chutney, a characteristically Indian relish, is compounded of fruits, herbs, and seasonings. Apart from its culinary use, chutney is considered a sensual stimulant.

Erotic ingenuities have devised variations in physiological relations. The Arab erotologist the Sheikh Nefzawi, in his *The Perfumed Garden*, alludes to this ingenuity in the case of Indian practices, where twenty-nine possible forms of intimacy were in vogue.

An eye-salve called collyrium was known among the Romans as, apart from its ophthalmological virtue, a sexual aid. Collyrium was so considered in India too, where it was also credited with possessing magic qualities that were applicable to erotic manifestations.

Macabre concoctions have been the stock in trade of the dispensers of philtres and excitants in all ages among all races. A prescription that is urged in Hindu erotological literature runs as follows: A compound consisting of flowers thrown on a corpse that is being carried to a burning ghat for disposal: along with a mixture compounded of the powdered bones of the peacock and of the jiwanjiva bird, and the leaf of the plant vatodbhranta. A genital application promises, in the opinion of the Hindu manuals, marked physiological vigor.

Many Oriental treatises on erotology deal with the physiological characteristics of men and women, temperamental differences, erotic postures in multiple varieties, and recommendations regarding local inguinal applications. The topic of potions as such is far less extensively treated, largely for the reason that the love-potion, innocuous and effectual, is actually rare. Yet each manual is hopeful and anticipatory in this respect.

The Ananga-Ranga, of which a French translation appeared in Paris in 1920, in the Bibliothèque des Curieux, was originally composed in Sanskrit in the sixteenth century by the poet Kalyanamalla. It covers cosmetic hints and amatory devices, hygienic suggestions, periapts and incantations designed to attract and retain affection. It discusses the four major types of women, their personal characteristics, the hours and days most propitious for intimacy. There are tables and statistics that go into minute detail on these points. There is a table classifying and differentiating the seats of passion, the erotogenic areas. There are several pages of tables that expound different types of embrace with different types of partners. Nothing is left to chance. Nothing is omitted. The text marches forward, with confidence and a sense of authority, from the uprising of the libido to the ultimate consummation.

The characteristics of men, their physiological frame, their capacities are evaluated, with a remarkable substantiation of tables and statistics and measurements. The temperaments of women are reviewed with equal thoroughness, and the regions of India are considered geographically and erotically in relation to this topic.

Aphrodisiacs, both external and internal, are treated: drugs and charms, magic unguents, fascinating incense, incantations and invocations.

An external application runs thus: Shopa or anise seed, that is, anethum sowa, reduced to a powder. An electuary is made with honey. This application, according to the Ananga-Ranga, promises effective results.

Or, Take Asclepias gigantea. Crush and beat in a mortar with leaves of jai, until the juice has been extracted. This too is an external application.

Again: The fruit of the Tamarinda Indica; crush in a mortar, with honey and Sindura.

The seeds of Urid, in milk and sugar. Expose for three consecutive days to the sun. Then crush to a powder. Knead into cake form. Fry in ghee. Eat this concoction every morning.

One hundred and fifty seeds of the inner bark of the Moh tree. Heap in a mortar and beat. Drink it in cow's milk.

On a Tuesday, extract the entrails of a blue jay—coracias indica—and put into the body a little kama-salila. Place the bird in an earthen pot and cover it with a second pot moistened with mud: keep it in an uncluttered spot for seven days. At the end of that time take out the contents and reduce them to a powder. Make pills, and dry them. One pill to be taken by a man or a woman: that will be sufficient to promote vigor and libido.

Magic verses will be equally effective: also the chanting of a mantra, for the efficacy resides in the Devata, the deity therein. Or pronounce formulas and utter invocations, such as:

Oh Kameshwar, submit this person to my will!

Utter the hallowed and mystic term Om! Mention the name of the woman who is the object of the passion. Then conclude with Anaya! Anaya!

Pulverize kasturi, which is common musk, and wood of yellow tetu. Mix with old honey, two months old, and apply genitally.

Sandalwood and red powder of curcuma and alum and costus and black sandalwood, together with white Vala and the bark of the Deodaru. Powder, and mix with honey: then allow to dry. This is now Chinta—mani Dupha: an incense that will promote your efficiency, dominate all thought, and, according to the promise of the manual, make you master of the entire universe.

To prepare a powerful and alluring incense, mix equal quantities of cardamom seeds, oliba, and the plant Garurwel, sandalwood, the flower of jasmine, and Bengal madder.

Pulverize bombax heptaphyllum: macerate in milk. Then apply the paste to the face. This will produce amatory reactions.

Take bibva nuts and black salt, leaves of lotus. Reduce to ashes and soak in solanum Jacquini. Apply with buffalo excrement and the result will be most favorable.

Mix equal parts of the juice of rosa glanduifera, expressed from the leaves, and ghee or clarified butter. Boil with ten parts of milk, sugar, and honey. Drink this concoction regularly. The result will be a state of active vigor.

Take saptaparna on a Sunday by mouth, with a prospect of renewed vigor.

Soak the seeds of Urid in milk and sugar: dry in the sun for three days. Reduce the whole to a powder. Knead into cake consistency. Fry in ghee. Eat this every morning. However old the patient may be, he will acquire great vigor.

The seeds of white Tal-makhana, macerated in the juice of the banyan tree. Mix with seeds of karanj and put into the mouth.

Vajikarana. This agent restores strength and physical vigor.

The Ananga-Ranga, like other Oriental erotic manuals, concludes devoutly: May this treatise, Ananga-Ranga, be dear to men and women, so long as the sacred River Ganges flows from Siva's breast with his wife Gauri by his left side: so long as Lakhmi shall love Vishnu: so long as Brahma shall be engaged in the study of the Vedas, and so long as the earth shall endure, and the moon, and the sun.

Curry is especially associated with Indian culinary preparations. It is a sauce compounded of a variety of spices in varying proportions: coriander seeds, cumin, ginger, cardamom seeds, turmeric, garlic, vinegar, and mustard seeds. In addition to its use as a condiment, curry has been held to possess a stimulative quality.

As a rule when physiological vigor is defective or ineffectual in some respect, stimulants are advised to remedy the condition. In a contrary sense, however, when the libido is too intense and too active, a Hindu recommendation, designed to modify the urgency, consists of a special application. This application is compounded of the juice of the fruits of the cassia fistula, eugenia jambolana, in a mixture of powder of vernonia anthelmentica, the soma plant, the lohopa—jihirka, and the eclipta prostata: all of these plants being native to India.

The plant botanically designated Emblica Myrabolens, states the Hindu manual Kama Sutra, is conducive to the vita sexualis, when the plant is compounded into an ointment.

The same manual, adding a goetic touch to a prescription, asserts the stimulative value of a bead formed from jujube seed or conch shell, over which an incantation had been uttered. The bead is attached to the hand.

For a diminution of physiological vigor, or for its total elimination in an amatory direction, Indian manuals suggested a long, rigid treatment. It consisted of the daily consumption of young leaves of mairkousi. Fakirs and other holy men were subjected to this regimen until full manhood was reached at the age of twenty-five.

Fennel, an aromatic plant, has long been in use in culinary preparations. It has also a reputation for inspiring energy in an aphrodisiac sense. In India, it is used for this purpose in the following form: The juice of the fennel plant is mixed with honey, milk, sugar, liquorice, and ghee or clarified butter.

This concoction is viewed with a certain religious respect and is associated with a drink fit for the gods.

Perfumes have at all times been included in the amatory pharmacopoeia. Among Indian erotologists, perfumed fumigation is considered a powerful excitant.

In India, ghee, which is clarified butter, is normally used in cookery. At the same time it is credited with amatory properties. A drink of boiled ghee, taken in the morning, in the spring time, is among the erotic recipes of the Hindu treatises.

As a frequent base for love recipes, ginger, which is also commonly used in the Orient for dietary purposes, is generally present as an amatory item, and is taken by mouth with pepper, honey, and other spices.

Every natural phenomenon, every product of the fields, whatever dwells on sea or is hidden underground: all such items have at some time or other been tested and recommended for their potential contribution to amatory functions. So even the breeze in spring time has had its eulogists in Hindu erotology as an amorous inspiration: also the flowers that are in bud, the songs and twitterings of birds, and the humming sibilance of bees. Similarly, music was recommended as promotive of desire. Even, on occasion, the touch of a person, an aroma, a taste, a sound, a form may stir longings. In a more earthy and domestic sense, leeks and garlic, beans and onions have been found useful as stimulants. Some concoctions are merely hinted at, without being given a nomenclature. Thus an ancient Greek historian is cited by the Greek encyclopedist Athenaeus himself, in his *Banquet of the Philosophers*, as authority for a certain Hindu preparation.

When applied to the soles of the feet, it created an immediate and powerful amatory reaction. But this specific, as so many others, has faded into oblivion.

The Kama Sutra recommends an ointment compounded thus: Xanthochymus pichorius, honey, ghee, tabernamontana coronaria, mesna roxburghii, nelumbrium speciosum, and blue lotus.

Another compound, to be taken by mouth, is blue lotus and powder of the nelumbrium speciosum, mixed with honey and ghee.

Amatory provocation may be induced by certain powders and ointments made from the following plants: Costus speciosus, tabernamontana coronaria, and flacourtia cataphracta, compounded together.

For genital potency, preparations, mechanical devices, electuaries, unguents, incantations, and brews have been urged in Hindu manuals. In addition to the variety of ointments herbs, spices, and animal secretions, surgical operations, hazardous both physiologically and emotionally, have been gravely prescribed.

An unusual procedure for strengthening vigor involves a mixture that is to be thrown at the person desired. The mixture is composed of powder of milk, kantaka plant, and the hedge plant, with the powdered root of the lanjalika plant and the excrement of a monkey.

A mixture of cowach and honey, along with the pulverized remains of a dead kite and the prickly hairs of a tropical plant. This is a means of amatory supremacy.

An application of Lechi, costus arabicus, kanher root, chikana, gajapimpali, and askhand, pulverized and mixed with ghee.

To strengthen and recover vigor, a drink is prepared as follows: Lechi, kuili powder, asparagus racemosus, cucumber, and kanta-gokhru: mixed with milk.

Applications that, in the estimation of the Ananga-Ranga, are of value as phallic stimulants, include leaves of the jai, rui seed, honey, lotus flower pollen, Hungarian grass, and anise.

Loha-Bhasma is a preparation of ferrous oxide and is used, according to Hindu erotologists, as a priapic stimulant.

An herb indigenous to India, known botanically as maerua arenaria, is considered beneficial in inducing amatory inclination.

Despite Hindu proscriptions against the consumption of meat, meat is frequently mentioned in Hindu texts as an erotic agent, particularly red, lean meat.

Arrack is an Indian liquor prepared from the flowers of the Moh tree, that are rich in sugar content. The Moh tree, botanically Bassia latifolia, is used in a recipe for physiological renewal. The pith is pounded and, with cow's milk, taken as a drink.

In India, opium, that is, papaver somniferum, has been used as a phallic excitation, although a sixteenth century Dutch traveler, Linschoten, who was familiar with the East and the West Indies, asserted that it diminishes the libido.

A phallic application is costus arabicus, powdered raktabol, which is myrrh, borax, aniseed, and manishil, mixed with oil of sesame.

A lotion of juice of the roots of the madayanlika plant, the anjanika plant, yellow amaranth, the shlakshnaparni plant, and the clitoria ternateea.

A help in amatory experimentation is the following: The sprouts of the vajnasunhi plant are cut into small strips. They are then dipped in a mixture of sulphur and red arsenic, and dried seven times. The resultant powder is now burned at night; when the smoke rises, if a golden moon is observed behind the fumes, success will attend the erotic encounter.

A composition of long pepper, seeds of the plant sanseviera roxburghiana, and seeds of the plant hedysarum gangeticum, pounded and mixed with milk.

Various soups are advised, in Hindu erotology, as strengthing ministrants. Particularly so, soups in which the ingredients are cheese, or fish, or celery, or mushrooms, or lentils, or onions.

Dill, which botanically is anthum graveolens, is an Eastern ingredient for furthering the libido.

To Hindu erotologists, all amatory acts, the cult of the phallus, and erotic performances, are under the aegis of the triune god Trimurti.

_____

Trapa bispinosa, which is a nut belonging in the water chestnut species, is frequently used in amatory composition. The paste is prepared from the seeds or roots of the trapa bispinosa, kasurika, tuscan jasmine, and liquorice, and a bulb called kshirakapoli. The whole is mixed with milk, ghee, and sugar: then boiled into a consistency.

_____

Wine, in India, is considered conducive to priapic performance. But only, as among the Greeks and the Romans and the ancient Hebrews, when taken in moderation. Otherwise, excessive drinking of wine is an object of condemnation. A rule in Hindu ritual establishes the criterion of sufficiency:

So long as the mind's light flickers not,

For so long drink! Shun the rest!

Whoso drinks still more is a beast.

_____

As a defensive measure against erotic aggressiveness, Hindu erotology suggests the following procedure. The woman who is the prospective object of an amatory approach should bathe in the buttermilk of a male buffalo. The milk is mixed with powder of yellow amaranth, the banu-padika plant, and the gopalika plant.

_____

Cinnamon is the dried inner bark of an East Indian tree. In addition to its use as a condiment, cinnamon has been credited with amatory implications.

_____

The _Atharva Veda_ is a Sanskrit text dealing with thaumaturgic procedures, magic formulas, incantations, and prescriptions affecting various emotional circumstances. A magic invocation, intended to excite feminine passion in a particular woman, runs this:

With the all-powerful arrow of Love do I pierce thy heart, O woman! Love, love that causes unease, that will overcome thee, love for me! That arrow, flying true and straight, will cause in thee burning desire. It has the point of my love, its shaft is my determination to possess thee!

Yea, thy heart is pierced. The arrow has struck home. I have overcome by these arts thy reluctance, thou art changed! Come to me, submissive, without pride, but only longing! Thy mother will be powerless to prevent thy coming, neither shall thy father be able to prevent thee! Thou art completely in my power.

O Mitra, O Varuna, strip her of will power! I, I alone, wield power over the heart and mind of my beloved!

A woman, on the other hand, may secure a man's love by the following supplication:

I am possessed by burning love for this man: and this love comes to me from Apsaras, who is victorious ever. Let the man yearn for me, desire me, let his desire burn for me! Let this love come forth from the spirit, and enter him.

Let him desire me as nothing has been desired before! I love him, want him: he must feel this same desire for me!

O Maruts, let him become filled with love. O Spirit of the Air, fill him with love. O Agni, let him burn with love for me!

A variant supplication directed toward a similar purpose is the following, from the same source as the two previous invocations:

By the power and Laws of Varuna I invoke the burning force of love, in thee, for thee. The desire, the potent love-spirit which all the gods have created in the waters, this I invoke, this I employ, to secure thy love for me!

Indrani has magnetized the waters with this love-force.

And it is that, by Varuna's Laws, that I cause to burn!

Thou wilt love me, with a burning desire.

In its religious traditions, India has affinities with the earliest known forms of sacred rites, concepts, and views. In Hindu religious mythology, the cosmic power of creation, of the generative capacity, is symbolized by the duality of the hermaphrodite, the male and female intertwined, sharing the properties of each other, representing the passive and active principles that pervade all Nature.

From the testimony furnished by bas-reliefs in caves such as the Ajanta caverns, by temple carvings, paintings, and sculptural adornments, the cult of the lingam, throughout India, appears to date back to a very remote and undetermined antiquity.

Among certain sects, the supreme power is worshipped in the phallic form. In wayside lodges, on facades and shrines, the genital figure of masculine dominance is everywhere on view. In many instances this omnipresence and insistence of the symbolic phallus assume monstrously obscene forms and positions, writhing and contorted in erotic frenzy, or entwined in serpentine coils and performing abominations of the utmost lubricity in the name and under the aegis of the cosmic creative force.

A remoter but still valid corollary is that the amatory urge derives from this universal generative process and strives to merge with it and hence seeks whatever erotic measures and manipulations may be favorable to such a consummation.

———

At Benares, Jagannath, and elsewhere in India, the deities of generation were held in great reverence, and were worshipped, notably by women, who symbolically, and more frequently actually, consorted with, for instance, Vishnu, at a nocturnal ceremony during the annual celebrations held in his honor.

———

The *Atharva Veda*, the Sanskrit magic text, contains an invocation whereby a woman appeals for a husband:

I seek a husband. Sitting here, my hair flowing loose, I am like one positioned before a giant procession, searching for a husband for this woman without a spouse.

O Aryaman! This woman cannot longer bear to attend the marriages of other women. Now, having performed this rite, other women will come to the wedding-feast of hers!

The Creator holds up the Earth, the planets, the Heavens.

O Creator, produce for me a suitor, a husband.

———

The *Atharva Veda* also recommends a talisman made from sraktya wood, to be used in supplication to all the divinities of the Hindu pantheon, with these words:

And this great and powerful talisman does strike to victory wherever it is used. It produces children, fecundity, security, fortunes!

Another Hindu invocation, in the text of the *Atharva Veda*, contains an amatory appeal for a wife:

I take upon myself strength, strength of a hundred men. I take up this power in the name of the spirit that comes here, that is coming, that has come. O Indra, give me that strength!

As the Asvins took Surya, the child of Savitar, to be a bride, so has destiny said that here shall come a wife for this man! Indra, with that hook of gold, of power, bring here a wife for him that desires a wife.

CHAPTER VI
VARIETIES AND OCCASIONS OF POTIONS

Alciphron, an Athenian writer who flourished during the second century A.D., composed a number of light, unpretentious letters dealing with simple daily occupations and subjects and characters of everyday life: farmers, courtesans, barbers, fishermen, parasites.

They deal with all sorts of intimate and personal matters, and are a marvelous reflection of the lower strata of antiquity. In one of these letters the girl Myrrhina writes to her friend Nikippe. Myrrhina complains that her lover Diphilus has abandoned her. He has been on a drinking spree for four days. To make matters worse, he has fallen for the jade Thessala.

Hence Myrrhina pleads with Nikippe to aid her in her perplexity. Nikippe, it appears, has a love-potion, that she has often used successfully on young but hesitant lovers. That is what Myrrhina now wants. It will banish Diphilus' interest in drink and rid him of his infatuation with Thessala.

Myrrhina is going to write an endearing, enticing letter to Diphilus. When, as a result, he comes to visit her, she will use the love-potion on him. She admits, however, that these love philtres are uncertain in their effects. Sometimes, she adds, they cause sudden death. But what does Myrrhina care? Diphilus must either live for Myrrhina or die for his Thessala.

Gestures and action, lascivious and lewd in intent, may be virtual potions in their immediate provocations. So Ovid, the arch-counsellor in amatory diversions, suggests in Book 3 of the *Amores*. Archness assumed, prudery, coyness, and an air of hesitation in acquiescence will prove all the greater stimulants:

Be more advised, walk as a puritan,

And I shall think you chaste, do what you can.

Slip still, only deny it when 'tis done,

And, before folk, immodest speeches shun.

The bed is for lascivious toyings meet,

There use all tricks, and tread shame under feet.

When you are up and dressed, be sage and grave,

And in the bed hide all the faults you have.

Be not ashamed to strip you, being there,

And mingle thighs, yours ever mine to bear.

There in your rosy lips my tongue entomb,

Practice a thousand sports when there you come.

Forbear no wanton words you there would speak,

And with your pastime let the bedstead creak;

But with your robes put on an honest face,

And blush, and seem as you were full of grace.

Deceive all; let me err; and think I'm right,

And like a wittol think thee void of slight.

Why see I lines so oft received and given?

This bed and that by tumbling made uneven?

Like one start up your hair tost and displaced,

And with a wantons tooth your neck new-rased.

Grant this, that what you do I may not see;

If you weigh not ill speeches, yet weigh me.

The erotic power, the essential property that possessed the virtue of enflaming desire and exciting sensual emotions, was believed, anciently and in later ages, to reside in growing things, in the produce of the earth, in the teeming abundance of the ocean, in metals, in essences, and in intricate and cunningly contrived combinations, mixtures, and amalgams of such matter.

The common onion, that normally was a part of a simple daily meal, acquired, among the Greeks, amatory virtues. The onion, in fact, rose from its lowly status as a gastronomic item to a mystically-endowed root, that could inspire and direct erotic sensations. Alexis, a writer of comedies who flourished in the third century B.C., dwells on its highly effective nature.

Another Greek comic writer, Diphilus, of the third century B.C., likewise says of onions: They are hard to digest, though nourishing and strengthening to the stomach. They are cleansing also, but they have a weakening effect on the sight. In addition, they stimulate sexual desire.

The pungency of pepper is relished gastronomically. But pepper had another use apart from its function as a condiment. It was pounded, then mixed with nettle-seed, and in this form it was regularly taken by the Greeks as a means of promoting intercourse.

Wine has for ages been lauded poetically and convivially, and a vintage meant, as a rule, a matter for gastronomic appreciation. But old wine, with the addition of ground pyrethron—which is botanically feverfew or pellitory, was known to the Hellenic people as a particularly powerful erotic potion.

Such draughts, however, had then more sinister applications as well, and not infrequently they were considered injurious physiologically. This was, in fact, the considered view of the Roman poet Ovid, of the first century B.C. In contrast to such a potion, he asserts, there are quite innocuous aphrodisiac stimulants, among them: eggs, wild cabbage, stone-pine apples, and honey.

To discover a plant that, unexpectedly and arousingly, 'kindles the flame of love,' must have been a revelation to the ancient Greeks. Such a plant was pyrethron, so named because it was such an inflammatory stimulant.

It was also known as pyrethrum parthenium, and was largely used for medicinal purposes.

In modern terminology, this plant is identified with pellitory.

In Arab countries pyrethrum was pounded and mixed with lilac ointment and ginger: and the resultant compound served to produce erotic stimulation in the genital area.

In his determined search for amatory satisfactions, man has probed deeply into the material world and also into conceptual zones. Thus erotic stimulation may be produced by an inspired dream. This is the situation in a comedy by the Greek poet Aristophanes, who flourished in the fifth century B.C. The play has survived in fragments only, but may be pieced together into some degree of cohesion, the theme being the problem of an old man who has a young wife. The aged husband makes a pilgrimage to the oracle of Amphiaraus. As a result of his visit, the solution of the marital perplexity is revealed in a dream, and the virility of the elder is restored. In the scattered fragments, there is a suggestion of the means adopted by the husband. It took the form of a dish of lentils.

A visual spectacle may virtually act as a potion. This is the view of a physician named Theodorus Priscianus. He flourished in the fourth century A.D., and was the author of a medical handbook, still extant, in which he gives realistic advice for a cure of incapacity. Let the patient, he counsels, in Book 2, be surrounded by beautiful girls or boys. Also, give him books to read that arouse lust and in which love stories are insinuatingly treated.

Virtually, such treatment approximates a visual love-potion.

Physical therapy may be as affective as a potion. Hence local massage, in the inguinal area, was often performed as an aid in inducing virility. This was a highly popular manipulation. It is alluded to in ancient writers, and particularly so in the Greek comic poet Aristophanes. Petronius, too, the author of the Latin novel entitled the *Satyricon*, describes such an operation performed by an old beldam on one of the characters, named Encolpius.

Blood has sinister and calamitous implications: yet it is also associated with erotic deviations. Blood, the mere visual presentation of it, may produce strong amatory symptoms. The public brothels in ancient Rome, for instance, were established over the Circus in which gladiatorial contests were on view. The sight of the violent scenes enacted in these conflicts manifestly bestirred the blood lust, and equally the sexual urge of the masses of spectators, who subsequently thronged the lupanaria. Similarly, in Spain, brothels were built in close proximity to the bull-rings. There was, here too, a manifest association between the frenzy of the tauromachia and the resultant lustful esurgence among the spectators.

Again, the perversion of flagellation involves blood. The resultant flow of blood, after whippings and lashings had been inflicted upon more or less willing victims by perverts and sadists, produced extraordinary erotic excitations. Scenes of this type are the stock in trade of the novelists the Marquis de Sade and Sacher-Masoch.

Describing an amorous intrigue with the maid Fotis, Lucius, the protagonist of the *Metamorphoses*, Apuleius' Roman novel, adds, in respect of the effect of wine;

We would eftsoones refresh our wearinesse and provoke our pleasure, and renew our venery by drinking of wine.

The primary, uncomplicated fact of life is its continuity through physiological relationships. But on this basis man has erected and developed ponderous and multiple ramifications of such functional associations, involving more than the primary purpose and activity of procreation. He has, in addition, an instinctual urge toward affection, love, desire, and lust. And these emotional manifestations have, in the course of time, become refined or coarsened or diverted into abnormal channels. In his efforts to achieve love or desire or lust and its consummations, he has exposed himself to the natural progressive degradation and impairment of his physiological capacities: and he has no less abused, weakened, or destroyed this force or energy.

Hence his febrile search for some undefined amelioration of his condition or some method or contrivance, however insecure, unwarranted, or barbaric, for recovering his instinctual erotic sensuality.

Gullibly and trustingly man has proceeded in this quest to restore the erosions and defects consequent on time and excess. What direction does this quest take? It is ubiquitous. It leaves no stone unturned, no faint possibility untested. It is prepared to make a trial of every novel fantasy, or any inspired scheme, any exploded myth, or every remote and fragile clue. In temples dedicated for the purpose he will repeat cryptic supplications to unknown, foreign, forbidding gods. Or he assumes on his person, in constant hope, periapts and amulets, inscribed with awesome symbols, gateways to the Mysteries. There arise occasions when he urgently consults aged and knowledgeable enchantresses, who reputedly possess the secrets of life and love. Or he is encouraged to drink certain fertilizing waters, drawn from mystic founts, from underground rivers. He may make silent prayers at wishing wells. Appeals to the deities associated with love or frantic lust, with prostitution and sexual deviations are his constant practices, in all countries, in Boeotia as well as in Bactria, in Egypt no less than in Mesopotamia.

Erotic stimuli sometimes sprang from the human figure itself, without the intrusion of contrived philtres or other adventitious aids. The Greeks, in particular, in drama and comedy, in poetry and sculpture, lavished endless praise on the seductiveness of various areas of the feminine person. The callipygian Greek girl was the subject of exultant erotic paeans. Contests were held in which callipygian rivals vied for public recognition and acclamation. There was no sense of shamefulness, no prudish primness, and, equally, there was no stimulated prurience, for beauty per se had no restrictions, no taboos, no amorality attached to it.

The theme of callipygia, in fact, runs through Greek life. The encyclopedist Athenaeus mentions two young country girls whose attractions in marriage rested with their callipygian forms. The citizens actually called these women *callipygoi*. Even Aphrodite, in her temple at Syracuse, was called Aphrodite Kallipygos. In one of the lively, revealing letters of Alciphron, two girls, Myrrhine and Thryallis, dispute over their own personal charms in this respect, while a number of poems, including one in the Greek anthology, laud the same area.

Sculptors and poets dwelt with an appreciative eye, free from personal lustfulness, on the rhythmic flow and alluring harmony of hip and thigh, of neck and ankles. The female breasts were figuratively described as apples, or the fruit of the strawberry tree. In the pastoral poet Theocritus, who belongs in the third century B.C. a young lover, Daphnis, speaks of the heaving apples of his girl friend.

There is the story of the famous Athenian courtesan Phryne, who was condemned to death in a court of law. Her life was saved, however, when her counsel, who was also her lover, Hyperides, exposed her beautiful bosom before the overwhelmed judges.

The term potion was in itself so closely associated with amatory proficiency or, on occasion, as a medicinal remedy for some other physiological condition, that its use was rarely questioned. The potion, however, might be deadly and might be concocted as a rapid means for the elimination of a rival, or a husband, or some enemy. Such a situation occurs in Book 10 of Apuleius' *Metamorphoses*:

The woman having lost the name of wife together with her faith, went to a traiterous Physitian, who had killed a great many persons in his dayes, and promised him fifty peeces of Gold, if he would give her a present poyson to kill her Husband out of hand, but in presence of her husband, she feined that it was necessary for him to receive a certaine kind of drink, which the Maisters and Doctours of Physicke doe call a sacred potion, to the intent he might purge Choller and scoure the interiour parts of his body. But the Physitian in stead of that drinke prepared a mortall and deadly poyson, and when he had tempered it accordingly, he tooke the pot in the presence of the family, and other neighbors and friends of the sick young man, and offered it to his patient.

To further the efficacy of potions, and also to act as indirect yet acknowledged reinforcements, aischrological and scatological allusions and references were frequent accompaniments of the actual act of imbibing the philtre.

Omar Khayyam, the wise old tentmaker, eulogized, in the Rubaiyat, food and love and wine in the memorable lines:

A loaf of bread,

A jug of wine

And thou, beneath the bough,

Were paradise enow.

The medieval Latin songs of the Goliards, the wandering students of the European universities, are full of paeans to drink and its amatory effects. Love and wine are inextricably mixed together in riotous and rollicking friendship. Everyone, exclaims one chant, is drinking: man and maid, master and serf, the sick and the healthy, young and old:

Bibit hera, bibit herus,

Bibit miles, bibit clerus,

Bibit ille, bibit illa,

Bibit servus cum ancilla,

Bibit velox, bibit piger,

Bibit albus, bibit niger,

Bibit constans, bibit vagus,

Bibit rudis, bibit magus,

Bibit pauper et aegrotus,

Bibit exsul et ignotus,

Bibit puer, bibit canus,

Bibit praesul, et decanus,

Bibit soror, bibit frater,

Bibit anus, bibit mater,

Bibit ista, bibit ille,

Bibunt centum, bibunt mille.

The intimate association between wine and love, as if by a chain of causality, has been established since proto-historical times. All ancient records, chronicles, supplications, ceremonials abundantly exemplify this thematic synthesis. Especially so in poetry, of all nations, and at all times.

Drink to me only with thine eyes

and I will pledge with mine

is merely a transposed symbolic formula for the same theme.

All kinds of foods have in the course of history been subjected to scrutiny and experiment for the purpose of extracting therefrom any indications of amatory incitements. Thus, out of the welter of magic undercurrents and legendary beliefs, superstitious rites and alchemical offerings, there arose a body of miscellaneous knowledge, largely orally transmitted but in time consolidated into a permanently durable form, dealing with periapts and panaceas that would bring back or conserve manly vigor and genesiac capacities.

Among such potential means were anchovies, credited with provoking lust, onion soup and herring roe, milk pudding. Angel water also was so considered. It was shaken together with rose water, myrtle water, orange flower water, distilled spirit of musk, and spirit of ambergris. To the genitalia of the stag were attributed amatory qualities. Rockets, cakes and pastries of phallic and genital design, chocolate and ices, pills compounded of vegetable extracts, burgundy and richly garnished game came under the same energizing category.

In South East Asia, particularly in what was formerly Cambodia, annual spring festivals were held during which a gigantic lingam was carried processionally through the streets. At the ghats in the holy cities of India, notably at Benares, the sacred lingam was displayed publicly by the Brahmin priests. Around these symbols clustered Hindu women on pilgrimage, wreathing the phallic shape in flowers, smearing it with ghee. And among the throngs strode the priests, bearing phallic forms for the adoration and prostration of the people. Temple girls, bedecked with tinkling anklets, and with beringed fingers, advanced, swaying and writhing voluptuously. In similar ceremonies there was food to be consumed, and drink flowed; followed, on the part of the initiates, by a general indiscriminate promiscuity that was intended to represent spiritual identification with the Hindu deities. The erotic urgencies never rested, never rest: and the act becomes a sublimation.

The phallic cult, as the basic recognition of the creative potency, is pervasively manifest, in every continent, throughout all distinctions of society. In New Guinea, huts are adorned with a phallus. In the South Sea Islands huge monolithic columns testify to the indigenous worship of the generative force. In some areas of Arabia tombs are adorned with the phallus and are treated with sacrosanct adoration by the women. The Druses, in ceremonial chants at night, pay honor and homage to the yoni, and particularly to the consummation on the sacred Friday, as enjoined by Islam. In Tahiti, secret rites are held, in a corresponding sense, in honor of the physiological act.

Greece had its processional mystai, male and female votaries of Bacchus, leading asses or goats, while young maids carried baskets of first-fruits and genital-shaped cakes. And a sequence of men, their heads wreathed in ivy or acanthus, bore a fig-wood triple phallus of the god.

From Phrygia the cult had anciently spread to Etruria, where the obscene deity, according to Augustine and Arnobius, was the phallic Mutunus with his consort Mutuna.

From Etruria the cult extended riotously to Rome and its far-flung frontiers, from Lambaesis to Dacia, from Bithynia to Pannonia.

CHAPTER VII
POTENCY OF PHILTRES

The potion is primarily the instrument of lust. Lust is the universal driving force, the cosmic mainspring. The pudenda muliebria, states the Bible, are among the insatiable things on this earth. Plato, the Greek philosopher, in his dialogue entitled *Timaeus*, confirms this eternally unappeased genital passion:

In men the organ of generation, becoming rebellious and masterful, like an animal disobedient to reason, and maddened with the sting of lust, seeks to gain absolute sway; and the same is the case with the so-called womb or matrix of women; the animal within them is desirous of procreating children, and when remaining unfruitful long beyond the proper time, gets discontented and angry, and wandering in every direction through the body, closes up the passages of breath, and, by obstructing respiration, drives them to extremity, causing all varieties of disease, until at length the desire and love of the man and the woman bringing them together and as it were plucking the fruit from the trees, sow in the womb, as in a field, animals unseen by reason of their smallness and without form; these again are separated and matured within; they are then finally brought out into the light, and thus the generation of animals is completed.

Of all potions, satyrion is associated, in legend and mythology, with the most numerous and consecutive effects. There was a story of an oriental king. It is related in Book 9 of the *Enquiry into Plants*, by Theophrastus, who flourished in the third century B.C. The king had sent a gift of satyrion to Antiochus, ruler of Syria. The slave-messenger who carried the plant was himself so affected by it that he performed seventy coital operations in succession.

In respect of this same root there was another anecdote about a certain Proculus. After drinking a satyrion concoction, Proculus performed on one hundred women in fifteen days.

Wines, liqueurs, and in general all kinds of spirits are, both in fictional contexts and in the chronicles of the eighteenth century, considered as salacious tonics, and were so used specifically. Even an occasional drink of wine had an erotic repute.

In the salacious and scatological novels of the Marquis de Sade, especially in Justine and in Les 120 Journées de Sodome, food is repeatedly stressed as immediately contributory to high amatory potency. Repletion, it appears, corresponds directly to amatory responses. De Sade describes, in lavish and appreciative detail, with a kind of personal gusto and even participation, dinner after dinner, in which courses follow each other in almost numberless and uninterrupted sequence: roasts of all varieties, game in season, and also out of season, hors d'oeuvre, pastries of fantastic shape and ingredients, ices and chocolates. Each course is accompanied with appropriate wines and brandies. Rhenish and Greek and Italian vintages, burgundy and champagne, tokay and madeira.

And, both synchronously with the meal, and as an aftermath of the banquets, the plenitude of food and drink and the total satiety of the diners produce an enormously exciting, urgent, and effective erotic reaction, in which not only the guests but the maidservants as well are involved.

A soup compounded of celery and truffles was a favorite and popular dish in eighteenth century France, when every possible aphrodisiac aid was eagerly sought and tested.

No less so was lentil soup in great demand for the same purpose. Bean soup, also, pea soup, and other vegetable assortments were regularly employed in culinary ways, but with a decided erotic suggestiveness.

Eighteenth century France, in fact, experimented in both amatory and gastronomic directions, for one practice was manifestly associated with the other. All manner of compounds, then, prepared for amatory vigor, were produced on a large scale. These concoctions invariably included vinegars, perfumed lotions, electuaries, and strengthening elixirs.

A Portuguese potion, that was in frequent use in the eighteenth century, consisted of a pint of rose water, shaken together with a pint of orange flower water and a half pint of myrtle water. To this were added two thirds of spirit of ambergris and two thirds of distilled spirit of musk. The result was reputedly a potent concoction.

Asiatic races were long known for their sexual prowess. Hence the West, through travelers and explorers and adventurers, was eager to acquire such knowledge in its own interests. In the case of the Asiatic Tartars, there were accounts of their strange practices. In one instance, they used the membrum of the wild horse for its reputed high content of vital fluid. The genitalia of the stag, itself considered an extremely libidinous animal, were similarly regarded.

In the case of highly responsive natures, a mere inhalation of a particular perfume, or the sight of a desired person, may produce extreme erotic symptoms. This was so with Antiochus, son of King Seleucus, who reigned in the third century B.C. Merely hearing the name of his mistress uttered aloud was sufficient to induce in him the ultimate amatory reactions.

The amatory urge has been, in the history of man, of such forceful and uninterrupted universality that, in special cases and in specific areas of activity, there have been devised anti-aphrodisiac means, formal prescriptions, herbal and other concoctions, and well-meant counsel. Verbena in a drink was formerly recommended as a specific preventive. Also dried mint and vinegar and the juice of hemlock. Cucumbers, too, and water melon have at various times been considered effective in diminishing or allaying sensual interests. In a general sense, whatever exhausts the body physiologically or mentally has been considered as a feasible amatory restriction. In this category are included laborious and persistent work that occupies all the waking energies: a minimum of sleep, or fasting, or a restricted diet, or exercise of the body: even castigation.

The problem was equally well known to the ancients, who advised, to counteract the heat engendered by passionate excitation, a prescription involving cold. Hence the cold bath was a common and recognized procedure and was adopted, centuries later, as a regular feature in Anglo-Saxon mores. Other Greeks, among them the philosophers Plato and his successor Aristotle, suggested that going barefoot would diminish the heat-producing physiological desire. Another suggestion was to wear sheets of lead, beaten out thin, near the kidneys or on the legs. Pliny the Elder, the Roman encyclopedist and author of the monumental *Historia Naturalis*, and the eminent Greek physician Galen, both coincided in this view.

A more difficult procedure, but one commended by the seventeenth century Sir Thomas Browne, was self-restraint in the 'flaming days,' as he calls them. Otherwise, there remains one other remedy, that was adopted by Origen, the third century A.D. Father of the Church. He cut the Gordian knot, freeing himself from all carnal inducements: Seeds genitalibus membris, eunuchum se facit.

Ingenious inventions, activities, devices for escaping from or suppressing compulsive amatory inclinations have been proposed in every age, from the arch poet of love Ovid himself to the knowledgeable Dr. Nicolas Venette.

Shun idleness, for idleness tends to amatory thoughts, warns the erotological poet. Be active, and you will not be endangered. Occupy yourself constantly: with agricultural pursuits, or fishing, or hunting. Or even take up the study of law.

Avoid food that tends to stimulate: and, in general, live an ascetic life removed from crowds, from visual provocations, from social parties and clamorous public spectacles and dramatic performances, from pictorial or sculptural objects that induce amatory images.

Snuff taking is suggested, as well as concentrated mental study, in later centuries. Or drink a concoction of the roots and seeds of the water lily. That is soothing and cooling, as the Turks seemed to have found it.

Aromatic herbs were, in ancient Rome, usually a preliminary to more active amatory adventures. The osphresiological sensitivity of men and women is such that in many cases particular aromas, strong unguents and cosmetics, arouse venereal impulses. In perverted and aberrational situations, in fact, even repellent but powerful effluvia and vapors, corporeal and genital, may create or induce erotic susceptibility. The Oriental manuals of erotology and certain anthropological studies confirm this view.

A strange personality who was himself European in origin but merged with the East was the writer Lafcadio Hearn. In the course of his essays, translations, and interpretations he produced a brief thesis on feminine osphresiological influence.

The Roman novelist Apuleius, who belongs in the second century A.D., was accused of marrying a wealthy widow named Pudentilla, by magic rites. He thus answered his accuser:

He said that I was the only one found capable of defiling her widowhood, as if it were virginity, by my incantations and love philtres.

Woman became so masterful, so pervasively dominant in her relations with her masculine counterpart, that she came to reflect man's primary physiological desire. She became equated with erotic passion and fulfillment, and her urgency grew so intense that all roads were directed toward her as the ultimate pleasure, the sensual summum bonum. She was in the medieval dialectical sense, matter in actu. And when the physiological and amatory capacities of the male became, through excessive practice or through incidental incapacities or aberrations and indiscretions, markedly weakened and deficient, there was instant and frantic resort to any means, to all means, whereby this defect or incapacity might be corrected or possibly completely remedied. Hence the febrile, the universal quest, in every land and at all cultural levels, for aids and persuasive spells and secret incantations, thaumaturgic formulas and brews, elixirs and anticipated panaceas.

Springs, rivers, lakes, wells, and fountains have had at various times a kind of miraculous or thaumaturgic repute as an efficacious amatory stimulant. The Khirgiz of Central Asia, for instance, have a legend that a princess, after bathing in a sacred lake, became enceinte. Waters may thus be fruitful and fecundating. Aristotle himself relates that a pool had the same effect on a bathing woman.

In the Middle Ages, the philosopher and occultist Albertus Magnus describes similar instances and similar potencies.

In India, barren women bathed in a sacred well. Similarly with the waters of Sinuessa in Greece. Springs in Germany and Morocco and in France were likewise venerated for their traditional erotic efficacy.

In Hindu mythology, there are instances of women bathing in the holy River Ganges and losing their sterility. So in the aboriginal myths of Australia. In the Fiji islands barren women bathe in the river and then take a drink of saffron and carob bean.

A similar tradition lingers in China, in the history of the Manchus. The lotus often appeared in their legends as a kind of confirmatory aid. In Egypt, in fact, the lotus was known as the wife of the Nile.

In both the West and the Orient, the personal will to be admired or loved is believed to be instrumental, in a perceptible degree, in producing a corresponding impact on the object of the desire. Various procedures are specified, each having its own effective possibilities. An offering of a bouquet of red flowers, breathed upon three times by the amorous giver, may prove highly favorable to his pursuit. Or a musical serenade, equally in vogue in the Latin countries, in medieval Europe, and in the Middle East.

CHAPTER VIII
INGREDIENTS OF POTIONS. RECIPES.
ANECDOTES.

Ingredients

What were the elements that, in combination, constituted the potion? Was there a formal, hieratic prescription for its composition, faithfully followed, scrupulously administered, uniformly conclusive? Or was it a more or less haphazard matter of collecting various essences and grasses, roots and drugs and far-sought items, and then hopefully thrusting them upon the tremulous suppliant, the desperate lover, the urgent princeling or vagrant poet? The ancients, both in the Mediterranean area and in the far-flung Asian territories, used virtually the same species of ingredients, the same or analogous roots and extracts, enwrapped, to strengthen the efficacy, in goetic chants, in awesome invocations, supplications, persistent pleas, and even menaces.

Sometimes the ingredients were abominable and repulsive in character, for all growing and living things were grist to the occultist's mill. Animal and human excreta and genitalia were frequently brought under contribution. Not rarely, exotic spices were garnered: or leaves from trees that grew in distant regions: or objects otherwise difficult to obtain? such as the hair, or nail parings, or even more intimate and less mentionable items from the human body. The traditions associated with the ingredients were manifestly read and studied and pondered over and memorized through the ages, and subsequently transmitted to later centuries. So that by the Middle Ages there had been accumulated an immense reservoir of available constituents: human and animal matter, herbs, genitalia, liquefied elements, excrement of ox and pig, of wolf, goat, dog, and goose, of sheep, hen, mice, pigeon, and cow. To ensure the validity of the potion, there would be a bewitchment of the entire compound, accompanied by certain formal rituals. Formulas would be inscribed on certain phials and objects. Frog's bones were popular in this regard. The mandrake, that mystic root that was associated with sinister human origins and characteristics, the plant that was reputedly endowed with male and female properties, was a popular ingredient in the love potion. Bryony was long used for the purpose, and, in later days, tobacco as well. Entrails of animals were no rarity. The more repellent the object, the more salacious and lewd and priapic would be the effect. For the gasping, excited recipient, nothing was too foul, nothing too obnoxious, nothing too horrendous. What did matter was its aphrodisiac value. Hence the powdered heart of a roasted humming bird had its potency. Or the liver of a sparrow. The kidney of a hare was a frequent addition to the sum total of decayed and decaying tissue. Or the womb of a swallow, that itself required minute preparation, was a prompt aid. Human blood came into the picture, and the human heart and the fingers, as well as viscera, excrement, and urine, brain and skin and marrow. Even the Roman poets give a literary shudder at the mention, and in the medieval chroniclers and encyclopedists there is equally a sense of repulsion yet attraction. For love and passion generated from death and offal, and desire sprang from decay. Sappho, that ancient Greek poetess of Lesbos, knew the supremacy of this passion. She called Aphrodite deathless, because love and life are co-eval and co-existent. The sweetest thing of all, she declares in one of her pieces, is to find one's lover. Ages later, Titus Lucretius Carus, the Roman Epicurean poet who, in the first century B.C., produced that remarkable, profound epic, *De Rerum Natura*, The Nature of Things, begins his poem with an invocation to fostering Venus, the delight of men and of gods.

The Orient, permeated by the same passions, had its own range of contributory aphrodisiac elements. Betel-nut, chewed and blood-red, was commonly a base for the philtre. Ambergris, touched with something mystic and elusive, played its creative, kinetic part. Some concoctions had more earthy associations: for instance, the brains of a hoopee, pounded into a cake, and devoured with hopeful zest. Or the wicks of lamps were inscribed with thaumaturgic invocations and then burned to ensure their amatory efficacy.

Despite the motivating force of love, it was, in some instances, an object of dread. For it was a widely disruptive agent, involving elements and features dangerous to the succumbing man and also to man's supremacy in his masculine context, his virile world. Hence in Euripides' tragedy *Medea* the chorus, speaking for the heroine, chants:

When in excess and past all limits Love doth come, he brings not glory or repute to man; but if the Cyprian queen in moderate might approach, no goddess is so full of charm as she. Never, O never, lady mine, discharge at me from thy golden bow a shaft invincible, in passion's venom dipped.

Again, in confirmation of this view of passion, in Sophocles' *Antigone* the tragic and cataclysmic impact of love is bewailed by the murmurous chorus:

Love unconquered in the fight, Love, who makest havoc of wealth, who keepest thy vigil on the soft cheek of a maiden; thou roamest over the sea, and among the homes of dwellers in the wilds; no immortal can escape thee, nor any among men whose life is for a day; and he to whom thou hast come is mad.

Thessaly, a region in northern Greece, was anciently known for sorcery and magic potencies. It was associated with witches and mystic practices, and its reputation for goety was so widespread, so deeply embedded in the region, that it continued far down into the Roman Imperial age.

At night, the dead had to be guarded with great care, as these witches were in the habit of tearing off pieces and shreds of flesh from the corpse, and using them in concocting their potions.

Necromancy, the multiple phases of the black arts, were normally believed to have come from Thessaly or to have found their sources there. Thessaly, in fact, is, throughout ancient Greek literature, the fountain-head of magic. The Greek tragic poet Sophocles, for instance, and, later, the comic writer Menander allude to Thessalian magicians.

The Thessalian witch became almost a stock character, in bucolic poetry, in the drama, in legend. She is the supreme adept, and is so acknowledged. Among the later Romans, in particular, her stature is established. The elegiac poets Tibullus and Propertius, as well as Ovid, Vergil, Horace, and Lucan cite her for her ubiquity, her constant participation in furtive manoeuvres, her intimacy with the foul and obscene and malevolent forces of the cosmos.

The Thessalian witch had notable skill in the selection and preparation of love potions. One of the most effective elements in such philtres was catancy, a plant often mentioned in this connection. It should here be observed that many factors in the composition of the potion are no longer completely identifiable. Organic matter of course has universal denotations: but obscure herbs, roots, spices, drugs belonged to a secretive traditional pharmacopoeia that is no longer available in its original intact form.

In the obscure depths and the furtive sinuosities of folk traditions and transmitted superstitions and rites and formulas that succeeding generations accepted and cherished, the sex motif was always pervasive, unalterably dominant. The quest for amatory power, for refreshment and recovery of the physiological apparatus, was uniformly directed to the tenebrous forces, the prescriptions and suggestions that would arouse the erotic faculties and effect consummation of the passions of love or affection or desire.

In the slow progression of time this oral corpus of knowledge and these secretive means of amorous enchantment and invigorating processes were coordinated. They became imprinted in the written word. They were now established, durable. These compilations, that were in essence erotic handbooks, were primarily intended for all the love-sick, the yearning youth, the disappointed and effete libertine, the persistent aged debauchee, the warped, distorted, and maleficent pursuers of Eros in his most naked identity, of Priapus exultant and self-perpetuating. Nor was this search for the remedial elixir delimited by time or circumstances. It has, on the contrary, been continuous, and has flowed down from shadowy ancientness through the complexities of the Middle Ages, the tumultuous era of the Renaissance, which made life and letters complementary concomitants, down into these very present days, when the search is no less unending, in the laboratories, in mystic and pseudo-mystic cults, in fantastic devices in the Chinese hinterland, in the steaming Congo, in Haiti and in scattered and sundered islands in the Pacific wastes.

In the misty ages, the formula for recovering or stimulating sexual vigor was comparatively simple. In Accadian and Chaldean, in Hittite and Sumerian rituals there was the spell, the enchantment involving mystic terms, a sacred logos, a philtre of recognized potency, a particular herb or food enwrapped in entreaty and threats and injunctions to the impalpable controlling forces and agencies.

Under the impact and influence of the esoteric science of the lands of Asia Minor and of Egypt, the prescriptions were extended, and assumed a variety of forms and ultimately were collected and embodied in corpora of relevant matter, destined for consultation, for succeeding ages.

Most of this matter, inscribed on papyrus, dates in the fourth century A.D., and is preserved in the Bibliothèque Nationale, in Paris.

A characteristic prescription gives directions for winning and ensuring a girl's love. Hecate is the motivating force: Hecate, the triple goddess, the sorceress, equated with the moon-goddess Selene, with Artemis, and with Persephone, the goddess of the Underworld. The goddess Hecate then is invoked with a plea: to ensnare the girl's love by means of torture, so that she will ultimately succumb to the urgencies of the panting lover.

Once the ingredients are accumulated, the next step is for the pleading lover to extol the effectiveness of the recipe. In the ancient Greek magic papyri, and in papyri containing particulars of love-charms, the offering itself is described in detail and its virtues are enumerated. Scrupulous adherence to the method of administering or treating the charm is enjoined. There is now the supplicative prayer to be intoned, while incense is sprinkled upon the sacrificial flames. Warnings are uttered, precautions are postulated, to prevent anything untoward from affecting the suppliant himself and bringing down upon his head any malefic consequences.

Directions are given for preparations of the potion. Prayers and chants to the goddess Actiophis follow. In her semi-oriental designation the goddess is again invoked: Actiophis Ereschigal Nebutosualethi Phorphorbasa Tragiammon. Emphasis is placed on wresting the girl into a state of unconditional passion.

In mythological contexts, certain divinities, such as Hecate, certain seers and warlocks, sorceresses and thaumaturgic adepts, are associated with rejuvenative powers. The ancient witch Medea belongs in this category. She is foremost in her capacity for restoring masculine virility and potency by means of her goetic techniques, her magical charms, potions, and incantations.

Medea, the cunning one, as her Greek designation indicates etymologically, is the universal witch par excellence. She can renew the youthful vigor of Aeson by boiling him in herbs endowed with special virtues. Thus she is described by the Roman poet Ovid in Book 7 of the *Metamorphoses*. She can re-create Aegeus, the aged king of Athens, and bestow virility on him by virtue of her secret philtres. In *Medea*, the tragic drama of the Greek poet Euripides, she makes such an assertion and a promise:

Medea: I am undone, and more than that, am banished from the land.

Aegeus: By whom? fresh woe this word of mine unfolds.

Medea: Creon drives me forth in exile from Corinth.

Aegeus: Doth Jason allow it? This too I blame him for.

Medea: Not in words, but he will not stand out against it. O, I implore thee by this beard and by thy knees, in suppliant posture, pity, O pity my sorrows; do not see me cast forth forlorn, but receive me in thy country, to a seat within thy halls. So may thy wish by heaven's grace be crowned with a full harvest of offspring, and may thy life close in happiness! Thou knowest not the rare good luck thou findest here, for I will make thy childlessness to cease and cause thee to beget fair issue; so potent are the spells I know.

———————————

Hedylus was a Greek epigrammatist of the third century B.C. In one of his pieces a girl makes her confession that she was overcome and succumbed to wine and words of love. The wine, in fact, was the operative potion.

Another Greek epigrammatist, chanting of love and women, warns that man's origin is lust itself.

The lyric poet Anacreon, who was born c. 570 B.C., suggests the attendant circumstances favorable to amatory exercise:

Sculptor, wouldst thou glad my soul,
Grave for me an ample bowl,
Worthy to shine in hall or bower,
When springtime brings the reveler's hour.
Grave it with themes of chaste design,
Fit for a simple board like mine.
Display not there the barbarous rites
In which religious zeal delights;
Nor any tale of tragic fate
Which History shudders to relate.
No—cull thy fancies from above,
Themes of heaven and themes of love.
Let Bacchus, Jove's ambrosial boy,
Distill the grape in drops of joy,
And while he smiles at every tear,
Let warm-eyed Venus, dancing near,
With spirits of the genial bed,
The dewy herbage deftly tread.
Let Love be there, without his arms,
In timid nakedness of charms;
And all the Graces, linked with Love,
Stray, laughing, through the shadowy grove;
While rosy boys, disporting round,
In circlets trip the velvet ground.
But ah! if there Apollo toys,
I tremble for the rosy boys.

Among the vast productions of the ancients, that included poetry and memoirs, biographies and chronicles, essays and dialogues, there are anecdotes, references of various kinds, subtle hints and mere verbal references to domestic or social life, from which we may glean items that are relevant to our present purpose.

This is the case with Plutarch, the Greek philosopher and biographer. He had a long, productive span of life, extending from c. 46 A.D. to 120 A.D. Primarily he is a biographer, and he is commonly so known. But he also produced a series of literary, political, religious, and ethical studies that are comprehensively included under the heading of *Moralia*.

One of these pieces consists of marriage precepts, Advice to Bride and Bridegroom: Polianus and Eurydice. It is, as Plutarch himself states, a compendium of marital conduct, and is packed with high ethical counsel, sober injunctions, sprinkled and reinforced with pertinent comments, apothegms, and anecdotes. Yet the matter of amorous stimuli is confronted straightforwardly and adroitly. The bride, Plutarch enjoins, should, according to the wise old statesman Solon, nibble a quince before getting into bed. It was an old tradition that quince, and particularly quince jelly, exercised erotic effects. Plutarch continues:

Fishing with poison is a quick way to catch fish and an easy method of taking them, but it makes the fish inedible and bad. In the same way women who artfully employ love-potions and magic spells upon their husbands, and gain the mastery over them through pleasure, find themselves consorts of dull-willed, degenerate fools. The men bewitched by Circe were of no service to her, nor did she make the least use of them after they had been changed into swine and asses.

Evidently the normal procedure in Plutarch's day was to employ the love-potion without hesitation. It must have been highly popular, a regular instrument of amorous stimulation. Further, in addition to sexual excitation, the potion manifestly induced other and less acceptable results, and it also intruded on normal physiological and emotional conditions. It was, in short, a malefic instrument. The most wholesome advice, then, that Plutarch could now offer was to shun such adventitious amatory aids, to rely primarily on the inherent amorousness of the two marrying partners.

In medieval Spain, in the thirteenth century, a certain Juan Ruiz, Archpriest of Hita, published a book entitled *Book of Good Love*. Good love, that is, *buen amor*, is spiritual love, divine love. *Loco amor* is the frenzied, carnal love of women that St. Thomas Aquinas terms *amor naturalis*.

Ruiz, familiar with the concept and practices of both types of love, refers to the large body of erotic stimulants, that the Arabs introduced into Europe. Among such potions and aphrodisiacs were: citrus fruits, ginger, cloves, cummin seeds, and carrots.

The actual composition of love-potions and analogous amatory fortifiers is not known in each case in specific detail. Erotologists, historians of ethnic mores, chroniclers, authors of amatory manuals, and writers on similar topics make frequent casual references to the fact of the potion itself, with the implication that the individual ingredients, their relationship to each other, the sources of supply, and the method of compounding them into one medicament are either so well established in public knowledge as to dispense with the enumeration of the component elements, or are merely in the nature of traditional information, transmitted to the reader without further comment, without the personal or necessary intrusion of the writer.

Despite such strictures, however, there remains a sufficiently substantial corpus of knowledge relative both to the potion as such and to the elements of such a compound elixir.

An immediate, rational, and fundamental explanation of the dearth of details about the potion is that the draught had a high economic value. The possessor of the mysterious ingredients collected and compounded and distilled for monetary gain. The selling of potions was a lucrative business: in the Middle Ages it was a flourishing industry, an indispensable production. And thus it was to the extreme advantage of the dispenser of the amatory cup to guard and retain the secret recipes with the most scrupulous care.

Perfumes and spices and aromatic roots were often included in the composition of philtres, to give a particular fragrance to the unguent or medicament. This was usually the case among the Romans, who often, in large and luxurious families, had special laboratories where the essences were distilled. These essences contained, among other ingredients, myrrh, cinnamon, marjoram, or spikenard.

Some philtres consisted of testicular and related matter, as: the sperm of deer and other animals, and even menstrual blood. The belief was that an intimate causal relationship existed between the elements of the philtre and the anticipated sexual implications.

One of the basic ingredients for a compound conducive to amatory vigor is mastic, recurrently recommended in the Arab manuals. Mastic is a gum or resin used nowadays in the manufacture of varnish. In some countries bordering the Mediterranean, particularly in Greece and Turkey, mastic is used to flavor a liquor.

The mastic shrub is an evergreen, multiple-branched, and indigenous to the Greek island of Chios. In the Orient mastic has been used as a kind of chewing gum. The fruit itself is a red berry. This fruit, crushed and pounded and mixed with honey, produces a drink that is reputed to be of great amatory potency.

Garlic, too, is an amatory stimulant, and has been so used in composition. It is repeatedly included in the enumeration of aphrodisiac elements, in both Western and Oriental erotic manuals. Among the aboriginal Ainu of Northern Japan, garlic has the same gastronomic status as nectar and ambrosia, the food of the gods, among the ancient Greeks.

Similarly with syrup of vinegar, and nutmeg, with cardamom, which, in a compound of onions, ginger, cinnamon and peas, is reputed to be particularly efficacious in Arab countries. Peppers, both white and red varieties, are credited with arousing intense sexual inclinations.

In the Arab manuals laurel-seeds are frequently mentioned: Indian cachou, cloves, gilly-flower. Instructions are given for pounding various items together into some consistency, then liquefying the compound with a broth, or honey, or goat's milk.

In all ages, alcohol has appealed to men for its aphrodisiac possibilities. In moderate amounts, it has been at various times and in varied circumstances commended as a stimulant. In excessive doses, however, it appears to act as a decided anaphrodisiac.

The French King Louis XIV, whose reign was marked by the utmost sexual liberties, was accustomed to encourage his amatory inclinations with a drink of alcohol sweetened with sugar.

Throughout the European countries, there was a folk tradition that required a bride and a bridegroom to consume cakes steeped in alcohol and sugar, to ensure nuptial consummation.

According to some authorities, small doses of spirits depress the higher centres of the brain and thus release emotional inhibitions.

Biblical literature is full of allusions to alcoholic drinks and spirits, and to their frequent use, but uniformly with the proviso of due moderation.

A relevant allusion occurs in Romans 14.21:

Give strong drink unto him that is ready to perish and wine unto those that be of heavy hearts. Let him drink, and forget his poverty, and remember his misery no more.

Since fish contain phosphorus and other elements highly productive in amatory inducements, brews and soups and chowders compounded of fish will equally contribute to aid energizing vigor.

Curries and sauces may act as excitants and hence be provocative, though by indirect means, of amatory urgencies.

The consumption of garlic, in any considerable quantity, may readily and normally repel intimate contacts. But in antiquity, and through the middle centuries, it was widely in use as a pronounced aphrodisiac. This was and still is especially so in the countries of the Mediterranean littoral. In a fluid form, as distilled oil of garlic, it appears that it has its use also, but with less invigorating effect.

Anise, which flourishes in the Eastern Mediterranean region, is used at the present time for gastronomic purposes. But it was also reputed to increase amatory excitation.

In the cyclic search for erotic reinforcements, the most horrific ingredients and means have been utilized. Even the human body. One medieval compound, for instance, consisted of the flesh of a human corpse, in a putrefied condition, along with ovaries and testes, both human and animal, soaked in alcohol.

The Marquis de Sade, author of Justine, Les 120 Journées de Sodome, and other novels dealing with sexual orgies and perversions, presents a character called Minski, a giant, who is himself anthropophagous and who eulogizes the consumption of human flesh, dwelling with inhuman relish on the texture, the taste, the continuous appeal of the human body in a sexual sense:

Minski's potency is such that, at the age of forty-five, his faculty for lubricity is able to induce in one evening ten manifestations. He admits that this physiological energy is largely due to the quantity of human flesh that he consumes. He advises this same regimen to those who would like to triple their capacity, apart from the strength and health and vigor that he will acquire through this diet. Once human flesh is tasted, one will disdain all other foods. No animal meat, no fish can compare with human flesh. Once the initial repugnance is overcome, one can never have enough of it.

That is the substance of Minski's argumentation. In this century, William Seabrook, the American writer who adventured in West Africa, the Caribbean Islands, and Arabia, himself describes the eating of human flesh in one of his personal narratives.

In the opinion of the medieval Italian physician Johannes Benedict Sinibaldus, author of the Geneanthropoeia, a compound of dried black ants was a frequent means of creating amatory desire. The ants were soaked in oil and stored for use in a glass jar.

Incense, particularly in the Orient, has immemorially been considered a priapic stimulant. In Biblical literature, in Exodus, the Lord gives directions for the preparation of a sacred, divine incense. It is to be composed of onycha and galbanum, stacte, pure frankincense, and spices: the whole to be reduced to a fine powder.

The most potent philtre or potion is the instinctive, natural, physiological desire. This maxim has been postulated by many erotologists and sexologists. It is forcefully so asserted by Robert Burton, the seventeenth century encyclopedist who, while searching for a clue to the cure of melancholy, in his Anatomy of Melancholy, simultaneously searched through all the chronicles, histories, and treatises of his predecessors.

Philtres, he asserts, and charms, amulets and figurines, periapts and unguents are basically unlawful means: they are, actually, the last resort in the amatory quest. Panders and bawds and the attendants on erotic provocations give some meagre aid in this respect. Beyond that, there is nothing but magic enchantments, Satanic assistance. 'I know,' confesses Burton, 'that there be those that denye the devil can do any such things, and that there is no other fascination than that which comes by the eyes.' He then quotes from Pietro Aretino, the Italian erotic poet, in relation to Lucretia's amatory power:

One accent from thy lips the blood more warmes,

Than all their philtres, exorcisms, and charms.

Lucretia's erotic faculty was such that she could accomplish, merely by kissing and embracing, her sole philtre, as she admitted, more than all the philosophers, astrologers, alchemists, necromancers, and witches.

Lucretia used neither potions nor herbs. With all my science, she said, I could never stir the hearts of men: only by my embraces, the warmth of my lips. I forced men to rave like wild beasts, and countless among them I drove into bestial stupefaction, with the result that they adored me and my love like an idol.

In the weird and confused history of human mores, there are noteworthy episodes and anecdotes, some apocryphal and traditional, others warranted by authenticity and verifiable historicity, relating to amatory experiences and their effects. Many of such anecdotes, prevalent in Oriental and classical literature, describe the amazing consequences of the consumption of love-potions and similar concoctions.

There is the story of the wayward and untrustworthy but brilliant Alcibiades, the fifth century B.C. political leader in Greece. His amorous bouts, his erotic intrigues, were so frequent, so forceful, and so indiscriminate that, as personal insignia, he bore the design of Eros, the god of love and son of Aphrodite. Eros was, in this instance, depicted as hurling lightning bolts. Of this same Alcibiades the tale ran, according to a later chronicler, that as a young man Alcibiades had the faculty of diverting wives from their husbands.

Alcohol, like wine, in moderation, has regularly been used as an amatory complement. King Louis XIV of France, for instance, was accustomed to take alcohol, with the addition of sugar, to arouse his jaded sensuality.

Brides and bridegrooms, too, in medieval Europe, followed a folk custom of eating a cake dipped in alcohol and sugar.

The embattled women known anciently as Amazons, on taking prisoners in battle, broke the captives' arms or legs. The belief was that, by the deprivation of a limb, the erotic functions of the captive would correspondingly be strengthened. One of the Amazon queens, Antiara by name, was the author of a kind of apothegm, that the lame best performed the amatory act.

Certain foods have urgent amatory reactions. Brillat-Savarin, the arch gourmet who is the author of The Physiology of Taste, a standard gastronomic classic, relates that as a result of a repast that included truffles and game, erotic manifestations among the guests were immediate and evident.

Although the mandrake root involved amatory performances, it was often used for analgesic effects. Theodoric, King of the Ostrogoths, who ruled in the fifth century A.D., used to order mandrake to be inserted in wine, and the drink to be administered to victims doomed to crucifixion.

In order to stimulate him doubly, both visually and fluidly, Anaxarchus devised a suitable diversion. He was a fourth century B.C. Greek philosopher, who was a friend of Alexander the Great, accompanying him on his Eastern expeditions. At the usual Greek symposium, which included drinking, entertainment, and discussion on various themes, Anaxarchus had his wine poured out for him by a young and beautiful female attendant, in puris naturalibus.

In classical antiquity, apples were associated with amatory connotations. Apples were regularly exchanged as gifts among lovers. This custom is mentioned by the Roman elegiac poet Catullus, and by Vergil in the Eclogues: Galatea is after me with an apple. Again:

I sent ten golden apples.

Propertius, the elegiac poet, similarly writes:

I gave her apples stealthily in the palms of my hands.

In the story of Ala-al Din abu-al, in the corpus of The Arabian Nights, there is an incident that relates how a druggist prepared a love-potion. He bought from a vendor of hashish two ounces of concentrated Roumi opium, and equal parts of cinnamon, Chinese cubebs, cardamoms, cloves, ginger, and mountain shiek—which is a lizard with aphrodisiac properties, and white pepper. After pounding these varied ingredients together, he boiled them in sweet olive oil, adding three ounces of male frankincense and a cup of coriander seed. The mixture was then macerated, and made into an electuary with bee-honey. The directions given by the druggist were as follows: After a dinner of house pigeon and mutton, well spiced, take a spoonful of this electuary, wash it down with sherbet of rose conserve, and await results.

King Henry IV of France, like other Gallic rulers, had pronounced erotic tendencies, resulting in the possession of many mistresses. On every occasion, before confronting one of them, he fortified his system with a glass of armagnac, a brandy distilled from wine.

An ancient Classical warning relating to the powerful dominance of love is contained in the tragic story of Arsinoe. Daughter of the King of Cyprus, she rejected her lover Arceophon. In a fit of dejection, he committed suicide. But Arsinoe was punished for her disdain. She was turned into stone by Aphrodite herself.

Certain animals, in classical and Oriental mythology, were associated with erotic symbolism. This was the case with the stag, the ass, the bull, the camel, the deer, the mare. During a festival in honor of Dionysus, god of wine and in general of fertility, Priapus, the god who represented the active male principle, was on the point of exercising his potency with the nymph Lotis. At the crucial moment, however, an ass brayed, and saved Lotis. As a consequence, the ass was doomed to become a sacrificial victim to Priapus.

Women were more rarely involved in experimenting with invigorating agents. One woman, however, has gained historical notoriety and infamy in this respect. She was the Countess Elizabeth Bathory, a seventeenth century Hungarian. In her passion for recovering her youthful energy, she was said to have strangled some eighty peasant girls and to have bathed in their blood. Retribution overtook her in the act, and she was sentenced to imprisonment for life.

Flagellation, as an erotic symbol, was known to the ancients and was frequently practiced in the Middle Ages. Galen of Pergamum, the Greek gladiator-physician who flourished in the second century A.D. under the Roman Emperors, asserts that slave merchants used this practice in order to make their slaves more appealing to prospective buyers.

Many historical personalities have been addicted to flagellation for their own purposes. Cornelius Gallus, administrator of the Roman province of Egypt and a friend of the Roman epic poet Vergil, resorted to scourging for the purpose of amatory excitation.

One Italian, a noted libertine of the times, had the scourge soaked in vinegar, to give the lashes greater pungency.

There is a strong probability that Abelard also used flagellation. For he declares, addressing Héloise:

Verbera quandoque dabat amor non furor, gratia non ira, quae omnium unguentorum suavitatem transcenderent. Again, he reminds her of his own lascivious and libidinous ways: With threats and scourges I often compelled thee who wast, by nature, a weaker vessel, to comply, notwithstanding thy unwillingness and remonstrances.

Tamerlane, the Asiatic master of the universe, the subject too of one of Christopher Marlowe's tremendous dramas, was both a flagellant and a monorchis.

Finally, Jean Jacques Rousseau, in his Confessions, acknowledges his condition:

I had discovered in pain, even in shame, a mixture of sensuality that left me with a greater desire, rather than a fear, of experiencing it again.

Sexual license, although restrained among the Semites, among the Greeks and Romans under certain conditions, and among other ancient nations, often broke all bounds under particular circumstances, with resultant orgies involving almost incredible erotic experiences. The Biblical episode of the Golden Calf illustrates this situation, for it was an absorption of pagan eroticism and then of pagan idolatry.

The wife of the Roman Emperor Antoninus Pius, Faustina, became enamoured of a gladiator. The Emperor consulted the court magicians, who suggested, to diminish or eliminate her passion, that she be required to drink the gladiator's blood. They promised that, as a consequence, Faustina would conceive a lasting hatred for her erstwhile lover. She drank the blood, and the magicians were justified in their prediction.

As an erotic performance, and, notably, as a means of curing sterility in women, certain practices associated with the phallic symbol were in force in many countries, in all ages. The women of Brittany practiced phallic rites for centuries, in order to end their sterility. In one town a public phallic figure was often the scene of a peculiar act. The women gathered some of the dust at the base of the image and swallowed it, anticipating, through this form of sympathetic symbolism, the favorable outcome of the priapic implications.

There was an old legend that King Philip of Macedon had been bewitched by a Thessalian maiden who had used philtres to effect her passionate purpose. When Olympias, the Queen, observed the girl's beauty and breeding and deportment, she declared that these qualities alone were the philtres that had ensnared King Philip.

Antiquity consistently associated sexual performances with sacred and divine rituals. So with the ancient Canaanites. The Hebraic tribes that lived in contiguous regions adopted this practice. They cohabited with the women of Shittim, and associated with the daughters of Moab. They went even further, and did obeisance to the gods of their neighbors, particularly to the god Baal-peor. The full text of this episode appears in Numbers 25, verses 1–3.

There was so much rivalry among the mistresses of King Louis XV of France that each one resorted to the most extreme means to hold his affection, or to regain his love. Madame de Pompadour, for example, used a tincture of cantharides. Cantharides is the beetle Mylabris or Lytta Vesicatoria. The active principle of this insect is a white powder called cantharidine: used as an amatory stimulant, but dangerous, and, when taken internally, fatal to the victim.

For Madame de Pompadour, however, and for many personalities notorious in history for their ruthless determination, there was the old but still meaningful adage about fairness in war and in love.

It is a popular belief that castration eliminates all amatory inclination as well as capacity. The Greek author of the encyclopedic Banquet of the Philosophers, however, Athenaeus, states that the Medes practiced this operation with their neighbors, for the purpose of arousing lustful excitations.

Pearls, and other precious stones, were anciently credited with amatory properties. In this connection, there was a legend that Cleopatra used to dissolve pearls in vinegar. She drank this mixture to excite her erotic sensualities.

Visual aphrodisiacs are virtually amatory philtres. The girls of ancient Sparta wore a short knee-length garment that was slit high at the side. The appellation given to these girls, thigh-showers, confirmed their amorous allurement.

There was an ancient Greek named Ctesippus, who had a notorious reputation for amorous exercises. He was so libidinous that, frantic in his lustful urgencies, he sold the stones from his father's grave to purchase the wherewithal for his pleasures.

Apuleius, the Roman philosopher and novelist, author of the romantic tale entitled The Metamorphoses, who flourished in the second century A.D., was involved in a public trial. Accused of practicing witchcraft to win a widow's love, he was also credited with preparing love-potions for this purpose. The love-potions, it was charged, contained as ingredients highly erotic elements: spiced oysters, sea hedge-hogs, cuttlefish, and lobsters. Apuleius, however, in a speech that is still extant, defended the innocuous nature of his offerings.

Dancing among the Romans had erotic implications. According to the Roman historian Sallust, a certain Sempronia danced with more zest than a respectable matron should.

Democritus, the Greek philosopher who belongs in the fifth century B.C., was credited with the preparation of love philtres.

The tyrant of Syracuse, in Sicily, Dionysius, who belongs in the fourth century B.C., was reputed to be an extreme libertine. He once filled a house with the fragrant herb thyme, which is an erotic stimulant, and with roses in profusion. Then he invited the young women of the city to participate in an orgiastic sequence of libidinous performances.

Madame du Barry, eager to retain the royal favor at the court of France, often prepared dishes that had amatory possibilities. These dishes involved: stewed capon, terrapin soup, crawfish, ginger omelettes, shrimp soup, and sweetbreads: all of which are reputed to be salacious provocatives.

The goddess of the dawn, who in Greek mythology was Eos, rhododactylos, rosy-fingered, was a divinity endowed with such amorous intensity that, whomever she observed favorably, she carried off for her amatory purposes. The youth Tithonus, who became her husband, was so treated. So with Clitus, Orion, and Cephalus.

There were, in antiquity, lascivious dances that were sexually provocative. One such dance was the Sicinnis, during which, in addition to lewd gestures, the clothes of the dancer were stripped off. Another dance was called the Dance of the Caleabides: also the Cordax, which involved amatory exhibitionism, denudation, and erotic motions.

Herodotus, the first major Greek historian, relates an episode connected with terpsichorean performances. Cleisthenes, ruler of Sicyon, had a daughter named Agariste. Her beauty brought her numerous suitors, all unsuccessful, in turn. Finally a wealthy young Athenian, a certain Hippoclides, appeared, as a guest at a banquet given by Cleisthenes. Having imbibed too generously, Hippoclides mounted on a table, and performed several lascivious dances. Cleisthenes was so shocked by the obscene movements that he declared to Hippoclides: You have danced away your bride.

Aphrodite, the Greek goddess of love, was widely worshipped throughout the Hellenic territories, both on the mainland of Greece, in Asia Minor, and in the Aegean Islands. At Paphos, in Cyprus, an annual festival, attended by both men and women, was held in her honor. The ceremonials conducted during the festival included frenzied sexual performances. In token of the goddess' favor, each member left for Aphrodite a coin, in return for which they received a phallus and some salt.

Phallic figures were a common feature in ancient religious cults. But even as late as the eighteenth century the phallus appeared in public demonstrations. At the annual three-day fair held in Isernia, in the Kingdom of Naples, reproductions of a phallus were on sale. The customers were usually barren women, who, through this phallic symbolism, anticipated a favorable outcome for their sterility.

In classical mythology, erotic inducements were used even by the divinities themselves. In the Greek epic poem the Iliad, Hera, wife of the supreme deity Zeus, employs such excitants, to arouse her husband. From

Aphrodite, the goddess of love, Hera secures Aphrodite's magic girdle of love and longing 'which subdues the hearts of all the gods and of mortal dwellers upon earth.'

Aphrodite 'loosed from her bosom a broidered girdle, wherein are fashioned all manner of allurements; therein is love, therein is longing and dalliance—beguilement that steals the wits of the wise.'

And, however wise he might be, Zeus' wits were thus stolen.

Although the search for amatory potency is one of the most dominant factors in human history, there are cases where the opposite effect was desired. A Roman matron, to cite one instance, named Numantina, wife of Plautius Sylvanus, was charged with having effected incapacity in her husband by magic means.

Magic played a part in medieval history too. Gregory of Tours, the sixth century A.D. churchman and historian, tells of a certain woman who was spell-bound by a number of concubines. She had become the wife of Eulatius, and had thus inspired the concubines of this Eulatius into jealous retaliation.

Again, according to the chronicles, the medieval king Theodoric was incapacitated by a magic spell.

Among the most lascivious women in all history was Catherine II of Russia. Married to the grandson of Peter the Great, and still childless, she was informed by her advisers that an heir was urgent in order to preserve the Empire.

Catherine consequently made a realistic decision. She ordered a sturgeon, and caviar, to be prepared for a banquet. Then she invited one of the officers of the Guard, named Sattikoff. The outcome of the invitation, and of the piscatory repast, was an heir to the Russian Empire.

The Emperor Saladin is concerned in a story that is pointed in confirmation of the amatory value of a fish diet. To verify the degree of continence of some holy dervishes, the Emperor invited two of them to an entertainment in his palace, at which rich food was served. Odalisques too took part in the banquet: but the dervishes succeeded in resisting the female blandishments. Saladin, however, dissatisfied with this reaction of the dervishes, and rather astonished, ordered another repast to be prepared. This consisted entirely of fish dishes. The dervishes were again invited, and the odalisques were present as entertainers. This time, Saladin was completely satisfied with his piscatory experiment, for the dervishes reacted to the odalisques as the Emperor had expected.

Francis I, King of France during the sixteenth century, was, apart from his cultural interests, noted for his erotic experiences, that he extended by provocative foods, drinks, and concoctions of various kinds designed to prolong his capacity. His mistresses were innumerable, and he died exhausted by his amatory excesses.

George IV, King of England, was a gourmet who appreciated the priapic properties of truffles. His Ministers at the Courts of Naples, Florence, and Turin were given special and unusual directions. They were to forward to the Royal Kitchen in London any truffles that they discovered to be of superior quality in delicacy or flavor or size.

King Edward VI of England was the victim, according to old historical chronicles, of bewitchment. The accused was the scholarly but tragic Lady Jane Grey, who was charged with concocting magic potions and employing amatory charms to the King's detriment.

An ancient view on incapacity derives from Hippocrates. This famous Greek physician, who died in the same year as Socrates, in 399 B.C., attributed the prevalence of genesiac incapacity among the Scythians to the fact of their wearing breeches. He considered this sartorial custom as at least a predisposing cause: and modern views largely confirm his postulate.

Glorification of the sexual motif manifested itself on the island of Cyprus, where the birth of Aphrodite was celebrated riotously. The divine image was bathed in the sea by the women of the island: then decked with garlands. There was a session of bathing in the river by both sexes: but this performance was a mere preliminary to subsequent orgiastic licentiousness.

Brasica eruca has long been considered a provocative agent. In a medieval monastery it was grown in the garden, and used by the monks in a daily infusion. The intention was to be roused from sluggish inactivity by this stimulating beverage. The concoction, however, had such physiological effects in an amatory sense that the monks climbed the walls of the monastery and pursued their urgencies at the expense of their devotions. They transgressed both 'their monastery walls and their vows,' comments the medieval chronicle.

Passion knows no bounds, no formalities, no conventions. An anecdote related by the Greek philosopher and biographer Plutarch illustrates this point. King Ptolemy II, who reigned in the third century B.C., was so enamoured of his mistress Belestiche that he built a temple in her honor. Then he dedicated it and named his mistress Aphrodite Belestiche, implicitly attributing to her divine characteristics.

Mixoscopy is an erotic perversion that involves secret observation of amatory performances.

In Homer's Greek epic, the Odyssey, there is an instance of this aberration, in the form of invited voyeurism. Hephaestus, the husband of Aphrodite, goddess of love, surprised his wife in intimacy with Ares, the war god. In revenge, he summoned all the deities to observe the sight of his wife in the amatory embrace of the god.

Another case of mixoscopy is related by Herodotus, the first major Greek historian. King Candaules, proud of his wife's beauty, persuaded his friend Gyges to hide in the sleeping chamber and observe the Queen while she was preparing for bed. The Queen caught Gyges in the act of observation and offered him this ultimatum: Either to kill the King and become her husband and the ruler of the Kingdom of Lydia: or to die on the spot. Gyges accepted the first alternative, slew the King, married the Queen, and became King of Lydia.

The sacred nature of the phallus as a symbol was transmitted from antiquity into modern times. In the Kingdom of Naples, for instance, at Trani, a Carnival was held in which there was carried processionally a huge figure of Priapus, ithyphallically posed, and termed by the participants in the celebration Il Santo Membro, The Holy Member. An ecclesiastical ordinance banished this pagan ceremony at the beginning of the eighteenth century.

In Greek mythology Orion, represented as a hunter or a monstrous giant, was so lascivious that when Oenopion, King of Chios, was his guest, he ravished the King's daughter. Orion's passion drove him to attack the goddess Artemis, who punished him by sending a scorpion, that stung Orion to death. There are other versions of this myth, but basically they represent the forcefulness and pervasiveness of the erotic motif in ancient Greek life.

The Duc de Richelieu, apart from his statesmanship, had other, more unique interests. One of these concerned amatory matters. He often entertained his guests and their mistresses at repasts called petits soupers. These little suppers provided dishes so prepared as to be conducive to amatory intimacies. In addition, the guests all appeared at the meals in puris naturalibus.

Osphresiological conditions often have amatory reactions. Henry III of Navarre, for example, inspired Maria of Cleves with intense erotic inclinations on account of a perspiration-soaked handkerchief. Such was the case also with Henry IV of France and Gabrielle.

In the seventeenth century Katherine Craigie, a Scottish witch, prepared love-potions for her clients. One such petitioner was a widow who had conceived a passion for a particular person. The witch promised her an herb that would make the man exclude all other interests, all other forms of affection, except love for the widow.

Titus Lucretius Carus, the first century B.C. Roman epic poet, author of the remarkable De Rerum Natura, was, according to legend and to the statement of St. Jerome, poisoned by a love philtre administered by Lucretius' own wife.

The Roman Emperor Caligula, according to ancient chronicles, was given a potion by his wife Caesonia. Her object was to induce in the Emperor amatory stimulation, but the drink threw him into a fit.

Even animals may be affected by amatory potions. There is an incident of a drake that belonged to a chemist. In the chemist's house there was some water in a copper vessel that had contained phosphorus. Phosphorus has aphrodisiac properties. When the drake drank the water, it was affected with amatory tendencies that manifested themselves until its death.

When Louis XIV of France approached old age and the disintegrating physiological effects associated therewith, he still retained his libidinous inclinations. As an invigorating drink, he was advised to take a mixture of distilled spirits, orange water, and sugar.

The lewd and perverted Roman Emperor Tiberius was so eager to experience all varieties of erotic possibilities that, when he became familiar with the plant known as Sandix ceropolium, he exacted from his Germanic subjects a tribute that was partly paid in the form of the plant.

The Assyrian King Sardanapalus was known for his forthright, unrestrained mode of living. He perpetuated his memory in an inscription on a stone statue of himself:

Sardanapalus, son of Anacyndaraxes, who conquered

Anchiale and Tarsus on a single day. Eat! Drink

Love! For all else is naught.

In Hindu erotology, there are legends concerning magic devices for overcoming sterility.

King Brihadratha, ruler of Magadha, was sensual and libidinous. But his great regret was the lack of an heir. He therefore consulted a holy ascetic, a certain Candakaucika. The latter presented the king with a juicy mango that had just fallen from its tree. The mango was given to the king's two wives. Each wife gave birth to half a child. The two parts, being brought together, thus produced a complete heir.

The Emperor Heliogabalus, according to the Historia Augusta, a Latin collection of the biographies of thirty Roman emperors, was notorious for his unsavory conduct: It was said that in one day he visited all the harlots in the circus, the theatre, the amphitheatre, and every spot in the city. He would cover his head with a muleteer's hood, in order to avoid recognition. After bestowing on all the prostitutes pieces of gold, without consummating his lusts, he would add: Let nobody know that the Emperor gave you this.

––––––––––––

The association of an Emperor and a harlot is described in the Latin collection of imperial biographies known as the Historia Augusta. The story concerns the Emperor Verus, who reigned in the second century A.D. At the instigation of a public harlot, he shaved off his beard while in Syria, an act that created much hostile talk in Syria itself.

––––––––––––

In the same Historia Augusta, the wild performances of the Emperor Heliogabalus are retailed:

He usually coaxed his friends into a state of drunkenness and suddenly at night let loose among them lions, leopards, and bears. When they woke up in the same chamber as the animals, and found lions, bears, and leopards around them, in the morning, or, what was worse, at night, they died of fright.

The Emperor would buy up harlots from all the pimps and then set them free. He gathered together all the prostitutes from the circus, the theatre, the stadium, and from everywhere, and brought them into the public buildings, and delivered military harangues, as it were, calling them fellow-soldiers.

At similar gatherings he addressed ex-pimps that he assembled from every quarter, as well as the most depraved boys and youths. When he went to the prostitutes, he dressed as a woman. At his banquets he and his friends performed with women.

The story went that he bought a well-known and very beautiful harlot for one hundred thousand sesterces.

In balneis semper cum muliebribus fuit, ita ut eas ipse psilothro curaret: ipse quoque barbam psilothro adcurans: quodque pudendum dictu est, eodem, quo mulieres adcurabantur, et eadem hora, rasit et virilia subactoribus suis, novacula manu sua, qua postea barbam fecit.

––––––––––––

The Historia Augusta makes many revelations about the intimate personal life of the Roman Emperors and their erotic mores. Among the later rulers, Commodus, who belongs in the second century A.D., defiled the temples of the gods with fornication and human blood.

––––––––––––

Of the Emperor Severus, who flourished in the second century A.D., the Historia Augusta says:

Domestically, he was indifferent, and kept his wife Julia, although she was a notorious adulteress and an accomplice in the conspiracy against his own life.

Heliogabalus, whose biography appears in the Historia Augusta and who ruled in the third century A.D., discovered certain kinds of lustful pleasures, as the chronicle states, to supersede the male prostitutes.

The younger Gordianus, the Roman Emperor who ruled in the third century A.D., was particularly fond of wine, and also of gastronomic delights. He had a great attachment to women, and was said to have twenty-two concubines assigned to him. He was called the Priam of his day, but the popular name for him was the Priapus of his times.

The Roman general Lucullus, who belongs in the first century B.C., was also a renowned gourmet, and held lavish and exotic banquets for his friends. The Greek biographer and philosopher Plutarch, and the Roman historian Cornelius Nepos both relate that Lucullus consumed love-potions, that made him unconscious.

The increase of libidinous inclinations, along with the physiological stimulus, was not invariably the sole, exclusive, and predictable effect of the love-potion. There were circumstances in which the potion might produce, for instance, temporary conditions of insanity. Such was the case, according to historical records, of the notable Roman administrator Gallus, who belongs in the first century B.C. He was driven mad through the excessive use of aphrodisiac philtres. Again, there is a tradition that Titus Lucretius Carus, the Roman poet who produced the remarkable epic entitled *The Nature of Things*, was the occasional victim of a potion administered by his wife with the intention of producing temporary insanity. So, too, with Lucullus, the Roman general and noted gourmet, who dates in the first century B.C. He succumbed to a poison that was contained as an ingredient in a love philtre.

In the Orient, the almond becomes an amatory agent: either eaten whole, or ground into a powder, or mixed with other ingredients. Powdered almonds with cream and egg yolks and chicken stock act presumably as a stimulant. So with honey taken with almonds and pine tree grains.

Minerals, precious stones have been constituents in exciting preparations. The medieval centuries in particular placed profound credence in their virtues. The agate was thus reputed to promote genesiac activity. So with molten gold taken in an infusion.

All sorts of brews are known and experimented with in the East. A stimulant that, although credited with amatory effects, produced at the same time violent reactions, was a Chinese concoction of opium and other ingredients, called affion.

Herbs were always a contribution in love drinks. An aromatic herb that was called by the Romans Venus' plant was known in the Middle Ages as Sweet Flag and was considered an erotic excitation.

Animal flesh and organs have immemorially formed part of the amatory apparatus. In the second century A.D. a physician of Alexandria recommended the flesh of lizard as a genesiac agent.

Cheese and cherries, dried shrimp and scallops, fried spinach and noodles: chestnuts boiled with pistachio nuts, pine kernels, sugar, rocket seed and cinnamon: chicken gizzard: a compound of juice of powdered onion and ghee, heated and then cooled and mixed with chick-peas and water: a cider drink: cinchona bark: a liqueur distilled from cinnamon: civet-perfumed candy: cod liver, and cod roe: cockles: all these disparate items, some centuries ago, others in our own contemporary times, East and West, have been in use as generative provocations: sometimes traditionally and hopefully: at other times, merely traditionally.

In the Hindu manuals there are enumerated and described such varied potions and unguents and drugs that masculine activity, according to legend, can be prolonged continuously to the extent of hundreds of individual and successive occasions.

In the South Seas a stimulating drink, consumed after wedding ceremonies and other notable occasions, is made from the roots of the plant kava piperaceae. The root is chewed and then the juice extruded into a bowl: the liquid is then strained and served.

In the Orient, from the bird known as King's Crow, the extracted bile is compounded into an amatory philtre.

A certain perfume popular among Arabs for amatory stimulus is known as dufz.

All sorts of drugs, both in their natural state and in synthetic preparations, dangerous in their application and fatal in their effects, have frantically been enlisted as erotic attendants. The venereal passion has thus frequently transcended health, sanity, and the continuance of life itself. Among such drugs, draughts, and preparations are: damiana, absinthe, yohimbine, adrenaline, brucine, aphrodisin, amanita muscaria, belladonna, borax, hashish, cocaine, bhang, mescaline, bufotenin, rauwiloid, harmine.

Among gruesome items used for libidinous purposes was human dried liver. The Romans were familiar with this ingredient, and Horace, the first century B.C. poet, makes mention of it in describing the dark operations of a witch.

Formerly used as a love charm was dragon's blood: a red resin extracted from the fruit of a palm tree called botanically calamus draco. Cast into a fire, dragon's blood was believed, when accompanied by a binding spell in the form of a rhyming couplet, to induce an errant lover to return to the object of his passion.

Dog-stones, tubers of the orchis species, are shaped like the testiculi canis, and hence are so called. At one time this plant was assumed to have an amatory virtue.

In the case of women, darnel grass was considered an amatory provocation, when mixed with barley meal, myrrh, and frankincense.

The comparatively innocuous cucumber, used domestically in salads, has sometimes been credited, mainly for its phallic shape, with venereal properties.

In the Orient, the aromatic plant cumin, which is used as a condiment, is also considered aphrodisiacally. So with the pungent berry cubeb, native to Java, and used in cooking and medicinally.

In the East, cubebs are chewed, sometimes powdered and mixed with honey: sometimes made into an infusion with cubeb leaves. The provocative virtues of cubeb peppers are widely known and esteemed, from Arabia to China, and have been used erotically since at least the thirteenth century.

Periapts and amulets of various types, both inanimate and organic, have been used with amatory prospects. Thus, in the Orient, betel nuts were so used. Or a lock of woman's hair, over which a spell had been uttered. Or the human liver, as in ancient Greece, was considered the source of all desire and hence became a fetish. Or, in the East, a hyena's udder, tied on the left arm, would induce the longed-for passion.

The aromatic plant basil, used as a condiment, was also credited with exciting reactions. So much so, in fact, that in Italy the herb was used by maidens as a love charm.

Beans, too, were thought at all times to be highly amatory in their results. Hence the Church Father St. Jerome forbade the use of beans to nuns.

Carrots, turnips, wild cabbage, and beets have also been included at various times in this category. Pliny the Elder, the Roman author of the Historia Naturalis, states that white beets are an amatory aid.

There was a long accepted tradition in the efficacy of certain fish, especially the barbel, which is mentioned by the Roman poet Ausonius in a poem dealing with various species of fish.

The fat of a camel's hump, melted down, and also camel's milk taken with honey are, in Oriental erotological literature, considered of marked venereal value.

The brains of certain animals were at various periods considered, apart from their food value, to possess erotic effects. So with the brains of sheep, pig, and calf. In some countries, notably in the Mediterranean area, animal brains are prepared as a gastronomic delicacy.

At one time the milk of a chameleon was treated as a generative excitation. The thirteenth century Arab physician and philosopher Avicenna so recommended it.

Rhubarb and cinnamon, ginger and vanilla, mixed in wine, produce a recipe that was prevalent in Italy, So with curaçao, mixed with madeira wine: to which were added pieces of sugar.

An old collection of unique recipes, entitled the Golden Cabinet of Secrets, was formerly but incorrectly included among the works of the Greek philosopher Aristotle. The collection itself was long popular for its putative authority. An amatory powder, described in the Cabinet, is compounded thus: Flowers of seeds of elecampane, vervain, mistletoe berries are crushed together and dried thoroughly in an oven. The powder is taken in a glass of wine, and the effects, it was urged, would be most gratifying.

Usually, amatory concoctions were prepared individually, for each suppliant. In the seventeenth century, however, an Englishman by the name of Burton, an apothecary, established a factory in the town of Colchester. Here he produced on a large scale aphrodisiacs compounded of the roots of sea holly.

There were for sale, in Rome, in the market place, in booths and emporia, and in quarters where people of all ranks and all ethnic origins congregated, philtres and brews, and articles putatively endowed with provocative and generative properties. Dried human marrow, and the sucking-fish, star-fish and intimate genital secretions, both male and female, were used in these concoctions. And over the preparations arose supplications and invocations and incantations directed to the divinities of the underworld, entreating efficacy in the purchased potions.

Among plants that have both culinary uses and at least presumed amatory implications are the artichoke and asparagus. In France, artichokes were sold by vendors who, in their street cries, added forthrightly that artichokes aroused the genital areas.

Similarly, in the Orient, asparagus, fried with egg yolks, and sprinkled with spices, constituted a decidedly amatory dish.

The egg plant, too, split and boiled with a flour paste, vanilla beans, pimentos, chives, and pepper-corns, and a concoction known as bois bandé or tightening wood, containing strychnine and hence highly dangerous, was commonly in use in the West Indies, where it was credited with excitant qualities.

In China, again, bamboo shoots, usually an appetizing culinary ingredient, are believed to have an aphrodisiac value.

A shrub that, since Roman times, was used for inciting desire was birthwort. In this respect it was quite familiar to the Middle Ages.

Bitter sweet, too, like many herbs, was at one time credited with erotic virtues.

The berry of the caper plant, that is, caperberry, belongs in the same category. Its potency was reputedly so great that the plant is equated, in Ecclesiastes, with erotic desire itself.

Paprika, which is Hungarian red pepper, is prepared from the plant capsicum annuum, and is both a spice and a traditionally credited amatory aid.

A plant similar to the artichoke, and equally prickly, is cardoon, considered a stimulating agent. In France, the fleshy parts of the inner leaves are consumed with this intent.

Caraway seeds, in the East, are valued erotically.

Stewed in milk sauce, carrots are endowed, in Oriental manuals, with stimulating characteristics. In ancient Greece the carrot, used as a venereal medicine, was called a philtron.

Rosemary, the aromatic shrub, has leaves that are used in perfumery, medicinally, and in cookery. Among the Romans, it has an amatory virtue.

Some amatory doses are of such a nature that excess may prove fatal. An urgent young man, invited to a dinner prepared by a courtesan, ate too heartily. He died on the following day, as all the dishes had been spiced with a potent stimulus.

Ferdinand of Castile, too, died from an administration of the same drug that had spiced the courses at the banquet.

———

A medieval powder that was an energizing potential, rejuvenating and refreshing, is described by the English dramatist Ben Jonson (c. 1573–1637) in his comedy Volpone. Volpone himself offers the beautifying powder thus:

Here is a powder concealed in this paper, of which, if I should speak to the worth, nine thousand volumes were but as one page, that page as a line, that line as a word; so short is this pilgrimage of man (which some call life) to the expressing of it. Would I reflect on the price? Why, the whole world is but as an empire, that empire as a province, that province as a bank, that bank as a private purse to the purchase of it. I will only tell you; it is the powder that made Venus a goddess (given her by Apollo), that kept her perpetually young, cleared her wrinkles, firmed her gums, filled her skin, colored her hair; from her derived to Helen, and at the sack of Troy unfortunately lost, till now, in this our age, it was as happily recovered, by a studious antiquary, out of some ruins of Asia, who sent a moiety of it to the court of France (but much sophisticated), wherewith the ladies there, now, color their hair.

———

The innocuous cress, that is regularly used in salads, was formerly consumed, either raw or boiled or as a juice, for its invigorating value. Cress was prescribed, in Roman times, in recipes intended to cure incapacity. In the Orient, this property of cress as an aphrodisiac is stressed in the erotic manuals.

———

Among many other herbs and plants that induce amatory conditions are valerian and coriander and violet: these are mentioned in this respect by Albertus Magnus, the medieval philosopher.

Another plant, botanically known as melampryum pratense and commonly called cow wheat, was given as fodder to cows. But it had also a reputation, according to Pliny the Elder and the Greek physician Dioscorides, as a rousing stimulus of passion.

The dried seeds of the Cola Nitida, a nut indigenous to Africa, furnishes a drink called cola. This beverage is also known as bichy. The cola nut itself, which is chewed, is credited, among the Africans, with promoting vigor.

A brew compounded of the Indian root called galanga, and cardamoms, laurel seeds, sparrow wort, nutmeg, cubebs, cloves, in a fowl or pigeon broth, was held to be a powerful stimulant, especially among Arabs.

Women esteemed, as an amatory incitement, the brains of the mustela piscis.

To a plant with a root shaped like a claw, called lycopodium, was formerly attributed the quality of inducing desire.

In Eastern countries, the fruit of the mastic-tree, pounded with oil and honey, makes a drink that is highly esteemed among Arabs as a venereal provocation.

The Arab erotologist Umar ibn Muhammed al-Nefzawi, author of *The Perfumed Garden*, a survey in amatory practices, discusses the entire range of erotic experiences and procedures among men and women. He treats of genital conditions, medical problems, potions, sexual ceremonials, circumstances favorable to amatory consummations, manipulations and contrivances and preparations that affect amatory potentialities. With all this mass of detail and particularization of venereal topics, the author emphasizes that his work is not an exposition directed toward lewd and libidinous ends, but a virtual glorification of the gifts bestowed upon men by divine graciousness and indulgent beneficence.

Plutarch, the Greek historian and philosopher, in his *De Sanitate Tuenda Praecepta*, Advice on Keeping Well, tells of an amatory incident:

When the young men described by Menander were, as they were drinking, insidiously beset by the pimp, who introduced some handsome and high-priced concubines, each one of them (as he says),

Bent down his head and munched his own dessert, being on his guard and afraid to look at them.

The inventive genius of man has included in the preparation of love philtres the most heterogeneous items, such as: human fingers, hoopee brains, tobacco, human excrement, snake bones, toads, skulls and intestinal fluids and organs. Horace and Catullus, Pliny the Elder and Apuleius, among the Romans, have frequent occasion to refer to philtres and their ingredients and effects.

So too the medieval and later physicians and demonographers have much to say on the subject: Martin Delrio and Sprenger, Reginald Scott and Bodin, Johannes Muller and Sinibaldus. A Roman recipe, composed by a witch, runs as follows:

Bring the eggs and plumage foul

Of a midnight shrieking owl,

Be they well besmear'd with blood

Of the blackest venom'd toad,

Bring the choicest drugs of Spain,

Produce of the poisonous plain,

Then into the charm be thrown,

Snatch'd from famish'd bitch, a bone,

Burn them all with magic flame,

Kindled first by Colchian dame.

John Gay, the eighteenth century playwright, in *The Shepherd's Week*, has one of the characters refer to a philtre in a casual and incidental manner, implying that the practice of this usage was in common vogue:

And in love powder all my money spent;

Behap what will, next Sunday after prayers,

When to the ale house Lupperkin repairs,

These golden flies into his mug I'll throw,

And soon the swain with fervent love shall glow.

Shakespeare, too, in *A Midsummer Night's Dream*, alludes to the love philtre:

Yet mark'd I where the bolt of Cupid fell,

It fell upon a little western flower,

Before milk-white, now purple with love's wound,

And maidens call it Love-in-Idleness.

Fetch me that flower; the herb I show'd thee once,

The juice of it on sleeping eyelids laid

Will make or man or woman madly dote

Upon the next live creature that it sees.

Again:

I'll watch Titania when she is asleep,

And drop the liquor of it in her eyes,

The next thing then she waking looks upon,

Be it on lion, bear, or wolf, or bull,

On meddling monkey, or on busy ape,

She shall pursue it with the soul of love.

Perfumes of all kinds, used on the person, on the genitalia, on clothes, in beds, in foods, were considered arousing stimulants. This procedure was in vogue both among the ancient Greeks and Romans, in the Orient, and during the Middle Ages: and is, of course, far from obsolescent these days.

The Greek playwright Aristophanes mentions perfumes in his comedy *Lysistrata* in connection with sexual enticements. Horace the Roman lyric poet tells of an old lecher 'scented with nard.'

Ambergris and civet were immensely popular. An ointment, extracted from spikenard, was known as foliatum: another, as nicerotiana. Cinnamon, sweet marjoram, myrrh, were in use. So with aromatic oils. Perfumes, in fact, are regularly mentioned in erotic and sexual situations and contexts. The corpus of the *Arabian Nights* contains many episodes involving the use and impact of scents. The Biblical *Song of Songs* too makes apposite reference to the subject:

a bundle of myrrh is my well-beloved unto me ...

ointment and perfumes rejoice the heart ...

perfumes and sweet spices ...

beds of aromatic spices ...

Ben Jonson, the English dramatist, has Volpone, in the comedy of that name, offer Celia perfumed baths:

The milk of unicorns, and panthers' breath

Gathered in bags, and mixed with Cretan wines.

Our drink shall be prepared gold and amber.

Onions in particular have for centuries possessed an aphrodisiac reputation. Onion is recommended for such intentions by the Greek and Roman poets. Ovid and Martial, and the later bucolic poet Columella urgently stress the eating of plenty of onions as both a rejuvenating and an animating agent. The Greek physician Galen also considered onions as having stimulating virtues.

In the East, onion seed is pounded, mixed with honey, and taken while one is fasting, in the hope of physiological urgency.

Among Arabs, onions boiled with spices, then fried in oil with egg yolks, are, if taken successively on a number of days, considered of high potency.

The seat of amorous passion was traditionally the liver. This concept is exemplified in *The Faithful Shepherdess*, by John Fletcher:

Amoret: Dear friend, you must not blame me, if I make

A doubt of what the silent night may do,

Coupled with this day's heat, to move your blood.

Maids must be fearful. Sure you have not been

Wash'd white enough, for yet I see a stain

Stick in your liver: go and purge again.

Perigot: Oh, do not wrong my honest simple truth!

Myself and my affections are as pure

As those chaste flames that burn before the shrine

Of the great Dian; only my intent

To drag you thither was to plight our troths,

With interchange of mutual chaste embraces,

And ceremonious tying of our souls.

For to that holy wood is consecrate

A virtuous well, about whose flowery banks

The nimble-footed fairies dance their rounds

By the pale moonshine, dipping oftentimes

Their stolen children, so to make them free

From dying flesh and dull mortality.

By this fair fount hath many a shepherd sworn,

And given away his freedom, many a troth

Been plight, which neither envy nor old time

Could ever break, with many a chaste kiss given

In hope of coming happiness; by this

Fresh fountain many a blushing maid

Hath crown'd the head of her long-loved shepherd

With gaudy flowers, whilst he happy sung

Lays of his love and dear captivity.

There grow all herbs fit to cool looser flames

Our sensual parts provoke, chiding our bloods,

And quenching by their power those hidden sparks

That else would break out, and provoke our sense

To open fires; so virtuous is that place.

Then, gentle shepherdess, believe and grant.

In troth, it fits not with that face to scant

Your faithful shepherd of those chaste desires

He ever aim'd at, and ...

Amoret: Thou hast prevail'd; farewell. This coming night

Shall crown thy chaste hopes with long-wish'd delight.

Perigot: Our great god Pan reward thee for that good

Thou hast given thy poor shepherd!

A medieval song, that appears in *The Maid's Tragedy*, by Beaumont and Fletcher, suggests that restraint in lust may occasionally be a desideratum:

I could never have the power

To love one above an hour,

But my heart would prompt mine eye

On some other man to fly.

Venus, fix mine eyes fast,

Or, if not, give me all that I shall see at last!

In *Philaster*, a play by Beaumont and Fletcher, mention is made of an amatory provocative that was in common use in the Middle Ages and later:

Cleremont: Sure this lady has a good turn done her against her will; before she was common talk, now none dare say cantharides can stir her. Her face looks like a warrant, willing and commanding all tongues, as they will answer it, to be tied up and bolted when this lady means to let herself loose. As I live, she has got her a goodly protection and a gracious; and may use her body discreetly for her health's sake, once a week, excepting Lent and dog-days. Oh, if they were to be got for money, what a great sum would come out of the city for these licenses!

Foods and herbs that have a gastronomic appeal are often empirically credited with amatory traits as well. For instance, eel soup and preserves and sundry pies have been brought into the field of such beneficial stimulants. Also the herb eryngium maritimum or Sea Holly, whose fleshy roots were candied and served hot in Elizabethan and later days. Figs and fennel soup: tunny fish and plovers' eggs, halibut, plaice, mackerel and mullet. So with apples and potatoes and garlic. Horseradish and sesame seeds, vanilla and turmeric, frangipane cream and purslane: frogs' legs and peaches. Ghee, ginger-fruit jam. Goose-tongues and grapes and guinea fowl. Hare soup and haricot beans. Soup seasoned with thyme, pimento, cloves, and laurel. Lentils and pomegranates and dates. Mutton, lamb, and rice. Mallows boiled in goat milk. Or the sap of mallows. Aromatic marjoram and marrow. Mint and onions, pineapple and mushrooms. Peas, and pastries kneaded into phallic and genital forms. All things, it appears, that are edible or potable come at some time or other under the classification of anticipatory amatory aids.

Messalina, the wife of the Roman Emperor Claudius, was infamous for her licentiousness, her intrigues, and her obscene amours. Historical testimony relates that she had amorous encounters with fourteen athletes, and in consequence assumed the honorific of *Invincible*. In commemoration of the episode she also dedicated fourteen wreaths to the Priapic god.

Apuleius, the Roman novelist who flourished in the second century A.D., alludes to an ancient Roman list of ingredients in the preparation of love-potions:

They dig out all kinds of philtres

from everywhere:

they search for the agent that

arouses mutual love:

pills and nails and threads,

roots and herbs and shoots,

the two-tailed lizard,

and charms from mares.

A certain philtre, according to the testimony of Girolamo Folengo in his *Maccaronea*, published in 1519, was composed of black dust from a tomb, the venom of a toad, the flesh of a brigand, the lung of an ass, the blood of a blind infant, the bile of an ox, and corpses rifled from graves.

It is unusual to discover a decided anti-aphrodisiac, recommended as an antidote, for banishing lust. The following prescription appears in the *Secrets of Albertus Magnus*, a medieval magic manual:

Turtur, a Turtle, is a birde very well knowne. It is called Merlon of the Chaldees, of the Greeks Pilax. If the heart of this foule be borne in a

Wolves skin, he that weareth it shall never have an appetite to commit lechery from henceforth.

In the same magic manual attributed to Albertus Magnus the medieval philosopher, there is a description of a philtre that has a number of properties, both medicinal and amatory:

The seventh is the herb of the planet Venus, and is called Pisterion, of some Hierobotane, id est, Sterbo columbaria et Verbena, Vervin.

The root of this herb put upon the neck healeth the swine pockes, apostumus behinde the eares, and botches of the neck, and such as cannot keepe their water. It healeth cuts also, and swelling of the evil, or fundament, proceeding of an inflammation which groweth in the fundament.

It is also of great strength in veneriall pastimes. If any man put it into his house or vineyard, or in the ground, he shal have great store of increase.

Another love charm, from Albertus Magnus' *Book of the Marvels of the World*, is designed to stabilize a woman's affection:

If thou wilt that a woman bee not visious nor desire men, take the private members of a Woolfe, and the haires which doe grow on the cheekes or eyebrowes of him, and the haires which bee under his beard, and burne it all, and give it to her to drinke, when she knoweth not, and she shal desire no other man.

Macrobius, a Roman writer who flourished c. 400 A.D., is the author of a symposium entitled *Saturnalia*, in which he states that hot drinks, particularly wine, are provocative of amatory exercise: deinde omnia calida Venerem provocant et semen excitant et generationi favent. Hausto autem mero plurimo fiunt viri ad coitum pigriores. That is, a long draught of unmixed wine is a decided stimulant to genesiac activity. On the other hand, like many of the ancient erotic poets, Macrobius adds that excessive and cold wine is a deterrent: vini nimietas ut frigidi facit semen exile vel debile.

The plant verbena officinalis was known to Hippocrates and later on to Pliny the Elder as an effective means of inducing virile potency.

An Indian plant named Datroa, the juice of which was used in a drink, was given as a physiological stimulant

---

In the eighteenth century an erotic concoction known as Diavolini was popular in Italy. In France, these Diavolini became equally popular under the name of diablotins—devil-pastilles.

The nettle, urtica urens, was a legendary and traditional stimulus, credited with promoting decisive potency.

Ocimum Basilicum is a plant with labiate flowers. It was known to the Egyptians and is mentioned by the Roman encyclopedist Pliny the Elder. It was used as an aphrodisiac as well as for other medicinal purposes.

Lycopodium Clavatum, a plant known by a variety of other names, was formerly used in amatory practices.

The amethyst was anciently considered a stone whose contact was a stimulus to passion.

In the Middle Ages there was in Germany a kind of humorous folk legend that was called the Old Wives' Mill. This legend extended into the eighteenth century. The theme was the rejuvenation of old women into young maidens and young women. There is an old print depicting the Mill, with elderly females being carried into the Mill and coming out young and comely.

The means of arousing erotic sensations and the devices contrived for the furtherance of weird or furtive amatory conditions have varied all the way from forthright bestialities, sacrificial blood rituals, as described by the poet Horace with reference to the witch Canidia's practices, down to more or less innocuous or ineffectual concoctions.

As far as ritual killing is concerned, and the extraction of human organs for amatory purposes, such methods were in vogue in Europe until far into the seventeenth century, notably in France.

A French preparation, that promised a renewal of physiological vigor, was known as Essence à l'usage des monstres.

Certain ancient Greek papyri contain suggestions and recipes intended to promote physiological vigor and by means of magic formulas to correct amatory deficiencies. These papyri now belong in the Louvre, in Paris, and in the British Museum.

Diagrams and symbols appear in the papyri. There are invocations, magic ritualistic prescriptions. There are, also, invocations and supplications to strange deities: among them, Sabazios, a Thracian-Phrygian god who had affinities with Dionysus, the god of wine, of fertility, and of procreation. He was also equated with the deity called Curios Sabaoth, mentioned in the Septuagint, and also Theos Hypsistos.

The Greek writer Lucian's *Lover of Lies* consists of a collection of sketches on various contemporary superstitions and practices. There are descriptions of magic statues endowed with animation, awesome apparitions, and also charms for bringing back a lover who has strayed.

The River Scamander, in Greece, was reputed to be such a potent amatory stimulus that maidens hopefully bathed in its waters. On one occasion, according to the testimony of the orator Aeschines, the beautiful Callirhoë, on her way to bathing in the sacred Scamander, was met by a young man who represented himself as an aide to the river god. The young man then substituted himself for the god and performed his divine function.

The medieval demonographer Martin Delrio, in his Disquisitionum Magicarum Libri Sex, discusses love charms, brews of all kinds, and other amatory inducements used by practitioners in the Black Arts. He mentions formulas and incantations, spells and alluring chants such as the seductive croonings of the ancient sirens, as well as the hypnotic music produced by Orpheus: also concoctions compounded of viscera and blood and other more intimate secretions.

Amatory inducements may be merely sensuous, or bodily proximity, as in dancing. Or excitation may be provoked by listening to an appealing voice, or visually observing a theatrical spectacle. Or recalling a fragment of song, a forgotten melody.

Particularly in the Orient, amatory preparations often run the gamut from oddities or puerilities to items that are monstrous in themselves, or so rare as to preclude the possibility of securing them: as, the scale of a tortoise, or the secretions of a stag, or a corpse, or a hyena's brains or whiskers.

Yet, in the East, these ingredients might well be furtively whispered to the love-sick suppliant by some aged crone who is the repository of legendary remedies, or by an obscure apothecary, whose pharmacopoeia is medieval, or by some wandering minstrel or trader.

Certain plants are associated with erotic consequences and have been resorted to by those in restless quest of amatory contentments. Among these plants are: the root of narcissus, vervain, water lilies, and bamboo.

In one Hindu erotic manual, a kind of Rake's Progress entitled The Harlot's Guide, certain ingredients are enumerated as contributing to the potency of philtres. Included in the items are fish soup, ghee, and indigenous herbs.

In former times, in France, a dish of the testes of a kid or a bull or a fox or a hare would be set before a man who intended to embark on amatory ventures.

Love stimulants may be both material and psychic. They may have physiological impacts that result in amatory capacity, or they may heighten and arouse the emotional awareness and sensitivity, with similar results.

Among the medieval investigators, philosophers, and alchemists and occultists, Albertus Magnus held a dominant position. He had a perception of scientific method, yet he also dealt in unwarranted and legendary fantasies. He wrote on physiology and astronomy. He investigated plant and animal life. He equated the characteristics and properties of certain stones, certain metals, certain creatures, with corresponding human traits and faculties. He felt that such stones, or the extraction of certain animal organs, would be conducive to the realization of the virtues of these minerals or viscera in relation to the human being. The lion's bravery resides in the lion's heart. Hence the eating of the heart, by a kind of sympathetic transference, will render the human consumer equally courageous. So the procedure extends throughout the entire amatory field. Certain animals and birds, as the pigeon and the ass and the goat and the bull, are known for their lubricity. The testes, therefore, and the genitalia of such animals will correspondingly endow the man who consumes them with equally intense capacity. Certain formulas, particular invocations and ritualistic procedures, diagrams and symbols and periapts will all contribute to the efficacy of the rite.

Thus, to stimulate desire in either sex, the genitalia of the animals of the opposite sex are consumed.

In the nests of eagles are found stones called echites. Worn on the left arm, these stones promote erotic sensations.

To ensure erotic continuance, the marrow of a wolf's left foot is advised. This is mixed with chypre and ambergris and the resultant unguent is rubbed on the object of affection.

Like a culinary direction, but usually with less promptness or ease, one is enjoined to take the liver of a sparrow, a swallow's womb, a hare's kidney, a pigeon's heart. Dry and crush into a powder. Add equal weight of one's own blood. Dry and mix in soup as an infallible potion.

For reinvigorating purposes, an ointment composed of ash of star-lizard, civet oil, St. John's wort oil is prepared. This is smeared on the toe of the left foot and the loins.

The fat of a young buck, together with civet and ambergris, is equally efficacious.

Goose testes and the stomach of a hare, well seasoned with spices, are amatory aids.

Also: a salad made of satyrion, rocket, and celery, soaked in oil and rose vinegar.

As, in rarer cases, an anaphrodisiac, on the other hand, the powdered genitals of a mild bull are recommended, in a soup containing veal, purslain, and lettuce.

The medieval grimoires, those manuals dedicated to sorcery, also treated of philtres and amatory brews.

Take two new knives. On a Friday morning—the day that is consecrated to Aphrodite—go to a spot where you can find earthworms. Take two, join the two knives together, then cut the two heads and the two tails of the worms. Keep the bodies. On returning home, smear them with sperm: dry, and pulverize them.

Again: Pull out three pubic hairs and three from the left armpit. Burn them on a hot shovel. Pulverize, and insert in a piece of bread, that will be dipped in soup.

Or: With the left hand pluck a bunch of vervain and repeat: I pluck you by the power of Lucifer, Prince of the Infernal Regions, and of Beelzebub, mother of three demons. Let her send Attos, Effeton, and Canabo to torment X so that, within twenty-four hours, she may do my will.

There is a prescription against cuckoldry, involving the organs, the skin, and the eyes of a wolf: pounded and calcined and composed into a drink.

Another prescription, designed for amatory purposes, involves a loaf of warm bread into which nine drops of blood are distilled. The bread is then dried, pulverized, and taken with coffee.

Another recipe requires the fat and the bile of a goat, dried, and mixed with oil. Its use will ensure faithful and continuous attachment to the person loved.

Another device for maintaining enduring love requires two turtle doves, male and female. After they are strangled, the blood is poured into a cup never before used. One's own blood is added, together with some hair of the woman. On the first white page of a new Bible there is now written with a gold pen dipped in the turtle doves' blood: Where you go, I shall go. Where you stay, I shall stay. Your people are my people and your god is my god. I shall die where you die. Only death shall separate us. The document is sprinkled with incense and placed under the nuptial pillow. The brew is poured into another cup, never before used, and mixed with wine. Each of the two persons concerned in the ceremony now takes a drink.

––––––––––––

An elaborate potion, that involves many ingredients, much time, and careful and scrupulous preparation, is as follows:

On the first Friday after a summer new moon, go at noon and look for a snake. Cut its head off, and carry it away in a new silk bag. Once home, throw the stick used for killing the snake toward the East, and hang the bag in a dark, warm corner. The following night, go barefooted to a meadow. Before midnight, gather two leaves of white clover, two of red clover, and six stems of spurge. Bring them back in a new basket. Then take a white bud from two rose bushes, a red bud and a young leaf of each, wrap in virgin parchment on which you write: Revarin myrtol her kulbata with a new goose quill dipped in your own blood.

The leaves, their contents, and the basket are set at the head of the bed, on a table on which a lamp burns for at least three hours. On waking up, spray the flowers and leaves with cold well water and set them in the place where the snake's head is drying. Wait until night. About eleven p.m. stretch out, on a table in the room, virgin parchment, draw thereon with a fresh heated point a six-branched star, by the light of an old church taper placed in a silver holder.

Procure a new chopper, two new knives, a new porcelain bowl, a new, well rinsed bottle, a black glass, a carafe of cold water, a stick of new wax, a seal, a mortar, and a new cork.

At midnight, make the sign of the cross three times. Then put the snake's head in the mortar with the leaves and flowers crushed into a paste. Heap up into a consistent mixture. Put the mortar on the flame until the contents are dry: then pulverize, while the mortar is heating.

With the new knives, let six drops of your blood fall into the cup: add water, pour the contents of the mortar into the cup, stir, and boil. Take three of your hairs, calcine them and throw into the cup. Do likewise with the parchment and the bag. Pour into the bottle, add water until it overflows. Cork it and seal it, place it in the bed, put out the light, pray and go to sleep.

After three days, after leaving it in the dark, by the window, on the third midnight the brew will be ready. Five drops for men, three for women, mixed with drink or food.

This elixir was reputed to be highly effective.

CHAPTER IX
MIDDLE AGES AND LATER

In the earlier Christian centuries, misogynistic attitudes were markedly prevalent, especially among the dogmatizing Church Fathers, and despite the traditions of the *agape*. Clemens and Ambrose, Tertullian and Athanasius were impassioned and vociferous, both in their oral denunciations, and in their written invectives against the essentially evil and malefic nature of woman.

Hence sexual love was anathema to them: and even marriage, grudgingly conceded but rarely accepted, was an object of horrified scorn. In consequence, it was not surprising that sexual interests and activities should go underground, as it were, and that amatory aids and encouragements likewise developed their secretive hiding places, their esoteric emporia, their identifiable but undisclosed havens.

The result was that, as the Middle Ages advanced, two basic views appeared to come into force. Laws that governed the marriage ceremonial and its consequent domestic involvements and possessive obligations. And laws that related to love as such, to the *amor naturalis*, as defined by St. Thomas Aquinas, both in its romantic sense as a kind of amatory but undefined ideal, and in its sexual implications that reached as far as adultery, under certain subdued, well-controlled, and unpublicized circumstances.

All these occasions created a hungry, frantic demand for philtres and phials and nostrums of all varieties, of all degrees of efficacy. They bloomed upon the markets, and gave employment and a vast impetus to quacks and adventurers, to alchemists and beldams, in furnishing the tantalizing apparatus of love.

One of the most dominant humanists during the Middle Ages was Albertus Magnus (1193–1280). Of Germanic birth, he was educated in Padua and Bologna. On account of his encyclopedic knowledge, he was generally known as the Doctor Universalis.

Professor of theology, scientist, teacher, he achieved, both by his voluminous writings and his lectures, an almost legendary reputation. In one of his treatises, *De Secretis Mulierum*, he expounds on feminine matters and then proceeds to discuss, in his *De Virtutibus Lapidum Quorundam Libellus*, the virtues and properties of certain precious and semi-precious stones. In an amatory direction, Albertus Magnus gives suggestions, as if they were prescriptive and categorically assertive, on how to win the favor and affection of a person:

Take the stone called Chalcedony. It may be black or red, and is extracted from the stomach of swallows. Wrap the red stone in a linen cloth or in calf skin and place it under the left armpit.

Although the philtre that is intended to inspire erotic excitations is normally a drink, a fluid, Albertus Magnus' recipe is virtually and in its ultimate sense a potion. He adds, on a later occasion in the same text:

If you want to promote love between two people, take the stone called Echites, by some termed Aquileus—because eagles place it in their nests. It is purple in color and is found on the sea shore: sometimes, too, in Persia. And it always contains within itself another stone that makes a sound when moved. The ancient philosophers say that this stone, worn suspended on the left arm, effects love between a man and a woman.

In the thirteenth century, a certain Arnold of Villanova, a physician who traveled widely throughout Europe and in Africa, was reputed to be a powerful karcist, believed to have occult contacts and interests. He dabbled, also, in alchemy, and, as legend rumored, was proficient in actual transmutations. In his medical practice he relied largely on herbal concoctions, on magic formulas, on amatory potions prepared according to traditional prescriptions.

Potions and love philtres pervaded all life, at all levels, throughout the middle centuries. Peasant and pilgrim resorted to aged creatures who were reputed to possess cryptic formulas, hidden resources transmitted to them orally by their forbears. Even in the Eucharistic rite the *poculum amatorium* made its contorted intrusion. In the Eucharistic rite, the wafer often became an ingredient in love potions and acquired a particularly efficacious renown.

Most dealings in love devices, secret formulas, erotic phials, were nameless, both the client and the practitioners remaining unknown by name to each other. Until the practitioner became so assertive, so prosperous and so much in demand that people flocked from remote regions, from distant cities, from foreign countries, to acquire the ultimate elixir. Count Alessandro Cagliostro was shrewd and unscrupulous enough to profit by such conditions. He was an Italian alchemist, magician, and hermetic, but basically his qualifications and capacities were at least dubious. What was not at all dubious was his facility in outwitting all Europe, in amassing great wealth from gullible clients, in escaping, on all but the ultimate occasion, from merited penalties. His original name was Giuseppe Balsamo, and his restless life extended from 1745 to 1795.

In the heyday of his quackery he became both known and notorious throughout Europe. He was *persona gratissima* among the most distinguished social circles and families. With the aid of his wife Lorenza Feliccani he amassed enormous wealth by the sale of alchemical compounds, magic elixirs, and love potions. Scandals followed his movements and implicated him in fantastic incidents, salacious episodes. Hence, for security or secrecy, he was constantly changing his abode. In his last years, he suffered imprisonment, in the fortress of San Leo. And with his death, the legends proliferated and multiplied. Strange feats were recorded of him. Mystic phenomena appeared at his potent will. According to such traditions, he was a necromancer, having exorcised a dead woman. At a public banquet he invoked the dead spirits of Diderot and Voltaire. And he was the founder of a secret organization known as The Egyptian Lodge, where goetic practices and sorcery were attempted and consummated.

Cagliostro had a kind of counterpart in the arcane arts. Catherine La Voisin was a notorious French fortune-teller, as well as a reputed witch. For the most part, she was a dispenser of love philtres, and plied her sinister trade in low and high circles. In this capacity she was intimately associated with the obscene and erotic operations of Madame de Montespan. Madame de Montespan, mistress of King Louis XIV of France, reached a point where her amatory offerings no longer aroused the King. Steps had to be taken, urgently and effectively, to recover that affection. With the aid of Catherine La Voisin, she concocted love philtres. She participated in magical rites, in amatory Masses, and even in child sacrifice, to gain her passionate purpose. In this sinister machination she enlisted the support of a notorious Abbé Guibourg. His scatological and lascivious activities in this respect brought about his arrest, and his summary execution.

The love-potion, then, could be, potentially, a tremendously evil force, a malefic and fatal weapon, an instrument of ruin and death. But usually the potion was associated with soft and luxurious dalliance, with amorous whisperings, with marital exchanges and sophisticated deceits. So it was in Italy in particular. In the sixteenth century, many Jewesses dabbled in love potions and amatory charms. They practiced their skill in Rome itself, and acquired an established reputation as purveyors of these physiological stimuli. Ferdinand Gregorovius, who produced a monumental history of Rome, declares that Jewish women brewed love philtres in the dark of the night, for their languishing customers, the ladies of Rome.

Lippold, a Jewish financier of the Elector Joachim II of Brandenburg, who also belongs in the sixteenth century, was accused, among other charges based on magic practices, of dispensing recipes for the concoction of love philtres. He was brutally tortured: then executed in Berlin.

The medieval era was a period of absorption of the past, with occasional tentative gropings and some experimentation in new directions. In the erotic sphere, the Middle Ages adopted this antique heritage, at times moulded and modified it, and sometimes made use of it in new contexts. Thus there was in use an aromatic herb called popularly Sweet Flag. This was the plant known anciently as acorus calamus, that the Romans believed to be endowed with erotic stimulus. It was appropriately known to them by the alternate name of the plant of Venus.

———

In their tenebrous laboratories, equipped with weird paraphernalia, lit by the glow of furnace fire, the experimenting alchemists busied themselves with their apparatus. On tables and benches stood, in confused array, retorts of fantastic shape, flasks and tubes, alembics and phials containing strange viscous multi-colored fluids, fungus growths, particles of obscene matter, unnameable secretions. Some liquids, under the influence of tiny flames, hissed and spluttered with cunning animation. All these brews were undergoing action by fire and intermingling of chemicals, were being forced into mutations and directions for horrendous ends: and, dominantly among these objectives, was the illusive mutation into gold, but also the discovery of the source of being, the elixir of life, the rejuvenating creative essence that would promote youthfulness and vigor, passion and potency.

———

The medieval occultist and the alchemist did not always remain, as tradition believed, secluded in their own ivory tower, or rather in their laboratories. In many senses, they were decided realists, and they made profitable use of their knowledge and experimentations in the direction of astrological horoscopes, fortune-telling, and the preparation of philtres. There was, particularly, a potion in great demand among amorous but disappointed swains of every degree and rank. It was, according to general hearsay, a beverage whose basic ingredient was gold. The preparation was consumed daily, over a space of time, as a kind of amatory potable gold.

Many types of potions were resorted to in the Middle Ages. Some acted as physiological excitants, but involved great circumspection in securing the ingredients. These ingredients were often organic fragments: hair of the beloved one obtained surreptitiously. Or nail parings. Or a shred torn from an intimately worn garment. Such items were then burned, and, when reduced to ashes, mixed with wine and used as a philtre.

In other cases, all sorts of putatively effective concoctions, never of course analyzed as to the contents by the passionate pursuer, were involved. They were freely sold in the market towns of medieval Europe, in battlemented castles, in remote hamlets. They were brought as elixirs by returning travelers from distant countries, and were eagerly purchased in the ports and capitals of the continent. Especially when these travelers reinforced their importations with tales and anecdotes that testified to the amazing virtues of their brews.

The Elizabethan Age is noted for its tremendous intellectual productivity, for its relish in living, its adventurous ways on the high seas, in exploration, in colonization, in discovery. In the drama, in the plays of Beaumont and Fletcher, of Marlowe and Ford and Ben Jonson and Thomas Dekker, the social and erotic phases of this tumultuous era play no mean or insignificant role. In palace and hut, in court and manor, the primary motif was love, in all its tantalizing manifestations. Love pervaded all. And the instruments for promoting love were all important, transcending domesticity and tranquillity, honor and ethics. The secretive drug, the rare pill, the poculum amatorium, the brew distilled by the wizened alchemist, the imported philtre, the dramatic potion are all made contributory to the furtherance of love and lust, to erotic subjugation, conquest, and mastery.

The corpus of Shakespearean plays, as an instance, contains a number of allusions to concoctions relating to amorous experiences. In *A Midsummer Night's Dream*, Act 3, Scene 2, Oberon, King of the Fairies, addresses Puck:

This falls out better than I could devise.

But hast thou yet latched the Athenian's eyes

With the love-juice, as I did bid thee do?

Puck: I took him sleeping—that is finished too— And the Athenian woman by his side; That, when he waked, of force she must be eyed.

Later, in the same play, another reference of the same kind appears:

Oberon: What hast thou done? thou hast mistaken quite,

and laid the love-juice on some true-love's sight.

Of thy misprision must perforce ensue

Some true love turned, and not a false-turned true.

Further on, in the same act, Lysander, in love with Hermia, addresses her thus:

Lysander: Thy love! out, tawny Tartar, out!

Out, loathed med'cine! O, hated potion, hence!

In *The Winters Tale*, Act 1, Scene 2, Camillo, Lord of Sicilia, addresses Leontes, King of Sicilia:

Camillo: Say, my lord,

I could do this, and that with no rash potion,

But with a ling'ring dram, that should not work

Maliciously like poison: but I cannot

Believe this crack to be in my dread mistress

(So sovereignly being honorable!)

T'have loved the ...

In *The Merry Wives of Windsor*, Act 3, Scene 1, the Host says to Caius:

Shall I lose my doctor? no; he gives me the potions and the motions.

In *Pericles*, Act 1, Scene 2, Pericles addresses Helicanus:

Thou speak'st like a physician, Helicanus,

That ministers a potion unto me

That thou would'st tremble to receive thyself.

In Part 1, Henry IV, Act 5, Scene 3, the Prince of Wales speaks:

The insulting hand of Douglas over you,

Which would have been as speedy in your end

As all the poisonous potions in the world.

And again, in Part 2, Act 1, Scene 1, Morton declares:

And they did fight with queasiness, constrain'd,

As men drink potions.

In these previously cited instances, in the Shakespearean contexts, it is evident that the term potion had often a malefic connotation, implying venom and destruction in its use. But it was equally a term of amatory and sensual significance, associated largely with physiological refreshment.

In *Dr. Faustus*, Christopher Marlowe's drama, the protagonist, passionately eager to embrace all knowledge that offers power, that is, the thaumaturgic and necromantic skills, exclaims:

'Tis magic, magic that hath ravished me.

He then proceeds, after his pact with Mephistopheles, to demand the implementation of the conditions. He is aroused erotically, and commands:

let me have a wife,

The fairest maid in Germany;

For I am wanton and lascivious,

And cannot live without a wife

Mephistopheles, virtually a pander, suggesting provocative amatory delights, promises:

Tut, Faustus,

Marriage is but a ceremonial toy;

And if thou lovest me, think no more of it.

I'll cull thee out the fairest courtesans,

And bring them every morning to thy bed;

She whom thine eye shall like, thy heart shall have,

Be she as chaste as was Penelope,

And as wise as Saba, or as beautiful

As was bright Lucifer before his fall.

In a later scene, Robin the Ostler appears with one of Dr. Faustus' grimoires:

Robin: Oh, this is admirable! here I ha' stolen one of Doctor Faustus' conjuring books, and i' faith I mean to search some circles for my own use. Now will I make all the maidens in our parish dance at my pleasure, stark-naked before me; and so by that means I shall see more than e'er I felt or saw yet.

Enter Rafe calling Robin.

Rafe: Robin, prithee, come away; there's a gentleman tarries to have his horse, and he would have his things rubbed and made clean: he keeps such a chafing with my mistress about it; and she has sent me to look thee out. Prithee, come away.

Robin: Keep out, keep out, or else you are blown up; you are dismembered, Rafe: keep out, for I am about a roaring piece of work.

Rafe: Come, what dost thou with that same book? Thou cans't not read.

Robin: Yes, my master and mistress shall find that I can read, he for his forehead, she for her private study; she's born to bear with me, or else my art fails.

Rafe: Why, Robin, what book is that?

Robin: What book! Why, the most intolerable book for conjuring that e'er was invented by any brimstone devil.

Rafe: Can'st thou conjure with it?

Robin: I can do all these things easily with it; first, I can make thee drunk with ippocras at any tavern in Europe for nothing; that's one of my conjuring works.

Rafe: Our Master Parson says that's nothing.

Robin: True, Rafe; and more, Rafe, if thou hast any mind to Nan Spit, our kitchenmaid, then turn her and wind her to thy own use as often as thou wilt, and at midnight.

Rafe: O brave Robin, shall I have Nan Spit, and to mine own use?

Frequently consulted on erotic difficulties were the ubiquitous witches who flourished in the Middle Ages throughout the European continent. In the literature of these middle centuries their amatory brews are used in a variety of passionate situations, to inspire love, to divert it into strange channels, and, sometimes, to crush it. On occasion the repulsive and abhorrent ingredients, both animal and human, are noted with a land of macabre relish. But the urgent suppliant, bent on his lustful self-appointed mission, rarely hesitated on that account. On the contrary, the rare or obscene nature of the brew was like an added spurt to his frantic libido: and the more distasteful the composition, the more intense the lustfulness that was so inspired.

It was not unusual for the philtres and preparations to contain animal testes, genitalia, human excremental matter, even fragments and shreds of human corpses, torn from graveyards and charnel-houses.

An extreme type of potion, administered in febrile cases, was actual blood, drunk by both man and woman.

The Middle Ages, particularly the eleventh century, was noted for its loose morality, its amorous diversions, its disregard of the old rigid domestic or social prohibitions and restraints. Achievement followed on desire, and sensuous and sensual whims met with ready acquiescence. Returning warriors, home from the Crusades in Palestine, or the campaigns in Spain, had, during the course of their embattled activities, come in contact with disturbing exotic women, so different, in both physical appearance and temperament, from the wives and women they had left in the châteaux and manors. These exotic women were brought back by the returning victors as captives. Once returned, the warriors looked back with something of nostalgia to their colorful days in foreign regions and in novel circumstances. Hence the captive women became a kind of live substitute for such meditations. The women consoled the warriors with murmurous love songs of their own country, sorrowful and prideful and exotic. And often the wives of these lords of the manor were unpleasantly surprised when these strange women were invited to domesticity as concubines. So that the medieval nobility became, in the course of time, a complicated series of relationships, tainted with harlotries and illegitimacies.

In these libidinous and licentious conditions, when exhaustion or age began to make perceptible appearance, amatory aids were sought, and philtres and brews were hopefully measured out by the furtive creatures, male and female, peripatetic vendors, sorceresses, quacks and occultists, who were always equipped, always prepared, to supply the passionate clamor.

The medieval passion for love aroused complications. Particularly, it aroused jealousy in the husband himself, however gallant or wayward he might be. Lovers or husbands, discovering the indiscretions and sportiveness of a mistress, a concubine, or a wife, exacted the utmost and not rarely the most barbaric penalties. A wife was compelled to eat her dead lover's heart. Another wife was forced to congregate with lepers because her conduct enraged her lawful spouse. One husband served up the heart of the slain adulterer in the form of a stew for his wife.

Yet the husband appeared to be exempt from any penalties inflicted for divergent amorous experiences in which he himself might be involved. For the man was dominant. The husband was equated with the ineluctable law. And the husband imposed that law upon his womankind. The male might consequently indulge with more than a fair chance of impunity in adultery, fornication, excessive lust.

And when these excitements seemed ultimately to approach physiological impairment, there was always the nostrum, and the extended hand of the aged crone, offering her mystic potion, her amatory panacea.

The permutations of amatory complications in the social frame of the Middle Ages, involving peasant and noble, troubadour and harlot, occasional damsels, poets, mistresses and concubines, resulted sometimes in a frantic movement toward chastity. Renunciation of carnal delights, of the amor naturalis that implied physical and sensual love only, became a pose, then a principle, then a habit, however, at times, it might be infringed or dishonored.

Chastity belts were devised by departing warriors to enforce continence upon their wives. Chastity tests, ingeniously contrived, became popular experiments in sexual restraints. It was the vogue, and the vogue became mores. Just as Tristan and Yseult slept with a naked sword between them.

And in excessive cases there was the weird but apparently effective device, for propagation purposes only, of the chemise cagoule.

And always, in the wake of these temporary waves of contrition or repentance, there followed, as a consequence of plague, violence, political unrest, banditry and war, a terrifying unleashing of all human inhibitions, a bacchanalian orgy of prolonged lechery and debauchery, reminiscent of Thucydides' dramatic account of the Athenian plague during the Peloponnesian War.

In the aftermath of these lecheries there arose perplexities, complications in erotic directions, incapacity through perversions and excesses: and a consequent hungry, voracious quest for remedial measures: drugs and drinks devised by itinerant traders, nostrums compounded by wily serfs and jongleurs, alchemical elixirs distilled in secret dens by putative adepts.

Women, in an amatory sense, were far from neglected in the Middle Ages. Many handbooks appeared that offered hints and guidance on dress, deportment, osculation and its limitations, social behavior, cleanliness, bathing and washing.

And if the object of the woman's passion was preoccupied elsewhere, or hesitant, or indifferent to her insistence or her personal charms, there was always recourse to the potion, by means of which she could have her way.

In France, in the Middle Ages, prostitution was so rampant and seeped into the life of the people and the nobility to such an alarming extent that the pious King Saint Louis, who flourished in the thirteenth century, promulgated a series of stringent decrees against prostitutes.

Yet Paris was notoriously populated with prostitutes. They practiced their occupation day and night, except on sacred days, in the most obscure rendez-vous, in inns and bath houses and cellars. François Villon, the poet of the brothel, and one of the chief sources for these days, casts a lurid but realistic light on this phase of the medieval scene.

Philtres were a common commodity in these circumstances, in spite of the spread of disease. For le mal de Naples, as it was virtuously called in France, but which the Italians as virtuously termed le mal français, was ravaging Europe. The disease, to give it its modern name, was syphilis.

Although the Middle Ages were intimately familiar with love and lust in all its lawful as well as its secretive phases, the amatory state itself occasioned such temperamental and physiological and characterial changes in the aspirant or the postulant that the question arose: Was love itself worth while?

This question was specifically asked by Andreas Capellanus, who belongs in the thirteenth century. He produced a handbook on the Art of Courtly Love, in which he listed rules, and gave directions, in connection with the conduct of the lover who is involved in a spiritual passion for the knight's wife, the queen, or a mistress of a manor.

Yet Andreas Capellanus also gives a sober, solemn warning against the ill effects of love, for of all disastrous results, it makes men old with untimely rapidity. Women, then, the source of this malefic consequence, should be shunned. They are avaricious. They are ruthless. They are faithless. They are dishonorable. This invective recalls a remarkably similar assault on women and their ways, the thunderous, condemnatory, bitter satire on women by the Roman satirist Juvenal.

In the Middle Ages amatory broths were in such demand that the most obscure, the most nauseating, and sometimes actually venomous items were indiscriminately compounded into philtres. Intimate human secretions, blood, animal semen and other discharges, formed the fluid basis for the incorporation of genitalia of animals, macerated sparrow brains, and analogous animal matter.

Such concoctions were designed to correct physiological disorders and natural weaknesses and defects in the person so affected.

One of the most significant treatises on love, applicable in its essential features to every age, although produced in the Middle Ages, is *Le Roman de la Rose*. It is an erotic allegory, begun in 1240 by Guillaume de Lorris, and completed in 1280 by Jean de Meun: a remote partnership that was nevertheless so effective as to make the book continuously popular for several centuries.

There are numberless precepts and suggestions regarding the material phases of love: personal appearance, social accomplishments, and in a more general way the requisite mode of behavior for the amatory suppliant. Above all, insistence is on giving free rein to passion and on indulging in every conceivable variety of erotic voluptuousness and sensual pleasure. And women, the treatise reminds one, are essentially as free as men in this respect. So that, when the passions subside and require increased fuel, the potion could be sought equally by men and women.

The philtre appears in imaginative literature no less than in actuality. The Wagnerian opera based on the Tristan and Yseult legend presents a heroine who is far from the submissive and dutiful medieval female, subservient to her amorous lord and master. She is highly selfish in her ways, and her love for Tristan is conditioned by the administration of a love-potion.

Medieval mortality distinguished between conjugal love and sexual love that extended, on the part of both husband and wife, beyond the domestic frontiers. Hence in many instances an insistent lover would resort to some provocative potion in order to bring the amatory objective into submission.

One of the most ravishing women in all history was Diane de Poitiers, who for some three decades was the mistress of the French king Henri II. Her beauty remained untarnished far beyond the usually allotted span. She was imitated by every woman: in her manner of walking, her hair styles, her general behavior. All society, all France was at her feet as the unattainable ideal woman. And she remained so long after her death.

Those who were particularly inquisitive about Diane de Poitiers' method of prolonged beauty, whispered, and general gossip supported the belief, that the continuance of her appealing and attractive charms was due to certain potent love philtres that she had regularly used.

Before her death, Diane de Poitiers revealed what was evidently the composition of the potion. Every morning, she declared, she had been in the habit of drinking a liquid consisting of molten gold and certain unrevealed drugs that had been recommended by alchemists.

It is curious to discover that sensual and sexual voluptuousness and amorous contests, whether accepted according to traditional principles or forbidden and experienced secretly, could find a vociferous, articulate opponent. Yet in 1599 such an attack on loose morality and licentious freedom was published under the title of *Antidote for Love, with a lengthy Discourse on the Nature and Causes thereof, together with the most singular Remedies for the Prevention and Cure of Amorous Passions.* The author was a Frenchman, a certain Dr. Jean Aubery.

To stimulate genital vigor, the French in the Middle Ages advocated, as a complement to physiological activity, verbal love making. Oral caresses, endearing diminutives, the poetic battery of language that was so familiar to the ancient poets, to Alciphron and Theocritus, to Plautus, to Catullus, to Horace, came into popular use again. One chronicler devotes himself to some extent to this phase of amorous conquest. He recommends erotic murmurings, whisperings, coaxings, endearments. And without question such recommendations were generally reinforced with anatomical and sexual terms, obscene and scatological references, that strengthened the lascivious gestures and contortions of the participants. Similarly, in Spain and in Italy perfumes began to acquire their amatory appeal and value, and added their subtle allurements and insinuations to a potion, or to an erotic phial.

Le Tableau de l'Amour Conjugal was a kind of amatory encyclopedia, first published in 1696. The author was a Frenchman, a Dr. Nicolas Venette. In addition to a great deal of matter on amatory subjects, the effects of excesses, the causes of the validity of marriage, continence and debauchery, there were also discussions on physiological conditions, sexual relations, theories on the humors, on male and female temperaments and peculiarities.

In respect of stimulants, Dr. Venette recommended, among other arousing potions, crocodile kidneys. These were to be dried, then pounded into a powder, to which was added sweet wine. The result, according to Dr. Venette, was amazingly effective.

In eighteenth century France, *la vie galante* had grown to such proportions socially that many clubs were established, devoted exclusively and fantastically to licentious erotic practices, to the dissemination of amatory gossip and tales of well-known personalities, prominent in contemporary life, who were addicted, orgiastically and with abandonment, to amorous mores. There were even publications that published spicy titbits about such characters, without disguise of name or circumstance.

Among such clubs were La Société Joyeuse, Les Sunamites, La Paroisse, and Les Aphrodites. One group, called Les Restauratrices, used the methods and manipulations and stimulating potions and drugs that are so vividly described in Petronius' Roman novel of the *Satyricon*. It was evident, then, that Les Restauratrices served men who had degenerated physiologically through age or extreme excesses.

These clubs recognized no amatory restraints whatever. They indulged in invented, ingenious permutations of amorous exercises, both privately and publicly, and even held competitions to decide the superior potency of members. The frequenters were ranked, in regard to prestige and distinction, according to the numerical extent of their encounters.

Birds and game were commonly used in amatory tonics. The medieval grimoires and manuals are packed with references to preparations that involve all parts of the bird as ingredients for erotic compounds. The philosopher and occultist Albertus Magnus, as an instance, who wrote on a vast number of allied subjects, prescribes, in one of his treatises, the brains of partridge, calcined into powder form, and steeped in red wine, as a prospective aid to vigor.

The licentious courts of France often experimented and used whatever lotion, concoction, or substance might prove effective in stimulating waning or exhausted capacities in the members of the court, both male and female. This quest grew to frantic and insidious proportions, for the entire court was tainted with perversions, sexual excesses, and exploratory monstrosities. For this purpose, then, ambergris, which is an ash-colored substance secreted in the intestines of the sperm whale, was used as a coating for chocolates, which were in the nature of titbits designed to arouse the courtiers, lechers, and gallants. As a perfume, ambergris was intended to provoke, through osphresiological channels, sensual attraction. Madame du Barry notoriously used ambergris as a means of ensuring Louis XV's amatory interest.

Early chroniclers, herbalists, and compilers of miscellaneous knowledge often refer to tonics, pastilles, and compounds as amatory specifics, but provokingly do not name them. Thus in the Geneanthropoeia, virtually a textbook on anatomy and sexology, produced in 1642 by an Italian professor of medicine named Johannes Benedict Sinibaldus, there is reference to a plant indigenous to the Atlas Mountains in North Africa. This plant was reputedly of great erotic virtue. The difficulty lies in its identification.

Allusion is similarly and frequently made to certain trees, shrubs, and herbs of India that have analogous properties.

The eighteenth century in Europe became an age of debauchery and gluttony. It was the age of licentious drama, of lewd poetry, of unbridled lusts, of the overthrow of all moral and social restraints. This was the situation notably in England, and in France.

It is known now, almost axiomatically, that foods, particularly meats and game, stimulate sensual desires. Hence, when there was an excess of sexual diversion, indiscriminate and pervasive through all classes of society as a result of over indulgence in food and equally in drink, there was correspondingly a resultant physiological reaction, a weariness and incapacity and expenditure of energy that clamored for renewal, for stimulants, brews and philtres to remedy this parlous situation.

Similarly, in the Orient, from Arabia to Japan, in the South Seas no less than in Africa, the basic sustenance is not animal flesh, but a diet that is largely though not exclusively vegetarian.

Such a diet does not encourage erotic tendencies. In consequence, in the East as well as in the West but for quite divergent reasons, there grew up, through the centuries, corpora and manuals of prescriptions, contrivances, suggestions, and a diversity of aids conducive to amatory functions. In essence, the development was along the lines of an entire aphrodisiac laboratory.

Every conceivable substance, every presumed juice or blossom or spice was worthy of a trial, of being tested for its impact on procreative activity. So with borax. Refined and compounded into a beverage, borax was, in the seventeenth century, reputed to pervade the entire organic frame, and to produce highly favorable physiological reactions in the genital areas.

At the same time, borax was considered extremely dangerous in the view of practicing physicians, and its use was urgently deprecated, on account of its concomitant poisonous effects.

The seventeenth century was the century of the French King, Louis XIV, Le Roi Soleil. And his reign and personal life, and the society that encircled his court, were an incessant round of lavish gaiety, gross and scatological obscenities, and the most flagrant immoralities. Among other infamous episodes that marked this period were the machinations of Louis' mistress, Madame de Montespan. She was involved, according to contemporary records, in poisoning one rival mistress and attempting the elimination of another by the same means. But chiefly Madame de Montespan is remembered for her febrile associations with sorceresses, reputed witches, whom she consulted for help in retaining King Louis' affection. The principal aide and accomplice in these furtive and insidious operations was Catherine La Voison, a professed witch, a poisoner, a dealer in love-potions. It was from La Voisin that Madame de Montespan secured amatory charms and philtres.

In the issue, Madame de Montespan lost her intimate status with the King, while La Voisin was burned alive in Paris.

In the seventeenth century there appears in France The Great Almanach of Love. It contained directions for arousing sensual feelings. It suggested music and songs, sonnets and madrigals. But it also recommended, as more earthy enticements, meals that included a dish of beans, turkey, and sweets. These items were virtually love philtres.

An old medieval custom, that lasted until well into this century in Europe, was in the nature of a nuptial love-potion.

After a wedding feast, members of the village community set water to boil in a pot. Into the pot were thrown, in addition to pepper, garlic, and salt—which are essentially aphrodisiac in character—,less appetizing contributions, such as spiders' webs and soot. The entire compound was stirred into an unsavory mixture, but both the bride and the groom were required to take at least a mouthful.

In essence, this brew was designed to arouse excitations on the part of the bridal pair, just as Plutarch refers to the bride nibbling fruit before retiring to bed.

In place of actual potions, the Middle Ages at times used what were essentially visual erotic stimulants. These were lewd pictures and drawings that were in great vogue, extensively so in the reign of King François I. Many among the French nobility made private collections of such provocative and scatological sketches that produced, in some cases, marked inflammatory erotic reactions. In certain country châteaux, also, stained glass windows depicted salacious episodes, libidinous postures and embraces, just as the caves of Ajanta in India portrayed amatory contortions in which human and animal performers were involved.

The subject of erotic practices, including perversions, abnormalities, flagellation, as well as philtres and amatory brews, was not limited to professional physicians. Many demonographers, including Martin Delrio, mentioned erotic techniques in their discussions and investigations of witchcraft and the furtive operations of occultists. In 1520 there was published a Latin text entitled *Fustigationes*, which involves references to love philtres. The author was a certain Grillandus, a Florentine and also a member of the Inquisition at Arezzo.

Through the centuries, there were sporadic appearances of pamphlets and miscellaneous pieces that had reference to amatory aids. For instance, *Le Jardin d'Amour*, published in 1798 by a certain Tansillo or Tanzillo.

Every century, every country, every religious sect, had its own monstrous obscenities, its peculiar orgiastic ceremonials, its gross and bestial manifestations, and its most unhallowed erotic permutations. Some of these phenomena were of a seclusive nature, confined to initiates only. Others, more liberated or more daring, were associated with royal courts, or temple worship, or even conventual life. Erotic acts, bestial performances, tribadism and fellatio and every other abnormality were all depicted in caves and church windows, woven in tapestries, or represented in ornamental furniture, etched in books, moulded in statuary.

The Middle Ages, in particular, were the milieu, but of course not exclusively so, of political cataclysms and internecine wars, of plagues and intrigues and famine, of splendor and tournaments, jousts and crusades, and also of servitude and witchcraft, gluttony and debauchery, monastic life and religious reforms, art and poetry and lewdness.

All through the ages, notably during these middle eras, this dichotomy was prevalent and manifest. And pervading and transcending all civic conditions, all national issues, was the erotic life of the teeming, inarticulate populace and the highly literate and cultured minorities: wanton prelates and easy princesses, libidinous serving maids and poetic gallants, romantic crusaders, lechers, perverts.

The history of these times is packed with religious lusts, with worship of the genitalia, with female devotees of Priapus, with amatory flagellations and erotic feasts, with sexuality rampant in full public view, with chastity belts and barbarous contraptions. The Latin chronicles and the Latin satirical writings, the Wandering Scholars' songs and the anecdotes and tales that amused these centuries are filled with abhorrent nudist practices, with adultery and incest, with prostitution and unholy commerce of holy devotees, with rape and sodomy. We hear of the most unbridled, the most shameless doings from the chronicles of Godefroy and of Froissart, of Benevente and Grecourt. We read of obscene banquets under kingly sponsorship, of brothels under royal patronage, of public gymnastic performances of harlots, of the debaucheries of monks and canons and students, adventurers and courtiers. We read of a monastery dedicated to prostitution, of parades of harlots, of foul sexual privileges exercised by the lords of the manor, of the ius primae noctis and the droit de cuisse, and, in short, of an array, colossal in bulk and unspeakable in content, of every conceivable erotic fact.

Through the ages, the knowledge of sexual and amatory artifices, contraptions, inducements grew and multiplied in such variety, through legend and experiment, through the accretions of poetic myths and hearsay, that a voluminous corpus was achieved. It comprehended incantations and fantasies, rare prescriptions, crude operative techniques, formulas and incisions, superstitions and alchemical products, astrological cryptograms and Satanic supplications that were all assumed to be effective in guarding or in increasing amatory potency.

Sexual procedures of all types and at varying levels were particularly prevalent in the Middle Ages. In addition, the clergy, according to the testimony of contemporary songs and monastic chronicles and incidental references in drama and satire and history, were not altogether immune to such diversions. To promote asceticism, therefore, to diminish carnal lusts, various plants and drugs and other medicaments were employed in monasteries to produce the desired anaphrodisiac condition. Agnus castus, for example, which is now identified with the chaste-tree or Abraham's balm, was credited with having decided cooling effects and eliminating physiological urgencies.

An ingenious device that resulted in stifling the amatory advances of a king is related in Boccaccio's *Decameron*: The Fifth Story of the First Day. King Phillippe of France, learning of the beauty of the Marchioness of Monferrato, journeys to her domain, in the absence of the Marquis. He is invited to a banquet:

The ordinance of the repast and of the viands she reserved to herself alone and having forthright caused collect as many hens as were in the country, she bade her cooks dress various dishes of these alone for the royal table.

The king came at the appointed time and was received by the lady with great honor and rejoicing. When he beheld her, she seemed to him fair and noble and well-bred beyond that which he had conceived from the courtier's words, whereat he marvelled exceedingly and commended her amain, waxing so much the hotter in his desire as he found the lady overpassing his foregone conceit of her. After he had taken somewhat of rest in chambers adorned to the utmost with all that pertaineth to the entertainment of such a king, the dinner hour being come, the king and the marchioness seated themselves at one table, whilst the rest, according to their quality, were honorably entertained at others. The king, being served with many dishes in succession, as well as with wines of the best and costliest, and to boot gazing with delight the while upon the lovely marchioness, was mightily pleased with his entertainment; but, after awhile, as the viands followed one upon another, he began somewhat to marvel, perceiving that, for all the diversity of the dishes, they were nevertheless of nought other than hens, and this although he knew the part where he was to be such as should abound in game of various kinds and although he had, by advising the lady in advance of his coming, given her time to send a-hunting. However, much as he might marvel at this, he chose not to take occasion of engaging her in parley thereof, otherwise than in the matter of her hens, and accordingly, turning to her with a merry air, 'Madam,' quoth he, 'are hens only born in these parts, without ever a cock?' The marchioness, who understood the king's question excellent well, herseeming God had vouchsafed her, according to her wish, an oportune occasion of discovering her mind, turned to him and answered boldly, 'Nay, my lord; but women, albeit in apparel and dignities they may differ somewhat from others, are natheless all of the same fashion here as elsewhere.'

The King, hearing this, right well apprehended the meaning of the banquet of hens and the virtue hidden in her speech and perceived that words would be wasted upon such a lady, and that violence was out of the question; wherefore, even as he had ill-advisedly taken fire for her, so now it behoved him sagely, for his own honor's sake, stifle his ill-conceived passion.

―――――――――

The medieval love poem, usually sung to an accompaniment on the lyre or other musical instrument, was often, in spite of its superficially innocuous tone, full of amatory innuendoes and erotic provocations. The love song, in fact, was virtually an amatory philtre intended to set the listener afire, or to inspire the object of the implicit passion with an equal fervor, or to divert a passion in the direction of the songster. The concluding story of the fifth day, in Boccaccio's Decameron, contains a song of this nature:

O Love, the amorous light

That beameth from yon fair one's lovely eyes

Hath made me thine and hers in servant-guise.

The splendor of her lovely eyes, it wrought

That first thy flames were kindled in my breast,

Passing thereto through mine;

Yea, and thy virtue first unto my thought

Her visage fair it was made manifest,

Which picturing, I twine

And lay before her shrine

All virtues, that to her I sacrifice,

Become the new occasion of my sighs.

Thus, dear my lord, thy vassal am I grown

And of thy might obediently await

Grace for my lowliness;

Yet wot I not if wholly there be known

The high desire that in my breast thou'st set

And my sheer faith, no less,

Of her who doth possess

My heart so that from none beneath the skies,

Save her alone, peace would I take or prize.

Wherefore I pray thee, sweet my lord and sire,

Discover it to her and cause her taste

Some scantling of thy heat

To-me-ward,—for thou seest that in the fire,

Loving, I languish and for torment waste

By inches at her feet,—

And eke in season meet

Commend me to her favor on such wise

As I would plead for thee, should need arise.

A similar song, from the maiden's viewpoint, appears at the close of the last story on the sixth day:

Then Pamfilo having, at his commandment, set up a dance, the king turned to Elisa and said courteously to her, "Fair damsel, thou hast today done me the honor of the crown and I purpose this evening to do thee that of the song; wherefore look thou sing such an one as most liketh thee." Elisa answered, smiling, that she would well and with dulcet voice began on this wise:

Love, from thy clutches could I but win free,

Hardly, methinks, again

Shall any other hook take hold on me.

I entered in thy wars a youngling maid,

Thinking thy strife was utmost peace and sweet,

And all my weapons on the ground I laid,

As one secure, undoubting of defeat;

But thou, false tyrant, with rapacious heat,

Didst fall on me amain

With all the grapnels of thine armory.

Then, wound about and fettered with thy chains,

To him, who for my death in evil hour

Was born, thou gav'st me, bounden, full of pains

And bitter tears; and syne within his power

He hath me and his rule's so harsh and dour

No sighs can move the swain

Nor all my wasting plaints to set me free.

My prayers, the wild winds bear them all away;

He hearkeneth unto none and none will hear;

Wherefore each hour my torment waxeth aye;

I cannot die, albeit life irks me drear.

Ah, Lord, have pity on my heavy cheer;

Do that I seek in vain

And give him bounden in thy chains to me.

An this thou wilt not, at the least undo

The bonds erewhen of hope that knitted were;

Alack, O Lord, thereof to thee I sue,

For, an thou do it, yet to waxen fair

Again I trust, as was my use whilere,

And being quit of pain

Myself with white flowers and with red besee.

Elisa ended her song with a very plaintive sigh, and albeit all marvelled at the words thereof, yet was there none who might conceive what it was that caused her sing thus. But the king, who was in a merry mood, calling for Tindaro, bade him bring out his bagpipes, to the sound whereof he let dance many dances.

Another song, sung by Pamfilo, who represents Boccaccio himself, refers to the author's amours with the Princess Maria of Naples—Fiammetta.

The song occurs at the end of the eighth day:

At last, the queen, to ensue the fashion of her predecessors, commanded Pamfilo to sing a song, notwithstanding those which sundry of the company had already sung of their free will; and he readily began thus:

Such is thy pleasure, Love

And such the allegresse I feel thereby

That happy, burning in thy fire, am I.

The abounding gladness in my heart that glows,

For the high joy and dear

Whereto thou hast me led,

Unable to contain there, overflows

And in my face's cheer

Displays my happihead: for being enamoured

In such a worship-worthy place and high

Makes eath to me the burning I aby.

I cannot with my finger what I feel

Limn, Love, nor do I know

By bliss in song to vent;

Nay, though I knew it, needs must I conceal,

For, once divulged, I trow

'Twould turn to dreariment.

Yet am I so content,

All speech were halt and feeble, did I try

The least thereof with words to signify.

Who might conceive it that these arms of mine

Should anywise attain

Whereas I've held them aye,

Or that my face should reach so fair a shrine

As that, of favor fain

And grace, I've won to? Nay,

Such fortune ne'er a day

Believed me were; whence all afire am I,

Hiding the source of my liesse thereby.

This was the end of Pamfilo's song, whereto albeit it had been completely responded of all, there was none but noted the words thereof with more attent solicitude than pertained unto him, studying to divine that which, as he sang, it behoved him to keep hidden from them; and although sundry went imagining various things, nevertheless none happened upon the truth of the case.

At the end of the ninth day, Neifile sings:

Supper at an end, they arose to the wonted dances, and after they had sung a thousand canzonets, more diverting of words than masterly of music, the king bade Neifile sing one in her own name; whereupon, with clear and blithesome voice, she cheerfully and without delay began thus:

A youngling maid am I and full of glee,

Am fain to carol in the new-blown May,

Love and sweet thoughts-a-mercy, blithe and free.

I go about the meads, considering

The vermeil flowers and golden and the white,

Roses thorn-set and lilies snowy-bright,

And one and all I fare a-likening

Unto his face who hath with love-liking

Ta'en and will hold me ever, having aye

None other wish than as his pleasures be;

Whereof when one I find me that doth show,

Unto my seeming, likest him, full fain

I cull and kiss and talk with it amain

And all my heart to it, as best I know,

Discover, with its store of wish and woe;

Then it with others in a wreath I lay,

Bound with my hair so golden-bright of blee.

Ay, and that pleasure which the eye doth prove,

By nature, of the flower's view, like delight

Doth give me as I saw the very wight

Who hath inflamed me of his dulcet love,

And what its scent thereover and above

Worketh in me, no words indeed can say;

But sighs thereof bear witness true for me,

The which from out my bosom day nor night

Ne'er, as with other ladies, fierce and wild,

Storm up; nay, thence they issue warm and mild

And straight betake them to my loved one's sight,

Who, hearing, moveth of himself, delight

To give me; ay, and when I'm like to say

"Ah come, lest I despair," still cometh he.

Again, on the tenth day, Fiammetta sings:

If love came but withouten jealousy,

I know no lady born

So blithe as I were, whosoe'er she be.

If gladsome youthfulness

In a fair lover might content a maid,

Virtue and worth discreet,

Valiance or gentilesse,

wit and sweet speech and fashions all arrayed

In pleasantness complete,

Certes. I'm she for whose behoof these meet

In one; for, love-o'erborne,

All these in him who is my hope I see.

But for that I perceive

That other women are as wise as I,

I tremble for affright

And tending to believe

The worst, in others the desire espy

Of him who steals my spright;

Thus this that is my good and chief delight

Enforceth me, forlorn,

Sigh sore and live in dole and misery.

If I knew fealty such

In him my lord as I know merit there,

I were not jealous, I;

But here is seen so much

Lovers to tempt, how true they be soe'er,

I hold all false; whereby

I'm all disconsolate and fain would die,

Of each with doubting torn

Who eyes him, lest she bear him off from me.

Be, then, each lady prayed

By God that she in this be not intent

'Gainst me to do amiss;

For sure, if any maid

Should or with words or becks or blandishment

My detriment in this

Seek or procure and if I know't, ywis,

Be all my charms forsworn

But I will make her rue it bitterly.

Scattered throughout the Decameron, there are other erotic songs too. At the end of the first day:

Emilia amorously warbled the following song:

I burn for mine own charms with such a fire,

Methinketh that I ne'er

Of other love shall reck or have desire

Whene'er I mirror me, I see therein

That good which still contenteth heart and spright;

Nor fortune new nor thought of old can win

To dispossess me of such dear delight.

What other object, then, could fill my sight,

Enough of pleasance e'er

To kindle in my breast a new desire?

This good flees not, what time soe'er I'm fain

Afresh to view it for my solacement;

Nay, at my pleasure, ever and again

With such a grace it doth itself present

Speech cannot tell it nor its full intent

Be known of mortal e'er,

Except indeed he burn with like desire.

And I, grown more enamoured every hour,

The straitlier fixed mine eyes upon it be,

Give all myself and yield me to its power,

E'en tasting now of that it promised me,

And greater joyance yet I hope to see,

Of such a strain as ne'er

Was proven here below of love-desire.

At the end of the second day, the ditty following was sung by Pampinea:

What lady aye should sing, and if not I,

Who'm blest with all for which a maid can sigh.

Come then, O love, thou source of all my weal,

All hope and every issue glad and bright

Sing ye awhile yfere
Of sighs nor bitter pains I erst did feel,
That now but sweeten to me thy delight,
Nay, but of that fire clear,
Wherein I, burning, live in joy and cheer,
And as my God, thy name do magnify.

Thou settest, Love, before these eyes of mine
Whenas thy fire I entered the first day,
A youngling so beseen
with valor, worth and loveliness divine,
That never might one find a goodlier, nay,
Nor yet his match, I ween.
So sore I burnt for him I still must e'en
Sing, blithe, of him with thee, my lord most high.

And that in him which crowneth my liesse
Is that I please him, as he pleaseth me,
Thanks to Love debonair;
Thus in this world my wish I do possess
And in the next I trust at peace to be,
Through that fast faith I bear
To him; sure God, who seeth this, will ne'er
The kingdom of His bliss to us deny.

At the end of the third day, Lauretta began thus:

No maid disconsolate hath cause as I, alack!
Who sigh for love in vain, to mourn her fate.

He who moves heaven and all the stars in air
made me for His delight
Lovesome and sprightly, kind and debonair,

E'en here below to give each lofty spright

Some inkling of that fair

That still in heaven abideth in His sight;

But erring men's unright,

Ill knowing me, my worth

Accepted not, nay, with dispraise did bate.

Erst was there one who held me dear and fain

Took me, a youngling maid,

Into his arms and thought and heart and brain,

Caught fire at my sweet eyes; yea, time, unstayed

Of aught, that flits amain

And lightly, all to wooing me he laid.

I, courteous, nought gainsaid

And held him worthy me;

But now, woe's me, of him

I'm desolate.

Then unto me there did himself present

A youngling proud and haught,

Renowning him for valorous and gent;

He took and holds me and with erring thought

To jealousy is bent;

Whence I, alack! nigh to despair am wrought,

As knowing myself,—brought

Into this world for good

Of many an one,—engrossed of one sole mate.

The luckless hour I curse, in very deed,

When I, alas! said yea,

Vesture to change,—so fair in that dusk wede

I was and glad, whereas in this more gay

A weary life I lead,

Far less than erst held honest, welaway!

Ah, dolorous bridal day,

Would God I had been dead

Or e'er I proved thee in such ill estate!

O lover dear, with whom well pleased was I

Whilere past all that be,—

Who now before Him sittest in the sky

Who fashioned us,—have pity upon me

Who cannot, though I die,

Forget thee for another; cause me see

The flame that kindled thee

For me lives yet unquenched

And my recall up thither impetrate.

At the end of the fourth day Filostrato sang:

Weeping, I demonstrate

How sore with reason doth my heart complain

Of love betrayed and plighted faith in vain.

Love, whenas first there was of thee imprest

Thereon her image for whose sake I sigh,

Sans hope of succour aye,

So full of virtue didst thou her pourtray,

That every torment light accounted I

That through thee to my breast,

Grown full of drear unrest

And dole, might come; but now, alack! I'm fain

To own my error, not withouten pain.

Yea, of the cheat first was I made aware,

Seeing myself of her forsaken sheer,

In whom I hoped alone;

For, when I deemed myself most fairly grown

Into her favor and her servant dear,

Without her thought or care

Of my to-come despair,

I found she had another's merit ta'en

To heart and put me from her with disdain.

Whenas I knew me banished from my stead,

Straight in my heart a dolorous plaint there grew,

That yet therein hath power,

And oft I curse the day and eke the hour

When first her lovesome visage met my view,

Graced with high goodlihead;

And more enamoured

Than eye, my soul keeps up its dying strain,

Faith, ardor, hope, blaspheming still amain.

How void my misery is of all relief

Thou may'st e'en feel, so sore I call thee, sire,

With voice all full of woe;

Ay, and I tell thee that it irks me so

That death for lesser torment I desire.

Come, death, then; sheer the sheaf

Of this my life of grief

And with thy stroke my madness eke assain;

Go where I may, less dire will be my bane.

No other way than death is left my spright,

Ay, and none other solace for my dole;

Then give it me straightway,

Love; put an end withal to my dismay;

Ah, do it; since fate's spite

Hath robbed me of delight;

Gladden thou her, lord, with my death, love-slain,

As thou hast cheered her with another swain.

My song, though none to learn thee lend an ear,

I reck the less thereof, indeed, that none

Could sing thee even as I;

One only charge I give thee, ere I die,

That thou find love and unto him alone

Show fully how undear

This bitter life and drear

Is to me, craving of his might he deign

Some better harborage I may attain.

Weeping I demonstrate

How sore with reason doth my heart complain

Of love betrayed and plighted faith in vain.

At the conclusion of the last story on the seventh day Filomena sings:

Alack, my life forlorn!

Will't ever chance I may once more regain

Th'estate whence sorry fortune hath me torn?

Certes, I know not, such a wish of fire

I carry in my thought

To find me where, alas! I was whilere.

O dear my treasure, thou my sole desire,

That holdst my heart distraught,

Tell it me, thou; for whom I know nor dare

To ask it otherwhere.

Ah, dear my lord, oh, cause me hope again,

So I may comfort me my spright wayworn.

What was the charm I cannot rightly tell

That kindled in me such

A flame of love that rest nor day nor night

I find; for, by some strong unwonted spell,

Hearing and touch

And seeing each new fires in me did light,

Wherein I burn outright;

Nor other than thyself can soothe my pain

Nor call my senses back, by love o'erborne.

O tell me if and when, then, it shall be

That I shall find thee e'er

Whereas I kissed those eyes that did me slay.

O dear my good, my soul, ah, tell it me,

When thou wilt come back there,

And saying "Quickly," comfort my dismay

Somedele. Short be the stay

until thou come, and long mayst thou remain!

I'm so love-struck, I reck not of men's scorn.

If once again I chance to hold thee aye,

I will not be so fond

As erst I was to suffer thee to fly;

Nay, fast I'll hold thee, hap of it what may,

And having thee in bond,

Of thy sweet mouth by lust I'll satisfy.

Now of nought else will I

Discourse. Quick, to thy bosom come me strain;

The sheer thought bids me sing like lark at morn.

Rabelais (1490–1553), in his *Gargantua and Pantagruel*, incorporates into his fantastic and satirical novel contemporary views and personal attitudes on a large variety of subjects—religious and cosmological, literary, metaphysical, and theological. Among the topics and discussions propounded by some of his odd characters is the problem of amatory stimuli:

When I say, quoth Rondibilis, that wine abateth lust, my meaning is, wine immoderately taken; for by intemperance proceeding from the excessive drinking of strong liquor, there is brought upon the body of such a swill-down bouser, a chilliness in the blood, a slackening in the sinews, a dissipation of the generative seed, a numbness and hebetation of the senses, with a perversive wryness and convulsion of the muscles; all of which are great lets and impediments to the act of generation. Hence it is, that Bacchus, the god of bibbers, tipplers, and drunkards, is most commonly painted beardless, and clad in a woman's habit, as a person altogether effeminate, or like a libbed eunuch. Wine, nevertheless, taken moderately, worketh quite contrary effects, as is implied by the old proverb, which saith,—That Venus takes cold, when not accompanied with Ceres and Bacchus.

On another point in erotic investigations, Rabelais continues:

The fervency of Lust is abated by certain drugs, plants, herbs, and roots, which make the taker cold, maleficiated, unfit for, and unable to perform the act of generation; as hath been often experimented in the water-lily, Heraclea, Agnus Castus, willow-twigs, hemp-stalks, wood-bine, honey-suckle, tamarisk, chaste-tree, mandrake, bennet, keck-bugloss, the skin of a hippopotamus, and many other such, which, by convenient doses proportioned to the peccant humor and constitution of the patient, being duly and seasonably received within the body, what by their elementary virtues on the one side, and peculiar properties on the other,—do either benumb, mortify, and beclumpse with cold the prolific semence, or scatter and disperse the spirits, which ought to have gone along with, and conducted sperm to the places destinated and appointed for its reception,—or lastly, shut up, stop, and obstruct the ways, passages, and conduits through which the seed should have been expelled, evacuated, and ejected. We have nevertheless of those ingredients, which, being of a contrary operation, heat the blood, bend the nerves, unite the spirits, quicken the senses, strengthen the muscles, and thereby rouse up, provoke, excite, and enable a man to the vigorous accomplishment of the feat of amorous dalliance.

Obstructions to such dalliance are now discussed:

The ardor of lechery is very much subdued and check'd by frequent labor and continual toiling. For by painful exercises and laborious working, so great a dissolution is brought upon the whole body, that the blood, which runneth alongst the channels of the veins thereof, for the nourishment and alimentation of each of its members, hath neither time, leisure, nor power to afford the seminal resudation, or superfluity of the third concoction, which nature most carefully reserves for the conservation of the individual, whose preservation she more heedfully regardeth than the propagation of the species, and the multiplication of human land.

Metropolitan Museum of Art

EVE

by Rodin

Metropolitan Museum of Art

ETERNAL SPRINGTIME

by Rodin

On the other part, in opposition and repugnancy hereto, the philosophers say, That idleness is the mother of luxury. When it was asked Ovid, why Aegisthus became an adulterer? he made no other answer but this, Because he was idle. Who were able to rid the world of loitering and laziness might easily frustrate and disappoint Cupid of all his designs, aims, engines, and devices, and so disable and appal him that his bow, quiver, and darts should from thenceforth be a mere needless load and burthen to him, for that it could not lie in his power to strike, or wound any of either sex, with all the arms he had.

Again:

The tickling pricks of incontinency are blunted by an eager study; for from thence proceedeth an incredible resolution of the spirits, that oftentimes there do not remain so many behind as may suffice to push and thrust forwards the generative resudation to the places thereto appropriated, and there withal inflate the cavernous nerve, whose office is to ejaculate the moisture for the propagation of human progeny.

The English herbalist John Gerarde, who wrote a Herbal that was published in 1633, suggests a stimulating drink composed of juniper berries steeped in water. The juniper shrub itself was used medicinally, in cordials, and as an element in philtres.

The medieval writer Andreas Cisalpinus states that the tree called gossypion produced a juice that aided amatory efforts.

Emblica honey was, in the opinion of the thirteenth century Arab philosopher Avicenna, endowed with venereal virtues.

A plant that is native to both North and South Africa produces as an exudation a gum resin called euphorbium, which was considered in the thirteenth century an invigorating agent.

The medieval philosopher Albertus Magnus mentions a stone called aquileus or echites, that is found near the Mediterranean littoral and in Persia, in eagles' nests. This stone contains a smaller one that has an amatory character.

Babio, a twelfth century Latin comedy, presents the priest Babio himself apostrophizing women: Oh! What a guilty thing is a woman! The worst thing on earth. A seducer. There is no guile in the world that is missing in her. There is no evil so wicked as a long sequence of evils. Nobody considers the perils of a snake that has long been kept crushed. My wife is a thief. My slave is my guard. It's a case of trouble and trickery. She is a she-wolf. He's a lion. She holds me, while he fetters me. She casts me to the ground, he crushes me. She presses on me, he strikes me. She kills me, he crunches me.

In the medieval centuries the gum resin known as scammony, native to the Middle East, was suggested as a stimulus when mixed with honey.

A medieval potion that had Oriental ingredients was the following compound: Amber, aloes, musk, powdered together and soaked in spirits of wine. Heated in sand, then filtered, distilled, and hermetically sealed. The prescription required from three to five drops, taken in a broth.

In a number of twelfth century Latin comedies, particularly *De Nuntio Sagaci*, The Wily Messenger, nubile age is presented as in itself a strong amatory provocation. The messenger says.

Nubere tempus erat: iuveni tua forma placebat.

This was the theme of the medieval students, so vociferously and consistently proclaimed in the Carmina Burana:

Iam aetas invaluit,

Iam umor incubuit,

Iam virgo maturuit,

Iam tumescunt ubera,

Iam frustra complacuit

Nisi fiant cetera.

Again, the same view is determinedly expressed:

Si puer cum puellula,

Moraretur in cellula,

Felix coniunctio.

Amore sucrescente,

Pariter et medio

Avulso procul taedio,

Fit ludus ineffabilis

Membris, lacertis, labiis.

Baucis et Traso, a Latin comedy belonging in the twelfth century, presents the methods used in the Middle Ages for the amatory enticements of the male. These methods, however, have never differed in essence: whether in the fifth century in Athens, in the second B.C. in Rome, or in contemporary days.

Baucis, who knows where her interests lie, urged by the hope of gain, acts as a counsellor to the maiden Glycerium. She summons Glycerium, adorns her, pays her little attentions. She shapes the girl's lips, draws her cheeks down, skilfully refreshes her beauty, gives her a wide brow, spreads out her hair in flowing tresses, makes her neck glow, makes shoulders narrow, lengthens her nails, makes her hands look shorter. With a needle, she shapes her arms, puts a girdle on her to produce an effect of slenderness. Baucis teaches her what she must do, how, and with whom.

And so Glycerium strolls up and down the streets, glances around, looks for lovers. In some cases, she encourages hope by her words, just as she herself has confidence in her guile. She gives warnings, invitations, asks them to observe her beautiful eyes. She promises them affection, delights, wine, food. They will have with this maiden conversation and intimacies, kisses and the final consummation itself.

Baucis gives the girl imaginary names. Sometimes she is called Glycerium, and again Philomena, as the whim takes her. By means of such changes of name she multiplies her gains.

Lovers come flocking in rivalry, some searching for Glycerium, others for Philomena.

While she regales the young men with her words, while she gives them a vain hope and meanwhile acquires monies, Thraso comes upon her.

Thraso's glory is drink. His stomach is his god. Venus is his ever-ready companion. Baucis catches sight of him and, overjoyed, she approaches:

Baucis: O soldier, nurseling of Cupid, love's honor, what is it you desire? Where are you off to? What fires inflame you? If you need a maiden, I have one at home. A flower, the true fruit of love. She has a maidenly glow, she shines with every adornment of beauty.

Thraso: Baucis, let me see her.

Baucis: She is asleep and I can't waken her. She is delicate and a delicate girl needs much sleep. If she stays awake too long, she is sick. If she sleeps badly, she suffers.

Thraso burns up with restrained passion. He groans and pleads. He gives his gold ring to Baucis. Baucis relents. He buys provisions at the market and follows her home.

Suddenly, Baucis vanishes. All her talk, all her manoeuvers have been designed merely to tantalize his libidinous urgencies, to bring him suppliantly into her clutches. Thraso is left lamenting:

Thraso: O woman, noxious flame, gnawing wound, enemy to friendship. Woman, the sum of evil. Woman, deserving of death. Woman, who produces the seeds of putrefaction, who produces death. Foul procuress, monstrous in appearance, the image of the Chimera.

Later on, Thraso approaches Glycerium herself, but she refuses his advances. She is too young and inexperienced, she pleads:

Sum rudis in Venerem nec adhuc mea nubilis aetas:

Intemerata manet dos mea virginea.

Non novi quid amor, quid amoris sentiat ictus.

Officium Veneris horreo, siste preces.

———————

In Jay Fletchers play *The Wild-Goose Chase*, there is mention of amber, a reputed amatory provocative. Mirabel, one of the leading characters, is offering a portrait of women:

Mirabel: Only the wenches are not for my diet;

They are too lean and thin, their embraces brawn-fallen.

Give me the plump Venetian, fat and lusty,

That meets me soft and supple; smiles upon me,

As if a cup of full wine leap'd to kiss me,

These slight things I affect not.

Pinac: They are ill-built;

Pin-buttocked, like your dainty Barbaries,

And weak i' the pasterns; they'll endure no hardness.

Mirabel: There's nothing good or handsome bred amongst us;

Till we are travell'd, and live abroad, we are coxcombs.

Ye talk of France—a slight unseason'd country,

Abundance of gross food, which makes us blockheads.

We are fair set out indeed, and so are fore-horses:—

Men say, we are great courtiers,—men abuse us;

We are wise, and valiant too,—non credo, signor;

Our women the best linguists,—they are parrots;

O' this side the Alps they are nothing but mere drolleries.

Ha! Roma la Santa, Italy for my money!

Their policies, their customs, their frugalities,

Their courtesies so open, yet so reserv'd too,

As, when you think y'are known best, ye are a stranger.

Their very pick-teeth speak more than we do.

And season of more salt.

Pinac: 'Tis a brave country;

Not pester'd with your stubborn precise puppies,

That turn all useful and allow'd contentments

To scabs and scruples—hang 'em, capon-worshippers.

Belleur: I like that freedom well, and like their women too,

And would fain do as others do; but I am so bashful,

So naturally an ass! Look ye, I can look upon 'em,

And very willingly I go to see 'em,

(There's no man willinger), and I can kiss 'em,

And make a shift—

Mirabel: But, if they chance to flout ye,

Or say, "Ye are too bold! Fie, sir, remember!

I pray, sit farther off—"

Belleur:'Tis true—I am humbled,

I am gone; I confess ingenuously, I am silenced;

The spirit of amber cannot force me answer.

In Ben Jonson's *The Alchemist*, there is reference to a means of securing amatory and rejuvenating capacity. Sir Epicure Mammon tries to impose his alchemical beliefs on Surly:

Mammon: I assure you,

He that has once the flower of the sun,

The perfect ruby, which we call elixir,

Not only can do that, but by its virtue,

Can confer honor, love, respect, long life;

Give safety, valor, yea, and victory,

To whom he will. In eight and twenty days,

I'll make an old man of fourscore, a child.

Surly: No doubt; he's that already.

Mammon: Nay, I mean,

Restore his years, renew him, like an eagle,

To the fifth age; make him get sons and daughters,

Young giants; as our philosophers have done,

The ancient patriarchs, afore the flood,

But taking, once a week, on a knife's point,

The quantity of a grain of mustard of it;

Become stout Marses, and beget young Cupids.

Surly: The decay'd vestals of Pickt-hatch would thank you,

That keep the fire alive there.

Mammon: 'Tis the secret

Of nature naturiz'd 'gainst all infections,

Cures all diseases coming of all causes;

A month's grief in a day, a year's in twelve;

And, of what age soever, in a month.

Past all the doses of your drugging doctors.

I'll undertake, withal, to fright the plague

Out o' the kingdom in three months.

Surly: And I'll

Be bound, the players shall sing your praises then,
Without their poets.

Mammon: Sir, I'll do it. Meantime,
I'll give away so much unto my man,
Shall serve th' whole city with preservative
weekly; each house his dose, and at the rate—

Surly: As he that built the Water-work does with water?

Mammon: You are incredulous.

Surly: Faith, I have a humor,
I would not willingly be gull'd. Your stone
Cannot transmute me.

Mammon: Pertinax Surly,
Will you believe antiquity? Records?
I'll show you a book where Moses, and his sister,
And Solomon have written of the art;
Ay, and a treatise penn'd by Adam—

Surly: How!

Mammon: Of the philosopher's stone, and in High Dutch.

Surly: Did Adam write, sir, in High Dutch?

Mammon: He did;
Which proves it was the primitive tongue.

Surly: What paper?

Mammon: On cedar board.

Surly: O that, indeed, they say,
Will last 'gainst worms.

Mammon: 'Tis like your English wood
'Gainst cobwebs. I have a piece of Jason's fleece too,
which was no other than a book of alchemy,
Writ in large sheepskin, a good fat ram-vellum.
Such was Pythagoras' thigh, Pandora's tub,
And all that fable of Medea's charms,
The manner of our work; the bulls, our furnace,
Still breathing fire; our argent-vive, the dragon:
The dragon's teeth, mercury sublimate,
That keeps the whiteness, hardness, and the biting;
And they are gather'd into Jason's helm,
Th'alembic, and then sow'd in Mars his field.
And thence sublim'd so often, that they're fix'd.
Both this, th' Hesperian garden, Cadmus' story,
Jove's shower, the boom of Midas, Argus' eyes,
Boccace his Demogorgon, thousands more,
All abstract riddles of our stone.—How now!

In another scene, amatory potency is expressed in lavish rhetorical imagery:

Mammon: Do we succeed? Is our day come? And holds it?

Face: The evening will set red upon you, sir;
You have color for it, crimson: the red ferment
Has done his office; three hours hence prepare you
To see projection.

Mammon: Pertinax, my Surly,
Again I say to thee, aloud, BE RICH.
This day thou shalt have ingots; and tomorrow
Give lords th'affront.—Is it, my Zephyrus, right?
Blushes the bolt's-head?

Face: Like a wench with child, sir,

That were but now discover'd to her master.

Mammon: Excellent witty Lungs!—My only care is

Where to get stuff enough now, to project on;

This town will not half serve me.

Face: No, sir? Buy the covering off o' churches.

Mammon: That's true.

Face: Yes.

Let 'em stand bare, as do their auditory;

Or cap 'em new with shingles.

Mammon: No, good thatch:

Thatch will lie upo' the rafters, Lungs.

Lungs, I will manumit thee from the furnace;

I will restore thee thy complexion, Puff,

Lost in the embers; and repair this brain,

Hurt wi' the fumes o' the metals.

Face: I have blown, sir,

Hard, for your worship; thrown by many a coal,

When 'twas not beech; weigh'd those I put in, just

To keep your heat still even. These blear'd eyes

Have wak'd to read your several colors, sir,

Of the pale citron, the green lion, the crow,

The peacock's tail, the plumed swan.

Mammon: And lastly,

Thou hast descried the flower, the sanguis agni?

Face: Yes, sir.

Mammon: Where's master?

Face: At's prayers, sir, he;
Good man, he's doing his devotions
For the success.

Mammon: Lungs, I will set a period
To all thy labors; thou shalt be the master
Of my seraglio.

Face: Good, sir.

Mammon: But do you hear?
I'll geld you, Lungs.

Face: Yes, sir.

Mammon: For I do mean
To have a list of wives and concubines
Equal with Solomon, who had the stone
Alike with me; and I will make me a back
with the elixir, that shall be as tough
As Hercules, to encounter fifty a night.—
Thou'rt sure thou saw'st it blood?

Face: Both blood and spirit, sir.

Mammon: I will have all my beds blown up, not stuft;
Down is too hard: and then, mine oval room
Fill'd with such pictures as Tiberius took
From Elephantis, and dull Aretine
But coldly imitated. Then, my glasses
Cut in more subtle angles, to disperse
And multiply the figures, as I walk
Named between my succubae. My mists

I'll have of perfume, vapor'd 'bout the room,
To lose ourselves in; and my baths, like pits
To fall into; from whence we will come forth,
And roll us dry in gossamer and roses.—
Is it arrived at ruby?—Where I spy
A wealthy citizen, or a rich lawyer,
Have a sublim'd pure wife, unto that fellow
I'll send a thousand pound to be my cuckold.

Face: And I shall carry it?

Mammon: No, I'll ha' no bawds
But fathers and mothers: they will do it best,
Best of all others. And my flatterers
Shall be the pure and gravest of divines,
That I can get for money. My mere fools,
Eloquent burgesses, and then my poets,
Whom I shall entertain still for that subject.
The few that would give out themselves to be
Court and town-stallions, and, each-where, bely
Ladies who are known most innocent, for them,—
Those will I beg, to make me eunuchs of:
And they shall fan me with ten ostrich tails
A-piece, made in a plume to gather wind.
We will be brave, Puff, now we ha' the med'cine,
My meat shall all come in, in Indian shells,
Dishes of agate set in gold, and studded
with emeralds, sapphires, hyacinths, and rubies.
The tongues of carps, dormies, and camels' heels,
Boil'd i' the spirit of sol, and dissolv'd pearl
(Apicius' diet, 'gainst the epilepsy):

And I will eat these broths with spoons of amber,

Headed with diamond and carbuncle.

My foot-boy shall eat pheasants, calver'd salmons,

Knots, godwits, lampreys: I myself will have

The beards of barbel serv'd, instead of salads;

Oil'd mushrooms; and the swelling unctuous paps

Of a fat pregnant sow, newly cut off,

Drest with an exquisite and poignant sauce;

For which, I'll say unto my cook, There's gold;

Go forth, and be a knight.

Face: Sir, I'll go look

A little, how it heightens. (Exit)

Mammon: Do.—My shirts

I'll have of taffeta-sarsnet, soft and light

As cobwebs; and for all my other raiment,

It shall be such as might provoke the Persian,

Were he to teach the world riot anew.

My gloves of fishes and birds' skins, perfum'd

With gums of paradise, and Eastern air—

Surly: And do you think to have the stone with this?

Mammon: No, I do think t'have all this with the stone.

Surly: Why, I have heard he must be homo frugi,

A pious, holy, and religious man,

One free from mortal sin, a very virgin.

Mammon: That makes it, sir; he is so. But I buy it;

My venture brings it me. He, honest wretch,

A notable, superstitious, good soul,

Has worn his knees bare, and his slippers bald,

With prayer and fasting for it: and, sir, let him

Do it alone, for me, still. Here he comes,

Not a profane word afore him; 'tis poison.

Again, in the same play, there is an enumeration of alchemical items, many of which were, both in ancient and in medieval times, used in amatory brews:

Subtle: Sir?

Surly: What else are all your terms,

Whereon no one o' your writers 'grees with other?

Of your elixir, your lac virginis,

Your stone, your med'cine, and your chrysosperm,

Your sal, your sulphur, and your mercury,

Your oil of height, your tree of life, your blood,

Your marchesite, your tutie, your magnesia,

Your toad, your crow, your dragon, and your panther;

Your sun, your moon, your firmament, your adrop,

Your lato, azoch, zernich, chilbrit, beautarit,

And then your red man, and your white woman,

With all your broths, your menstrues, and materials

Of piss and egg-shells, women's terms, man's blood,

Hair o' the head, burnt clouts, chalk, merds, and clay,

Powder of bones, scalings of iron, glass,

And worlds of other strange ingredients,

Would burst a man to name?

———————————————

A number of herbs, some of which were reputed to produce amatory benefits, are mentioned in Ben Jonson's *Volpone*:

Lady Politic Would-Be: Alas, good soul! the passion of the heart.

Seed-Pearl were good now, boil'd with syrup of apples,

Tincture of gold, and coral, citron-pills,

Your elecampane root, myrobalances—

Volpone: Ay me, I have ta'en a grasshopper by the wing!

Lady Politic Would-Be: Burnt silk and amber. You have muscadel
Good i' the house—

Volpone: You will not drink, and part?

Lady Politic Would-Be: No, fear not that. I doubt we shall not get
Some English saffron, half a dram would serve;

Your sixteen cloves, a little musk, dried mints;

Bugloss and barley-meal—

In Ben Jonson's *Volpone* Nano the Dwarf sings some verses, in Act 2, scene 2, extolling an elixir that has remarkable medicinal and amatory properties:

You that would last long, list to my song,

Make no more coil, but buy of this oil.

Would you be ever fair and young?

Stout of teeth, and strong of tongue?

Tart of palate? quick of ear?

Sharp of sight? of nostril clear?

Moist of hand? and light of foot?

Or, I will come nearer to 't,

Would you live free from all diseases?

Do the act your mistress pleases,

Yet fright all aches from your bones?

Here's a med'cine for the nones.

An amatory appeal is made in a scene from *Bussy D'Ambois*, a drama by the English playwright George Chapman (c. 1559–c. 1634). Monsieur, brother of King Henry III of France, addresses the Countess Tamyra:

Monsieur: And wherefore do you this? To please your husband?

'Tis gross and fulsome: if your husband's pleasure

Be all your object, and you aim at honor

In living close to him, get you from Court;

You may have him at home; these common put-offs

For common women serve: "My honor! Husband!"

Dames maritorious ne'er were meritorious.

Speak plain, and say, "I do not like you, sir,

Y'are an ill-favor'd fellow in my eye;"

And I am answer'd.

Tamyra: Then, I pray, be answer'd:

For in good faith, my lord, I do not like you

In that sort you like.

The love charm in the form of a spell was a belief current in the Elizabethan age. In the drama *Friar Bacon and Friar Bungay*, by Robert Greene, Bacon, conceived as a thaumaturgist, declares:

Thou com'st in post from merry Fressingfield,

Fast-fancied to the Keeper's bonny lass.

Fast-fancied is an Elizabethan expression meaning bound by love.

The Elizabethan Fair, and all such traditional occasions for barter, commercial interchange, and public gossip were also and always an opportunity for amorous interludes. This is the view expressed in *Friar Bacon and Friar Bungay*, by Robert Greene (c. 1560–1592). Margaret, the fair maid of Fressingfield, enters:

Margaret: Thomas, maids when they come to see the fair

Count not to make a cope for dearth of hay;

When we have turn'd our butter to the salt,

And set our cheese safely upon the racks,

Then let our fathers price it as they please.

We country sluts of merry Fressingfield

Come to buy needless naughts to make us fine,

And look that young men should be frank this day,

And court us with such fairings as they can.

Phoebus is blithe, and frolic looks from heaven.

In a scene from the Elizabethan dramatist George Peele's *The Old Wives Tale*, Zantippa is in search of a husband. She and her ugly sister Celanta go to a well for water. A Head, speaking from the well, promises her a love charm, 'some cockell-bread':

Zantippa: Now for a husband, house, and home: God send a good one or none, I pray God! My father hath sent me to the well for the water of life, and tells me, if I give fair words, I shall have a husband. But here comes Celanta, my sweet sister. I'll stand by and hear what she says.

Enter Celanta, the foul wench, to the well for water with a pot in her hand.

Celanta: My father hath sent me to the well for water, and he tells me, if I speak fair, I shall have a husband and none of the worst. Well, though I am black, I am sure all the world will not forsake me; and, as the old proverb is, though I am black, I am not the devil.

Zantippa: Marry-gup with a murrain. I know wherefore thou speakest that: but go thy ways home as wise as thou camest, or I'll set thee home with a wanion.

Here she strikes her pitcher against her sister's, and breaks them both, and then exit.

Celanta: I think this be the curstest quean in the world. You see what she is, a little fair, but as proud as the devil, and the veriest vixen that lives upon God's earth. Well, I'll let her alone, and go home and get another pitcher, and, for all this, get me to the well for water. Exit.

Enter two Furies out of the Conjurer's cell and lay Huanebango by the Well of Life and then exeunt.

Re-enter Zantippa with a pitcher to the well.

Zantippa: Once again for a husband; and, in faith, Celanta, I have got the start of you; belike husbands grow by the well-side. Now my father says I must rule my tongue. Why, alas, what am I, then? A woman without a tongue is as a soldier without his weapon. But I'll have my water, and be gone.

Here she offers to dip her pitcher in, and a Head speaks in the well.

Head: Gently dip, but not too deep,

For fear you make the golden beard to weep.

Fair maiden, white and red,

Stroke me smooth, and comb my head,

And thou shalt have some cockell-bread.

In an old Elizabethan play there is reference to lunary or moonwort as a contributory factor in amatory thoughts:

I have heard of an herb called Lunary that being bound to the pulse of the sick causes nothing but dreams of weddings and dances.

In *Endymion*, a drama by the Elizabethan playwright John Lyly (c. 1554–c. 1606), Endymion soliloquizes:

As ebony, which no fire can scorch, is yet consumed with sweet savors, so my heart which cannot be bent by the hardness of fortune, may be bruised by amorous desires.

In the drama *The Old Wives Tale*, by George Peele, the Elizabethan playwright, Frolic and Fantastic sing an erotic chant:

Whenas the rye reach to the chin,

And chopcherry, chopcherry ripe within,

Strawberries swimming in the cream,

And school-boys playing in the stream;

Then, O then, O then, O my true-love said,

Till that time come again

She could not live a maid.

In *Endymion*, the Elizabethan drama by John Lyly, Sir Tophas describes a desirable woman:

Sir Tophas: I love no grissels; they are so brittle they will crack like glass, or so dainty that if they be touched they are straight of the fashion of wax: animus maioribus instat. I desire old matrons. What a sight would it be to embrace one whose hair were as orient as the pearl, whose teeth shall be so pure a watchet that they shall stain the truest turquoise, whose nose shall throw more beams from it than the fiery carbuncle, whose eyes shall be environ'd about with redness exceeding the deepest coral, and whose lips might compare with silver for the paleness! Such a one if you can help me to, I will by piecemeal curtail my affections towards Dipsas, and walk my swelling thoughts till they be cold.

In *Philaster*, a drama by Francis Beaumont (1584–1616) and John Fletcher (1579–1625), Megra, a Lascivious Lady, is thus described:

Dion: Faith, I think she is one whom the state keeps for the agents of our confederate princes; she'll cog and lie with a whole army, before the league shall break. Her name is common through the kingdom, and the trophies of her dishonor advanced beyond Hercules' Pillars. She loves to try the several constitutions of men's bodies; and, indeed, has destroyed the worth of her own body by making experiment upon it for the good of the commonwealth.

In *Endymion*, John Lyly's drama, Epiton and Sir Tophas have a verbal bout on love:

Epiton: Sir, will you give over wars and play with that bauble called love?

Tophas: Give over wars? No, Epi, Militat omnis amans, et habet sua castra Cupido.

Epiton: Love hate made you very eloquent, but your face is nothing fair.

Tophas: Non formosus erat, sed erat facundus Ulysses.

Epiton: Nay, I must seek a new master if you can speak nothing but verses.

Tophas: Quicquid conabar dicere, versus erat. Epi, I feel all Ovid De Arte Amandi lie as heavy at my heart as a load of logs.

In *The Lady of Pleasure*, a play by the English dramatist James Shirley, Lady Bornwell is rebuked for her amorous diversions by her husband Sir Thomas:

Another game you have, which consumes more

Your fame than purse; your revels in the night,

Your meetings called the "Ball," to which repair

As to the Court of Pleasure, all your gallants

And ladies, whither bound by a subpoena

Of Venus, and small Cupid's high displeasure;

'Tis but the Family of Love translated

Into more costly sin!

Amatory enticement is illustrated in a scene in *The Lady of Pleasure*, by James Shirley:

Lord: Have you business, madam, with me?

Madam Decoy: And such, I hope, as will not be
Offensive to your lordship.

Lord: I pray speak it.

Madam Decoy: I would desire your lordship's ear more private.

Lord: Wait i' th' next chamber till I call.—
Now, madam.

Exit Haircut.

Madam Decoy: Although I am a stranger to your lordship,
I would not lose a fair occasion offer'd
To show how much I honor, and would serve you.

Lord: Please you to give me the particular,

That I may know the extent of my engagement.
I am ignorant by what desert you should
Be encourag'd to have care of me.

Madam Decoy: My lord,
I will take boldness to be plain; beside
Your other excellent parts, you have much fame
For your sweet inclination to our sex.

Lord: How d'ye mean, madam?

Madam Decoy: I' that way your lordship
Hath honorably practis'd upon some
Not to be nam'd. Your noble constancy
To a mistress hath deserv'd our general vote;
And I, a part of womankind, have thought
How to express my duty.

Lord: In what, madam?

Madam Decoy: Be not so strange, my lord. I know the beauty
And pleasures of your eyes; that handsome creature
With whose fair life all your delight took leave,
And to whose memory you have paid too much sad
Tribute.

Lord: What's all this?

Madam Decoy: This: if your lordship
Accept my service, in pure zeal to cure
Your melancholy, I could point where you might
Repair your loss.

Lord: Your ladyship, I conceive,
Doth traffic in flesh merchandize.

Madam Decoy: To men
Of honor, like yourself. I am well known
To some in court, and come not with ambition
Now to supplant your officer.

Lord: What is
The lady of pleasure you prefer?

Madam Decoy: A lady
Of birth and fortune, one upon whose virtue
I may presume, the lady Aretina.

Lord: Wife to Sir Thomas Bornwell?

Madam Decoy: The same, sir.

Lord: Have you prepar'd her?

Madam Decoy: Not for your lordship, till I have found your pulse.
I am acquainted with her disposition,
She has a very appliable nature.

Lord: And, madam, when expect you to be whipt
For doing these fine favors?

Madam Decoy: How, my lord?
Your lordship does but jest, I hope; you make
A difference between a lady that
Does honorable offices, and one
They call a bawd. Your lordship was not wont
To have such coarse opinion of our practice.

Lord: The Lady Aretina is my kinswoman.

Madam Decoy: What if she be, my lord? The nearer blood
The nearer sympathy.

In *A New Way to Pay Old Debts*, by the English dramatist Philip Massinger (1583–1640), there appears a description of a love philtre:

Furnace: Here, drink it off; the ingredients are cordial,

And this the true elixir; it hath boil'd

Since midnight for you. 'Tis the quintessence

Of five cocks of the game, ten dozen of sparrows,

Knuckles of veal, potato-roots and marrow,

Coral and ambergris. Were you two years older

And I had a wife, or gamesome mistress,

I durst trust you with neither. You need not bait

After this, I warrant you, though your journey's long;

You may ride on the strength of this till tomorrow morning.

Allworth: Your courtesies overwhelm me: I much grieve

To part from such good friends.

Later, in Act 3 of the same play, Allworth, the young page, describes the amatory lure of Margaret:

Allworth: My much-lov'd lord, were Margaret only fair,

The cannon of her more than earthly form,

Though mounted high, commanding all beneath it,

And ramm'd with bullets of her sparkling eyes,

Of all the bulwarks that defend your senses

Could batter none, but that which guards your sight.

But when the well-tun'd accents of her tongue

Make music to you, and with numerous sounds

Assault your hearing, (such as if Ulysses

Now liv'd again, howe'er he stood the Syrens,

Could not resist,) the combat must grow doubtful

Between your reason and rebellious passions.

And this too; when you feel her touch, and breath

Like a swift western wind when it glides o'er

Arabia, creating gums and spices;

And, in the van, the nectar of her lips,

Which you must taste, bring the battalia on,

Well arm'd, and strongly lin'd with her discourse,

And knowing manners, to give entertainment;—

Hippolytus himself would leave Diana,

To follow such a Venus.

Lord Lovell: Love hath made you poetical, Allworth.

In another scene, between Sir Giles Overreach, an extortioner, and his daughter Margaret, the father gives his daughter amatory but sinister advice that is tantamount to the prescriptions of the *Kama Sutra* and similar manuals:

Margaret: There's too much disparity

between his quality and mine, to hope it.

Overreach: I more than hope't, and doubt not to effect it.

Be thou no enemy to thyself, my wealth

Shall weigh his titles down, and make you equals.

Now for the means to assure him thine, observe me:

Remember he's a courtier and a soldier,

And not to be trifled with; and therefore, when

He comes to woo you, see you do not coy it:

This mincing modesty has spoil'd many a match

By a first refusal, in vain after hop'd for.

Margaret: You'll have me, sir, preserve the distance that

Confines a virgin?

Overreach: Virgin me no virgins!

I must have you lose that name, or you lose me.

I will have you private—start not—I say, private;

If thou art my true daughter, not a bastard,

Thou wilt venture alone with one man, though he came

Like Jupiter to Semele, and come off, too;

And therefore, when he kisses you, kiss close.

Margaret: I have heard this is the strumpet's fashion, sir,

Which I must never learn.

Overreach: Learn any thing,

And from any creature that may make thee great;

From the devil himself.

Margaret (aside): This is but devilish doctrine!

Overreach: Or, if his blood grows hot, suppose he offer

Beyond this, do not you stay till it cool,

But meet his ardor; if a couch be near,

Sit down on't, and invite him.

Margaret: In your house,

Your own house, sir! For Heaven's sake, what are you then?

Or what shall I be, sir?

Overreach: Stand not on form;

Words are no substances.

Margaret: Though you could dispense

With your own honor, cast aside religion,

The hopes of Heaven, or fear of hell, excuse me,

In worldly policy this is not the way

To make me his wife; his whore, I grant it may do.

My maiden honor so soon yielded up,

Nay, prostituted, cannot but assure him

I, that am light to him, will not hold weight

Whene'er tempted by others; so, in judgment,

When to his lust I have given up my honor,

He must and will forsake me.

Overreach: How! I forsake thee!

Do I wear a sword for fashion? or is this arm

Shrunk up or wither'd? Does there live a man

Of that large list I have encounter'd with

Can truly say I e'er gave inch of ground

Not purchas'd with his blood that did oppose me?

Forsake thee when the thing is done! He dares not.

Give me but proof he has enjoy'd thy person,

Though all his captains, echoes to his will,

Stood arm'd by his side to justify the wrong,

And he himself in the head of his bold troop,

Spite of his lordship, and his colonelship,

Or the judge's favor, I will make him render

A bloody and a strict account, and force him,

By marrying thee, to cure thy wounded honor!

I have said it.

As late as the eighteenth century, in Italy, phallic amulets, in the form of the fascinum itself and the obscene digital gesture called in French *la figue*, were in common use. They were worn by children as protective periapts. Chapels too were decorated with wax images of phalli, dedicated by devout women worshippers.

An esoteric club existed in England in the eighteenth century that was associated with the British Navy. It was called *The Very Ancient and Very Powerful Order of Beggars Benison and Merryland*. On the seal of this Society, among other and naval designs, was a phallic symbol. The intent of the Society is still obscure, especially the relation between naval matters and the phallus.

Amulets in the form of the male mandrake came into vogue in the Middle Ages, especially in Central Europe, for apotropaic and amatory purposes. These charms were associated with incantations and magic formulas and recitatives.

The phallus or fascinum, too, especially in France, was used, as a meaningful protective agent, on buildings and even on churches.

Phallic and other genital forms were also used for cakes and breads: and are still so used, especially in Germany and France.

In the Middle Ages Priapus assumed Christian characteristics and in time was even endowed with sanctity, although he still retained his functional properties. In many cities of Southern France, for instance, Saint Foutin was virtually a transferred Priapus. He aided sterile women and renewed the amatory vigor of men. Images of genitalia were included among the sacrificial objects dedicated to this saint.

In medieval France a certain Saint Greluchon was a cryptic Priapus, venerated among the members of the saintly canon. When women made supplication to this saint, they scraped off minute particles from the stone genitalia and compounded these scrapings into an amatory potion, and also as an aid to counteract sterility.

Other saints to whom were attributed the virtues and functions of Priapus were: Saint Guignolet, Saint Regnaud, Saint Gilles.

In Belgium, Priapus became Ters, equally venerated by women. Ters, in Antwerp, was actually a synonym for fascinum.

Among the gods of Northern Europe was Frikko, who may be equated with Priapus, the phallic deity. The Saxons had a similar god, called Frisco, endowed with the same functions. An analogous deity was Frigga, goddess of voluptuousness. Before the worship of this symbolic or actual phallus was the worship of the sun, represented by the phallus as the creator of cosmic and human fecundity.

Clauder

A German medieval scholar presented for his doctoral thesis a brief monograph on Philtres, their essential characteristics, the dangers involved in their use, the contents, the purpose of their employment. The thesis, in Latin, is entitled De Philtris, and was published in Leipzig in 1661. The author is Johannes Clauder.

Although philtres were frequently used for erotic purposes, the author asserts, the result rarely corresponded to the intention. The reason for this was that the philtre was concocted under evil auspices, without appeal to divine aid and protection. Another reason for the inefficacy of the potions was improper and defective preparation. The result, he declares categorically, was very often madness for the victim, or even death itself.

Some philtres are associated with Satanic and magic practices, and are essentially poisons. Whores and panders resort to such philtres, although some use what might be termed natural remedies.

The best philtre, however, according to Clauder, is love itself. In this regard, he quotes confirmatory statements from the Romans. Seneca the philosopher, in one of his 124 Epistles, advises: I shall show you a love philtre, without medicaments, without herbs, without a witch's incantations. It is this: If you want to be loved, love. Martial, the Roman epigrammatist, has something similar to say: Marcus, in order to be loved, love.

And Ovid had already advised: Banish every evil, be lovable, in order to be loved.

Paracelsus, the medieval scholar and alchemist, is quoted in relation to the philtre and its content. Or, as Clauder suggests, the amatory inducement may take the form of a magic inscription on a key, or a ring, or a necklace, or an armlet. As for herbs, the Romans preferred the laurel and the olive, in infusions. Vegetable and mineral and organic matter is also in use; perspiration, urine, spittle. But there is a sinister and hazardous element in such practices. Prostitutes in particular, Clauder threatens, use philtres that rob the victim of mind and soul and leave him a shallow husk. So corroborates Paracelsus. There is one potion, however, called Charisia, that may be innocuous. It has not been identified. But possibly the name may have been invented etymologically on the basis of the Greek *charis*, which means grace or gratitude: and hence the nomenclature is wishfully proleptic in significance.

With respect to a variety of lustful and amatory circumstances, the Middle Ages were marked by strange social mores, by monstrous obscenities and erotic barbarities. There were practices designed primarily to preserve chastity and marital and domestic purity, but they actually resulted in greater indecencies than the circumstances that induced these inventive prophylaxes. There was, first of all, the girdle of chastity, a mechanical device to prevent indiscriminate and unlawful lustful consummations in the absence of the husband. The putative inventor of the device was Francesco da Carrara, Provost of Padua, who belongs in the latter part of the fourteenth century. He himself, it was said, met with a miserable death, being strangled on the scaffold for his many cruelties, in 1405, by order of the Senate of Venice.

There was, too, the Congress, a kind of judicial body that determined marital questions, quarrels, incompatibility, by viewing the two participants *in actu sexuali*.

Men and women taken in adultery were compelled to march through the public streets naked, sometimes mounted on an ass, for centuries the bestial symbol of lust.

There was the libidinous *ius primae noctis*, the *droit de cuisse*, exercised by the lord of the manor, and on occasion by monks and prelates, in the case of a newly wedded couple.

In France, in the city of Toulouse, there was a notorious brothel called The Great Abbey. There were, dispersed through France, many such pseudo-abbeys, the madame of which, in each case, was called Abbess. Such terms and such practices, of course, heightened the lewd obscenity. There was a similar type of dissolute haven that had an infamous reputation in England.

This perversion, in which devout elements are linked with the extremes of lust, to heighten the amatory impulse, is described in abundant and salacious detail in the novels of the Marquis de Sade and in other instances of erotic literature.

Prostitution reached such a social importance, and the practitioners acquired such influence in various directions, that, in Paris, a kind of trade union was formed, to which the practicing prostitutes prescribed. They established their own procedures, their working hours, and similar regulations.

At many royal banquets, public entertainments, and processional ceremonials, in Italy and in France, prostitutes were prominent participants, some half-naked, often entirely so.

There were, of course, fulminations against such and similar indecencies, but without much immediate or effective results. Preachers thundered, to no avail, against the erotic provocations to adultery and fornication engendered by the sight of women who, by the subtlety of their dress, exposed various parts of their person. There was public debauchery. There were genesiac performances in the presence of the children in a household. There were poems and tales, called fabliaux, that, reflecting the mores of the age, dealt with nothing but cuckoldry and fornication, adultery, sodomy, bestiality, and all the multiple varieties of physiological perversions.

Furthermore, houses, manors, large estates were decorated with tapestries, paintings, sculpture, all depicting the greatest obscenities. Even churches and chapels and abbeys contained scenes, figures, statues of the utmost lewdness in posture, presentation, and implication.

Among the barbarities of the medieval centuries, many performances, processions, and rites contained an amazing mingling of ecclesiastical elements and dissolute blasphemies and libertinage: just as the Greek satyr plays and the comedies of fifth century Athens were composites of functional representations by human actors of the libidinous and irreverent actions of the deities themselves.

The medieval scene contained secular and monastic lubricity, and processions and rites in which the performers, under the guise of nuns and prelates, presented shameless and unspeakable obscenities. In addition, flagellation was inflicted on penitents. In Germany, France, England, and Italy, all ranks, of all ages, underwent phallic castigation as an act of devotion.

In Girolamo Folengo's *Maccaronea*, published in 1519, there is mention of manuals that provide magic instruction and prescriptions favorable in inducing or diverting erotic urges:

He opens the manuals, or reads all that are open:

How to write arcane spells:

How to compel love;

How a husband can find out his wife's adultery;

How virginal maidens can be forced to love;

How to make a hated husband impotent.

During the Italian Renaissance the women of Italy played a dominant and sometimes sinister part in both social and political life. Courtesans, particularly in Rome, had a position somewhat analogous to that of the

Greek hetairae. One such courtesan, Imperia, had skill in composing sonnets. Most of them were literate and interested in intellectual pursuits as well as in erotic interludes. Caterina di San Celso played and sang. Many women of this type are described by Giraldi in the novels of the *Hecatommithi* and by Pietro Aretino in his *Ragionamenti*.

The Italian Renaissance was marked by both literary and social indecencies and lewd lubricities and all kinds of scatological productions and performances. In the lavish public entertainments, in the Carnivals and Masques, apart from contests, reviews, pantomimic presentations, the emphasis was consistently on scandalous songs, with lascivious undertones, innuendoes, suggestions.

In literature, the moral atmosphere of this period is reflected in the depiction of the most common Renaissance features—adultery and cuckoldry, all kinds of illicit amours, lusts resulting in secrecies, gallantries, murder. To satisfy her lusts, a woman poisons her husband. An adulteress has her lover kill her husband, without hesitation, without compunction. Love and lust, poison and death, infidelities and vengeance followed each other in an abandoned, frenzied, amoral sequence.

The Italian strega or witch was a powerful intermediary in amatory affairs of all sorts. With her preparations, her thaumaturgic skills, her secret concoctions, she aided men and women in consummating erotic urges, arousing lustful sensualities, securing the love of hesitant objects of passion, promoting vigor and virility, arranging furtive amatory assignations: acting, in short, as an amatory midwife, an empirical guide in debauchery.

By her magical skill the strega was able to aid men and women bent on amatory consummations. Some of these skills were transferred to the prostitutes. Acquiring these techniques, and discovering the secrets of preparing potions, they were able to retain a lover, to lure a new admirer. For their concoctions and brews they used human teeth and the eyes of dead men, skulls and ribs, scraps of the flesh of corpses, hair and nails boiled in oil. They made a fire of burning ashes, in the form of a heart. Piercing the heart, they chanted their goetic invocation, anticipating the surrender of the hesitant lover by this means of sympathetic magic. In this sphere, in fact, the Italian Renaissance had taken over, as it were, the entire corpus of ancient magic rites, love brews, and concomitant procedures in the art of erotic control.

A solemn love conjuration appears in a medieval manual called the *True Grimoire*. The invocation itself is preceded by special preparations during the waxing or the waning of the moon. An inscription is written on virgin parchment, by the light of a taper. The supplication runs:

I salute thee and conjure thee, O beautiful Moon, O most beautiful Star, O brilliant light which I have in my hand. By the air that I breathe, by the breath within me, by the earth which I am touching: I conjure thee. By all the names of the spirit princes living in you. By the ineffable Name On, which created everything! By you, O resplendent Angel Gabriel, with the Planet Mercury, Prince, Michiael, and Melchidael.

I conjure you again, by all the Holy Names of God, so that you may send down power to oppress, torture, and harass the body and soul and the five senses of her whose name is written here, so that she shall come unto me, and agree to my desires, liking nobody in the world, for so long as she shall remain unmoved by me. Let her then be tortured, made to suffer. Go, then, at once! Go, Melchidael, Baresches, Zazel, Firiel, Malcha, and all those who are with thee! I conjure you by the Great Living God to obey my will, and I promise to satisfy you.

A technique involving the separation of husband and wife, the converse of a love-potion intended to attract or cement passion, appears in the following invocation from a magic grimoire called the *Sword of Moses*:

I conjure you, luminaries of heaven and earth, as the heavens are separated from the earth, so separate and divide N from his wife N, and separate them from one another, as life is separated from death, and sea from dry land, and water from fire, and mountain from vale, and night from day, and light from darkness, and the sun from the moon; thus separate N from N's wife, and separate them from one another in the name of the twelve hours of the day and the three watches of the night, and the seven days of the week, and the thirty days of the month, and the seven years of Shemittah, and the fifty years of Jubilee, on every day, in the name of the evil angel Imsmael, and in the name of the angel Iabiel, and in the name of the angel Drmiel, and in the name of the angel Zahbuk, and in the name of the angel Ataf, and in the name of the angel Zhsmael, and in the name of the angel Zsniel, who preside over pains, sharp pains, inflammation, and dropsy, and separate N from his wife N, make them depart from one another, and that they should not comfort one another, swift and quickly.

.

National Gallery of Art

DIANA

by Renoir

Metropolitan Museum of Art

PYGMALION AND GALATEA

by Rodin

In the middle centuries prostitution as a civic institution had its distinction and its privileges. In Venice, all kinds of secondary favors were granted to these practitioners. They were favored with an indulgent and even eulogistic Latin testimonial: nostrae bene merentes meretrices.

In France, there were orgiastic ceremonies in which the participants performed in the nude. These rituals were associated in a contorted sense with primal creation and were known as Fêtes d'Adam.

In one of Boccaccio's tales there is an instance of a script intended as an erotic provocation:

Quoth Bruno, 'Will thy heart serve thee to touch her with a script I shall give thee?'

'Ay, sure,' replied Calandrino; and the other, 'Then do thou make shift to bring me a piece of virgin parchment and a live bat, together with three grains of frankincense and a candle that hath been blessed by the priest, and leave me do.'

Accordingly, Calandrino lay in wait all the next night with his engines to catch a bat and having at last taken one, carried it to Bruno, with the other things required; whereupon the latter, withdrawing to a chamber, scribbled divers toys of his fashion upon the parchment, in characters of his own devising, and brought it to him, saying, 'Know, Calandrino, that, if thou touch her with this script, she will incontinent follow thee and do what thou wilt.'

In Turkey, under the Sultanate, and notably in the sixteenth century, erotic relations in the seraglio were stimulated by a preparation known as pastilles de sérail.

In the sixteenth century there was a religious-erotic cult in Europe whose members were called Loïstes. Their rituals were marked by sexual orgies and erotic aberrations.

The corpus of Shakespearean plays contains numberless allusions and comments on sexual and amatory topics. The language, however, in which these references are couched is sometimes figurative, euphemistic, and seemingly innocuous and ingenuous. Sometimes, again, they are so expressed in the contemporary Elizabethan idiom as to have an immediate and illuminating impact on the contemporary audience: but, on a cursory perusal, the context may not spontaneously reveal the underlying currency.

There is, throughout the plays, mention of the functional processes and their media, of the organs of the human body, including what are usually termed pudenda. Shakespeare touches on the normal sexual functions and also on deviations, on tribadism and coprophilia, on lust and cuckoldry, on adultery and eunuchs, on all manner of erotic encounters, embraces, and circumstances.

In *Troilus and Cressida*, to take an example, lust, libido, and potency are illustrated:

Cressida: They say all lovers swear more performance than they are able, and yet reserve an ability that they never perform: vowing more than the performance of ten, and discharging less than the tenth part of one. They that have the voice of lions and the act of hares, are they not monsters?

Act 3.2

Again:

Troilus: This is the monstrosity of love, lady—that the will is infinite and the execution confined; that the desire is boundless and the act a slave to limit.

Act 3.2

Troilus: What will it be

When that the watery palate tastes indeed

Love's thrice repured nectar?—death, I fear me,

Swooning distraction, or some joy too fine,

Too-subtle potent, tuned too sharp in sweetness,

For the capacity of my ruder powers:

Act 3.2

There are similar references in *The Merry Wives of Windsor*, *Twelfth Night*, and *A Midsummer Night's Dream*.

In *Pericles* Priapus is mentioned as a symbol of virility:

Pericles: Fie, fie upon her!

She's able to freeze the god Priapus.

François Villon, the fifteenth century French lyric poet, was not too happy in his loves. In his *Double Ballade* he makes his personal confession on amatory exercises, and gives due admonitions as to the possible effects of erotic practices:

Then love until you have your fill,

Follow the ball and midnight feast,

The end will bring you naught until

You break your head, to say the least;

For foolish loves make man a beast:

Idolatrous was Solomon,

And thereby Samson's vision ceased.

Happier those who all this shun!

And Orpheus, sweet troubadour,

Who piped his flute among the dead,

Risked mortal peril on its spoor

From Cerberus of the triple head;

And beautiful Narcissus fled,

Because of love too lightly won,

To seek his peace in a watery bed.

Happier those who all this shun!

Sardana, once a valiant knight,

Who conquered all the realm of Crete,

Aped woman's form and took delight

In girlish chores and things effete;

And David, quitting wisdom's seat,

Forgot his fear of God for one

Whose perfumed thighs aroused his heat.

Happier those who all this shun!

And Amnon, drunk with carnal power,
Feigning to gorge himself the while,
Plucked lovely Tamar's virgin flower,
A deed incestuous and vile;
Herod—and here I use no guile—
Had John the Baptist's head undone
For a dance, a song, a dancer's smile.
Happier those who all this shun!

Of my poor self I wish to speak:
Beaten like washing in a stream,
Entirely nude—no tongue in cheek—
Who made me chew such sour cream
But Kate Vausselles? Noël I deem
Made up the three to share the fun.
Such wedding mittens costly seem.
Happier those who all this shun!

But is this hot, young blood to spurn
Their tender love and flee their sight?
May God forbid! Such ought to burn
As witches do who ride the night.
Sweeter than civets their delight,
But not to put your trust upon:
For be they brown or be they white,
Happier those who all this shun!

As late as the eighteenth century, in Central Europe, there were secret cults
that drew their basic tenets from ancient priapic rites. Some of these orders
practiced nudism but rejected marriage. Some encouraged promiscuities in
their ritualistic assemblies. The Ebionites, for instance, were of this type.
Also the Basilidians, a Gnostic sect that followed the principles of the

founder Basilides, a Gnostic who flourished in Alexandria in the second century A.D.; also the Nicolaitans, an early Christian sect.

In Italy, in the eleventh century and the twelfth, there was a similar sect known as the Patarini. They made obscene obeisance to a black cat, evidently a variant Satanic form, then abandoned themselves to scenes of frantic lubricity.

So too in many regions of France that still recalled ancient pagan Gaul similar orgiastic performances occurred under cover of darkness.

Even the Knights Templars, the military-religious members of the Order that was founded early in the twelfth century and was suppressed at the beginning of the fourteenth century, were reputed to have aligned themselves with foul obscenities that involved anal osculation, as in the case of the witch members of the Satanic Sabbat, and desecration of Christian ritual accompanied by erotic perversions.

Sympathetic magic and the use of wax images were common means of securing amatory ardor compulsively. The ancients were intimately familiar with the procedures. And the grimoires current in medieval times were similarly repositories of dark and occult amatory techniques, and likewise recommended a variety of rituals. Involved in the ceremonials were of course darkness, the burning of incense, the construction of special pentagrams and magic circles, the shaping of the figurine, and the Latin invocation which gave final assurance to the erotic effects.

Amatory intimacies, especially but not exclusively in the Middle Ages, were believed possible between human beings and disembodied creatures, incubi and succubi, sylphs and undines or water spirits, salamanders, various types of Satanic emissaries and subordinates in the infernal hierarchy, such as Isheth Zemunin, who presided over prostitution.

Some of these mystic, occult unions, on the other hand, were associated with beneficent spirits, with angelic embodiments, saints, and similar personalities.

In the malefic traditions of the Black Arts and demoniac relationships, there was widespread credence in intercourse between witches and the members of the Satanic legions, between sorceresses and Satan himself, and between the practitioners of magic and all kinds of bestial and obscene creatures. The medieval demonographers are soberly voluble in recounting many such instances. They chronicle, with precise supporting confirmatory testimony, tales that brought the participants, the old and the young women so accused of diabolic intimacies, to trial, to torture, and finally to the gallows.

Ready and voluminous evidence comes from Guazzo and Johannes Anania and Jean Bodin, from Henri Boguet and Delrio, from Tartarotti, Stridtbeckh, Sinistrari and Ricardus, Molitor, de L'Ancre, Elich, and Daugis.

At the Sabbats, the assemblies of witches and Satanic forces, there were, according to the medieval chroniclers and the old European folk traditions, frantic performances of the most obscene nature, monstrous rituals, weird banquets, culminating in lewd orgies characterized, according to the grave testimonies of the demonographers, by copulation of witches and materialized demoniac spirits.

The Aphroditic force and influence are all-pervasive. Hence, in the field of astrological lore, Venus represents love, in its most extended sense, normal, illicit, and aberrational. Certain symbols, creatures, forms are regularly associated with her functions. The lubricities of the goat and the bull are under her sway, while, botanically, many plants, among them vervain and myrtle, are endowed with aphrodisiac qualities.

CHAPTER X
MODERN TIMES

Eros is triumphant in the twentieth century, in every social frame, in every milieu, and in every country. Henri Bergson, the French philosopher who is associated with the concept of *l'élan vital*—the vital urge, or, as George Bernard Shaw termed it, the life force, declared that this twentieth century has become aphrodisiac.

The love-potion is not a matter of academic history only: it is still flourishing. It still has its devotees. It is still encountered in obscure places, where furtive secrecy is of the essence of the amatory preparations. In the folk mind in particular the love-potion can still be efficacious, sometimes grim in its attendant effects, but unquestionably an accepted and often employed means of directing erotic feelings, imposing amatory impulses, on a beloved victim, on the indifferent libertine, on the wayward and flighty girl.

Ottokar Nemecek in his *Die Wertschätzung der Jungfräulichkeit* (Verlag A. Sexl. Vienna, 1953) gives interesting instances of erotic practices, rituals, religious ceremonials, culled from many ethnic groups. In Fernando Po, for example, a prayer is offered: May the woman and the man become as erotically entwined as the creepers in the forest entwine around the tree trunks.

In Ethiopia a phallic provocation was the wearing on the head of a band to which a horn was attached. Similarly among many African tribes, where the chief wore a phallus-crown with the same intention. As in Hellenic antiquity, in ancient India and in modern India also, the phallus is the symbol of might, of masculine sovereignty, of cosmic creativeness.

Such customs and rites, such implicit amatory instigations, have not died out. They appear in many forms and guises, sometimes decorative, on other occasions in fanciful culinary shapes. Amulets and figures in phallic and genital form were sold, as late as 1894, in the shops of Tiflis, in Caucasia, and in the United States migrants from the Central European countries still reproduce, in their bake shops, festive genital formations.

Traditional potions, aphrodisiacs, and similar means of arousing genital impulses are in use even at the present time. Carrots, for instance, were long listed by the Arabs as a stimulant. In medieval Spain they were commonly consumed for such a purpose. And in the United States carrots are still reputed to have a marked erotic potency.

—————

Current magazines of the more popular sort, contemporary drug stores have their amatory allurements. Some periodicals advertise exotic perfumes, sultry essences, seductive cosmetics and similar feminine accessories, or insidious unguents and lotions, whose avowed purpose is to attract men in an amorous direction. In the drug stores, hormones and gland extracts, transplantations and rejuvenative manipulations and operations are publicized for similar purposes.

—————

Among some primitive tribal communities in New Guinea, powerful love charms take the form of genital secretions. Such secretions are then used in magic ceremonials affecting both man and beast: the underlying intent being procreational encouragement.

—————

Virility and its concomitants have no frontiers, no temporal restrictions. In Central India, in areas that have not yet been significantly affected by the encroachments of modern ways and procedures, virility has not become a tribal or personal problem. It is so normal, in fact, and sexual indulgence is so released from emotional or social inhibitions and taboos that erotic encouragement in the shape of unguents, liquids, potions is rare: although there is, as a prelude to erotic excitations, a preliminary mamillary exercise.

—————

In the Orient, especially in the islands off South Eastern Asia, erotic frustrations may be solved by resorting to the tribal magician, who holds the communal secrets, the traditional ways of the society, within his memory and his jurisdiction. A maiden may be recalcitrant to the advances of her lover. He will then approach the magician, who will present him with an amulet, a disc or token. The girl who has amatory intentions in the direction of a particular male will likewise be given a disc to wear, on which there is a design of a crescent moon, a moon-coin, as it is termed, fashioned, according to indigenous traditions, by the ancient gods themselves, indulgent to help mortals in their erotic perplexities.

In extremely stubborn cases, love charms associated with magic incantations and formulas are brought into operation: certain fruits, such as bananas or cocoanuts, or even a child's tears.

The love-potion, in respect of its ingredients, is often conditioned by geographical situation. The flora and fauna of a particular region become the elements for the amatory goblet. Mediterranean reeds, roots, nuts, and plants naturally become useful for the philtre. It is only in extreme cases that exotic items, rare drugs, inaccessible roots are the object of any particular composition. So, in Sikkim, a state situated in the Eastern Himalayan region, water in which a bird called indigenously Ken fo, or a chameleon, has defecated, forms a potent love philtre. So powerful, in fact, that it produces a condition of priapism in the male and nymphomania in the female.

Absinthe is a popular drink in European countries, predominantly in France. It is a liqueur distilled from a bushy plant, that has a silk-like stem and small yellow flowers. The plant is found among the valleys and foothills of Europe and on the North African littoral, and prefers to flourish among hedges and ditches.

The botanical name of the plant is Artemisia absinthium: that is, wormwood. Wormwood itself was sacred to the Greek divinity Diana, who was also Artemis: hence the designation Artemisia.

Absinthe itself, distilled from the plant, is a green liqueur to which are added aniseed oil, marjoram, and similar aromatic elements.

Used regularly, absinthe is not only dangerous, but when taken in large quantities produces insanity. Yet it has been reputed to stimulate amatory excitation.

Many noted French writers, poets, and painters have been addicted to the drink, notably the artist Amedeo Modigliani.

The drink was first concocted by a Frenchman, a certain Dr. Ordinaire, who resided in Switzerland. In 1797 the recipe was sold to a M. Pernod. The name Pernod has since then been continuously associated with the drink.

In the hinterland of folklore, in antique traditional sagas transmitted through the ages to recent times, in areas that have been for centuries more or less unaffected by developments, changes, and innovations, that is, largely, in rural and secluded regions, old beliefs still cling. Old ways are still followed. Old remedies, beverages, potions are still used with anticipations of effective results. This view is illustrated in the French film entitled

L'Éternel Retour. As its pervasive theme it stressed the rooted belief, among the French peasantry, in the efficacy of the love-potion.

Currently, a great deal of writing appears constantly in the press, in learned journals, in periodicals of a professional nature, and in complete encyclopedias, all devoted to erotic studies, analyses of society in terms of sexual life, and investigations into sexual morality and sexual abnormalities.

In France, the Polish sponsored Biblioteki Kultury has been established. This Press has recently produced a study of Pornography and its involvements, by Witold Gombrowicz. In France, too, many surveys on erotic practices in the field of films, the stage, art have likewise made their appearance, in addition to a History of Eroticism. Lavishly produced folios are also on the market, in which maisons closes are the subject of detailed treatment and description. Their policies and mores are freely expounded, and the texts are reinforced with photographs and illustrations of persons and places and towns, along with paintings by recognized artists.

A major project in this field is the Illustrated Encyclopedia Erotica, to which a number of noted European sexologists and erotologists have contributed. Published in ten volumes, under the sponsorship of the Institute for Sexual Research of Vienna, this comprehensive compendium is now reprinted in a new edition by the Verlag für Kulturforschung of Hamburg.

There are some 22,000 articles and 12,000 illustrations. The contents range over all aspects of human sexual activity, in their relation to psychology and biology, medicine and jurisprudence, sociology and psychotherapy. Folklore and ethnography, marriage, prostitution, fertility rites, rites of initiation, the deviations of society, secret amatory sects, flagellation and biographical memoirs comprise the introductory matter.

Other subjects discussed and examined include: erotic sculpture, sex mythology, criminology and forensic medicine as they affect perversions, and contemporary developments along the lines of research.

Liquid and also solid nourishment, when essentially compounded of wholesome ingredients, will unquestionably, in the contemporary consensus of medical opinion, promote amatory capacity.

To go one step further, any nourishing food or beverage will, to the extent of its wholesomeness as an acceptable and normally consumed commodity, contribute to the general organic euphoria of the subject, and consequently to his physiological vigor.

In a general sense, therefore, the fantastic or repellent compounds, brews and stews, lotions, electuaries, ointments, and philtres that, for long centuries, were transmitted either in folk legend or imprinted in grave treatises, are, according to medical authority, brusquely deprecated, and in many cases entirely discounted.

Yet, as is well known, legend and saga, folklore and tradition, often retain within themselves accumulated knowledge based on tested validities.

With the increase in experimentation along medical, pharmaceutical, and culinary lines, there is a corresponding emphasis on food and preparations that promote physiological well-being and act as tonics and stimulants.

For these purposes, extracts of the gonads or sex-glands, and pituitary extracts, are medically recommended in certain cases of physiological weakness.

In a more gastronomic direction, there are wholesome broths and soups, such as: mushroom soup, lentil soup, celery soup, as well as salads, lobster dishes, and curries: all of which contain elements that are traditionally reputed to aid in increasing vigor.

In a novel by John Brophy entitled *Windfall*, and published in London in 1951, the hero arrives in New York, where he is confronted with the fact that the drive for erotic aids is as urgent as ever:

It was true: where Broadway converged on, before it crossed, the undeviating straightness of Sixth Avenue, the wide double roadway was surrounded by theatres, cinemas, hotels and restaurants and newspaper offices, indiscernible behind huge, colored, epileptically moving signs advocating, pictorially or by blunt lettered exhortation, whiskies and pea- nuts, cigarettes, motor-cars, night-clubs, patent medicines and proprietary brands of sexual stimulants.

In the same novel there is a description of a New York Night Club, the Freudian Frolics. Here are presented amatory stimulants and visual and palpable inducements in a contemporary setting, basically identical with the Aristophanic performances, the satires of Lucian, the sketches of Alciphron and the more boisterous narratives of the Middle Ages, the Renaissance, and, dominantly, eighteenth century France. The scene is introduced with a generalization that marks the activities of the place:

Beyond the swing-doors almost every erotic taste not utterly perverted could be if not gratified at least stimulated ... the majority made straight for the primary erotogenic zones.

Again, there is a wildly farcical description of amatory reinforcements. The character concerned is a degenerate multi-millionaire, an American named Mirabel Jones XVIII. His problem is to achieve an heir to his vast interests. For this purpose, he is undergoing a multiple variety of treatments at the hands of his physician and his psychiatrist. He is subjected to daily injections. He consumes all sorts of tablets. He is regulated by calisthenic exercises, by vitamin pills, by radio-therapy, by baths. All these various means are regimented methodically into prospective erotic channels. As a climax, he travels constantly, from one country to another, to secure a climate favorable to his condition, from South America to California to England.

The possibilities of the love-potion still intrude into modern times. In a series of light sketches of Scottish life, entitled *Christina*, the author, J. J. Bell, presents young Christina herself, who is living with an aunt who runs a small village store. To further a possible courtship between the aunt and the commercial traveler Mr. Baldwin, Christina conceives a plan to help the shy and hesitant Miss Purvis. The book itself was published about forty years ago:

Christina greatly enjoyed looking at the shops without supervision or restriction. She had made up her mind to purchase a gift for her aunt, whose birthday fell about a month later.

Christina enters a barber's shop, because she has seen the ideal gift:

She moistened her lips, and, in a tremulous whisper, said—

"I want a—a potion."

"A lotion, miss?"

"A potion."

"A lotion—for the hair?" He smiled dreadfully—so it seemed to Christina. Once more she all but fled.

Christina had been reading about potions, in a periodical devoted to love stories. She tells her aunt, Miss Purvis, about it. "It was a magic potion. A lass got it frae a—a sosserer to gi'e to a young man that wasna heedin' aboot her. She gi'ed it to him, an' it charmed him, an' afore she could say

'Jack Robinson' he was coortin' her like fun, an' their nuptails was celebrated in—"

Now Christina is ready to employ the same means in behalf of her aunt.

To the barber, then, Christina whispers: "A potion. What—what's the price o' yer—yer Spirit o' Love?"

The barber, momentarily nonplussed, finally smiled with understanding:

A moment later he was brushing a cobweb from a small bottle containing a yellowish fluid. A soiled and faded label of floral design was affixed to the bottle, and on it appeared, as in letters of fire, the words "Spirit of Love."

"One shilling, miss."

"Would it—charm a lady?"

"Certainly! I have sold hundreds of bottles of 'Spirit of Love' to gentlemen for that very object. Charms them like magic!"

"Like magic?"

"Like nothing else, miss. Do you wish the bottle for a sick friend? Just so! In that case a few drops on the pillow will prove a real charm."

Christina nearly dropped. It was too wonderful!

He must be a sosserer!

Christina administers the potion in her own way. While her aunt is asleep, she pours a few drops on the pillow, but, disturbed by the sudden squalling of a cat, lets the phial fall. It empties itself on the pillow.

The aunt, a sceptic, throws the empty bottle into the fire, with the remark "Spirit of Fiddlesticks!"

———

Experimentation and research in the direction of rejuvenating processes and invigorating vigor continue all the time, without cessation. Some procedures involve surgical operations: others are associated with the administration of various hormones and extracts and glandular compositions. Proprietary medicines are on the market, particularly in France and in England. An advertisement in a weekly magazine advocates The Royal Jelly Rejuvenating Food Supplement.

———

In the early nineteenth century, in Edinburgh, there were on sale Luckenbooth Brooches. They were in the nature of amatory periapts. These brooches were sometimes engraved with a lover's initials. Or a plea or an amorous inducement might appear thereon, such as:

Let me and thee

most happy be.

Or:

My heart ye have and thir I creve.

I fancie non but the alon.

Wrong not the heart whose joy thou art.

Analogous to philtres and similar amatory concoctions is the indirect stimulus derived from reading teacups. A popular Scottish weekly paper says: It's fun, and there's a good deal in it, too, if the signs are read aright.

In relation to Love and Friendship, the column declares that a 'human' figure seen in the form of the tea leaves, whether man or woman, or the outline of a letter of the alphabet, indicates that the love and feeling of affection will concern the person whose name begins with the tea leaf letter.

This is, in essence, an innocuous variation of an amatory inducement.

Among contemporary proprietary preparations reputed to have amatory value is aphrodisin. This is a compound of yohimbine, a substance indigenous to Central Africa and derived from the bark of the yohimbe tree, along with extract of miura pauma, aronacein, and other ingredients.

There are many instances of women, concubines, mistresses, and harlots, who have become historically famous or notorious through their own personal practices, or for the influence they have exerted socially and politically. A French courtesan who rose from minor and humble circumstances was Céleste Mogador, who was born in 1824 and who died in 1909. She was a dancer, an actress, and an equestrienne: and ultimately became the Comtesse Lionel de Moreton de Chabrillan. She gained some additional réclame by the publication of her Memoirs.

Charles Baudelaire (1821–1867), the French poet, in his *Les Fleurs du Mal*, has a sequence of poems on passion, macabre, violent, distorted, filled with fantastic imagery, touched with the symbol of death, and putrefaction, and unsated human longings. There are hymns to beauty that border on disaster and cruelty, on ugliness and inhumanity. There is a paean to exotic perfumes, a laudation of a woman's dark tresses. But these poetic effusions are stamped with bitterness and a sense of reality aghast, unholy revelations. There appears an entire distant, remote world, far-flung and almost extinct, where the poet sees an aromatic forest, where he dwells in the woman's depths. She pleads with her lover, for she is unsated and insatiable. He peers through those two dark eyes, the windows of your soul. O ruthless demon, he clamors, pour less flame upon me. I am not the dread and furtive Styx, capable of embracing you nine times.

A putrescent carcass, seen on a summer morning, is a poetic memento mori, like an Egyptian skeleton at the feast, a warning that lust and beauty and passion have their brief day and are grimly evanescent, and an indirect injunction, on the poet's part, to adhere to the Roman poet Horace's hedonistic *carpe diem*.

In *The Vampire* Baudelaire exclaims at being enslaved by a hateful but alluring woman, while in another piece he stresses the potency of perfumes.

These poems, then, symbolize, in a comprehensive sense, the intrusions of lust and passion in human relationships, and the intimate contacts and associations of these lusts with malefic forces and ominous impacts.

Ballads, street songs, and broadsides, belonging to a wide and usually comparatively uncultured level, in all ethnic communities, deal largely with physiological and scatological functions, sexual and erotic intrusions and experiences and experiments, without restraint, without reflection and without moralizing corollaries thereon, but with a forthright, direct verbal impact. Hence there are, dispersed through such unsophisticated uncontrived versified episodes, many matters relating to amatory enticements and means of erotic provocations and challenges affecting both male and female, in all types of occupation, in many gradations of society, at every age level, from young and urgent milkmaids and their swains to debauched lechers and libertines.

Pastoral pieces, soldiers' rollicking ditties, sailors' chanties, all the rhythmic, chthonic, usually crude but outspoken exuberance of folk ways and currents, of peasantry and burgher, tinker and servant, tipplers, ploughmen, and innkeepers—that is the colorful and various component of the popular muse.

Sometimes the erotic impact is suggested by indirection: sometimes by an innocuous expression used in a double entendre context. Sometimes the idiom has the immediacy of the Greek functional and genital significance exemplified in the Aristophanic comedies.

Rakes and panders rub shoulders with guileless innocence and feminine wiles, with lordly arrogance, authority, and wealth, with humility and beggarliness, with want and starvation. And pervasive through all the insinuating permutations of street life and market place, of court and manor, of fields and ocean, battle and stress, there runs the urgency of amatory attraction: lust and passion and allurement, and the means of satisfying and sating and continuing and maintaining such erotic capacities, such animal lustfulness and unbridled salaciousness and lewd ardor, prurience and perverted depravities.

Yet there are instances, sudden outbursts, occasional spurts of deeper feelings, brusque awareness: some latent though possibly dishonored principle, a touch of wry humor, in which blatant reality and some remote consciousness of betterment peer through the vernacular crudities.

In one collection of such ballads, entitled *Drolleries*, the amatory theme returns again and again, always lusty, always sensual. The burgess who is off to the fair while her good man is absent from home: the coy mistress: the country maid on a visit to the City: the old lecherous beau unrepentantly persistent: the lustful squire, the libidinous courtier, the wayward maid: widows and lords, fiddlers and coopers, cobblers and miners, merchants all conniving in adultery and incest, in concocting potions for reluctant lovers, in beseeching hesitant favors, in besmirching marriage and domesticity and exultantly and indifferently glorifying all the varieties of amatory diversions and perversions.

In *Today*, a popular British weekly magazine, an article appeared early in 1962, by a woman, accusing the contemporary man of having lost his virility. She spoke of 'sexually moribund men,' of man's failure, in consequence, as a marriage partner, and of his amatory deficiencies.

A response to these challenges appeared in a later issue. It was written by a factory worker who, from his own experience and that of his acquaintances and fellow-workers, refuted the first attack. He denied physical exhaustion. He asserted that the typical worker, by virtue of his constant application to his job, is kept continuously physically fit and capable. His knowledge, too, of the range of amatory procedures and practices has been widened by war contacts, by interchange of views and attitudes with many groups, foreigners, visitors, refugees. He added that the freedom of expression on such matters was an additional encouragement toward enlightenment. If anything, this typical worker concluded, it was the woman who was hesitant, indifferent, and un-cooperative.

In Gilbert and Sullivan's *The Sorcerer*, a farcical treatment of the Black Arts, there is a scene involving love philtres and their effects:

Mr. Wells: Love-philtre—we've quantities of it ...

Alexis: I have sent for you to consult you on a very important matter. I believe you advertise a Patent Oxy-Hydrogen Love-at-first-sight Philtre?

Mr. Wells: Sir, it is our leading article. (*Producing a phial*).

Alexis: Now I want to know if you can confidently guarantee it as possessing all the qualities you claim for it in your advertisement?

Mr. Wells: Sir, we are not in the habit of puffing our goods. Ours is an old-established house with a large family connection, and every assurance held out in the advertisement is fully realized. (*Hurt*).

Aline (*aside*): Oh, Alexis, don't offend him! He'll change us into something dreadful—I know he will!

Alexis: I am anxious from purely philanthropical motives to distribute this philtre, secretly, among the inhabitants of this village. I shall of course require a quantity. How do you sell it?

Mr. Wells: In buying a quantity, sir, we should strongly advise you taking it in the wood, and drawing it off as you happen to want it. We have it in four-and-a-half and nine gallon casks—also in pipes and hogsheads for laying down, and we deduct 10 per cent for prompt cash.

Alexis: I should mention that I am a Member of the Army and Navy Stores.

Mr. Wells: In that case we deduct 25 per cent.

Alexis: Aline, the villagers will assemble to carouse in a few minutes. Go and fetch the tea-pot.

Aline: But, Alexis—

Alexis: My dear, you must obey me, if you please. Go and fetch the tea-pot.

Aline (*going*): I'm sure Dr. Daly would disapprove of it.

(*Exit Aline*).

Alexis: And how soon does it take effect?

Mr. Wells: In twelve hours. Whoever drinks of it loses consciousness for that period, and on waking falls in love, as a matter of course, with the first lady he meets who has also tasted it, and his affection is at once returned. One trial will prove the fact.

Enter Aline with large tea-pot.

Alexis: Good: then, Mr. Wells, I shall feel obliged if you will at once pour as much philtre into this tea-pot as will suffice to affect the whole village.

Aline: But bless me, Alexis, many of the villagers are married people!

Mr. Wells: Madam, this philtre is compounded on the strictest principles. On married people it has no effect whatever. But are you quite sure that you have nerve enough to carry you through the fearful ordeal?

Alexis: In the good cause I fear nothing.

Mr. Wells: Very good, then, we will proceed at once to the Incantation.

In the South Sea Islands amatory aids and spells are still in vogue. The following love incantation involves the love-sick girl Taratake:

Mr. Hair-of-his-head, Mr. Hair-of-his-head,

Go you to him, to Taratake!

Whisper my name when he dreams,

when he wakes.

When he walks among the women.

Draw him by the hand,

Draw him by the foot,

Draw him by the heart and entrails to me.

He thinks only of me;

He dies for love of me;

There is no woman for him but me,

no love but mine,

no love-making but mine.

He comes to me, he comes, he is here with me,

With me, Laughter-of-Waves-o-o-o!

As recently as 1956, in the *Flute of Sand*, Lawrence Morgan describes an experience among the Ouled-Naïl dancers of North Africa:

Interwoven into their lives were sorcery, black magic, and, most common of all, the use of love-philtres with which they believed they could enslave any man. In the pot of mint tea in Yacourte's room had been a philtre intended to help the erring lover to make up his mind.

The term bayadère is derived from the Portuguese baladeira, associated with bailar, to dance. Originally, the expression was applied to a Hindu dancing girl, noted for erotic performances. The bayadère, in fact, like the nautsch dancers, could be equated with prostitution.

The European newspapers and magazines, notably in Germany, Austria, and France, until quite recent times, advertised, in the interests of readers, all kinds of elixirs, remedies, philtres, concoctions, and unguents, to correct sexual deficiencies or to promote physiological capacity. There was a cream called Vigor. Dragées des Fakirs were 'scientific and immediate.' A Parisian aphrodisiac powder announced itself as 'durable.' It could be forwarded by mail, from the Scientific Laboratories. Clients could be interviewed at specified hours. Renox was a concoction that was urged very persuasively: so too with the contrivance Heureka. There was another contrivance called Samson, implicitly suggesting a Biblical valor. Sexine and Stimulol and Dragées de Vénus were both harmless and effective, according to the laudatory testimony of the manufacturers themselves.

There was a highly advertised preparation, called Testogan, that implied stimulating amatory reactions.

A contrivance under the name of Amor Star was formerly advertised in Europe as very effective, making the agent another Casanova. In Paris, a preparation called Mono promised rejuvenation for the male.

Many European restaurants practiced a dual role. In addition to their culinary purpose, they were in a basic sense amatory rendez-vous. During the First World War German eating-places, variety halls, dance palaces, and cabarets advertised, with appropriately alluring illustrations:

Wein, Weib Gesang

In other instances, Teutonic gaiety was eulogized as being highly imitative of Gallic ways. Leben à la Paris—ran the posters:

Damenklub

Maskenbälle

Lustiger Abend

Café Dorian Gray.

These spots were instigations to perversions, amatory practices, and promiscuities.

Numerous collections of erotica exist in varying degrees of seclusion, in libraries, state archives, and museums. To a large extent, such compilations were made during the eighteenth and nineteenth century. The bibliophile, on his death, usually bequeathed his books and manuscripts and erotic objects and artifacts to a state or national library. Among English specialists in this genre were James Campbell, the pseudonym of J. C. Reddie, William S. Potter, Henry Spencer Ashbee, better known under his pseudonym of Pisanus Fraxi. In France, the Bibliothèque Nationale, in its section known as L'Enfer, houses a large collection of erotic matter.

In cosmopolitan cities like London and New York, the sex theme is predominant in certain types of rather furtive bookstores. They deal largely with paperbacks, stressing sexual relationships, erotic magazines, and treatises, both authoritatively written and, in some cases, barely literate, on erotic mores and variations of perversions. The paperbacks, flaunting jackets that play a significant role in the attraction of the text, range from lust to rape, from masochism to tribadism, with all possible intermediate permutations. Such fictional productions not infrequently transcend the ingenuities of the Marquis de Sade.

Contemporary witches, sorceresses, and spell-binders of varying degrees of reliability still use, as love potions, old, traditional ingredients. One of these is hippomanes. Hippomanes was well known among the ancients. It is a fleshy excrescence that appears on a foal's head at birth. When dried, and swallowed by the person in search of the amatory excitation, it produces, according to these dark practitioners, a result that cannot be questioned.

The erotic merit of this equine aposteme is confirmed by a number of authorities, from Vergil himself, the Roman epic poet, to Pausanias, the second century A.D. Greek geographer, and to the sixteenth century Neapolitan alchemist and occultist Gambattista della Porta.

SELECTIVE BIBLIOGRAPHY

Benoit, H. The Many Faces of Love. New York: Pantheon, c. 1955.

Bibliotheca Erotica Moniacensis. A German collection of erotica.

Bibliotheca Roloffiana. A collection of erotica published in Germany in the eighteenth century.

Blondeau, Nicolas. Dictionnaire Erotique. Paris: Isidore Liseux, 1885.

Clauder, Johannes. De Philtris. Leipzig, 1661.

Decle, L. Three Years in Savage Africa. London: Methuen, 1898.

Dufour, H. Histoire de la Prostitution chez tous les Peuples du Monde. Bruxelles: 1857.

Dulaure, Jacques-Antoine. The Gods of Generation. English translation by A.F.N. Privately printed. New York: Panurge Press, 1934.

Ellis, Havelock. Studies in the Psychology of Sex. 2 volumes. New York: Random House, c. 1938–1942.

Epton, N. C. Love and the French. London: Cassell, 1959.

Epton, N. C. Love and the English. London: Cassell, 1960.

Epton, N. C. Love and the Spanish. London: Cassell, 1961.

Flacelière, Robert. Love in Ancient Greece. Trans. by J. Cleugh. London: Muller, 1962.

Gilbert, O. P. Men in Women's Guise. London: John Lane, 1926.

Gilbert, O. P. Women in Men's Guise. London: John Lane, 1932.

Goncourt, E and J De. La Femme au dix-huitième Siècle. Paris, 1902.

Gregorovius, F. A. Der Ghetto und die Juden in Rom. Berlin: Schocken Verlag, 1935.

Hervé-Piraus, F.R. Les Temples d'Amour au XVIIIe Siècle. Paris, 1910.

King, L. W. Babylonian Magic and Sorcery. London: 1896.

Laurent, E. Magica Sexualis. New York: Anthropological Press, 1934.

Mantegazza, Paolo. English translation under the title Sexual Relations of Mankind. Privately printed. New York: Anthropological Press, 1932.

Rodocanachi, E. P. La Femme italienne: avant, pendant et après la Renaissance: sa vie privée et mondaine, son influence sociale. Paris: Hachette, 1922.

Wolff, J. F. Dissertatio de Philtris. Wittenberg, 1726.

Booksophile
Your Local Online Bookstore

Buy Books Online from
www.Booksophile.com

Explore our collection of books written in various languages and uncommon topics from different parts of the world, including history, art and culture, poems, autobiography and bibliographies, cooking, action & adventure, world war, fiction, science, and law.

Add to your bookshelf or gift to another lover of books - first editions of some of the most celebrated books ever published. From classic literature to bestsellers, you will find many first editions that were presumed to be out-of-print.

Free shipping globally for orders worth US$ 100.00.

Use code "Shop_10" to avail additional 10% on first order.

Visit today
www.booksophile.com

Milton Keynes UK
Ingram Content Group UK Ltd.
UKHW011117281123
433341UK00025B/774

9 789357 390408